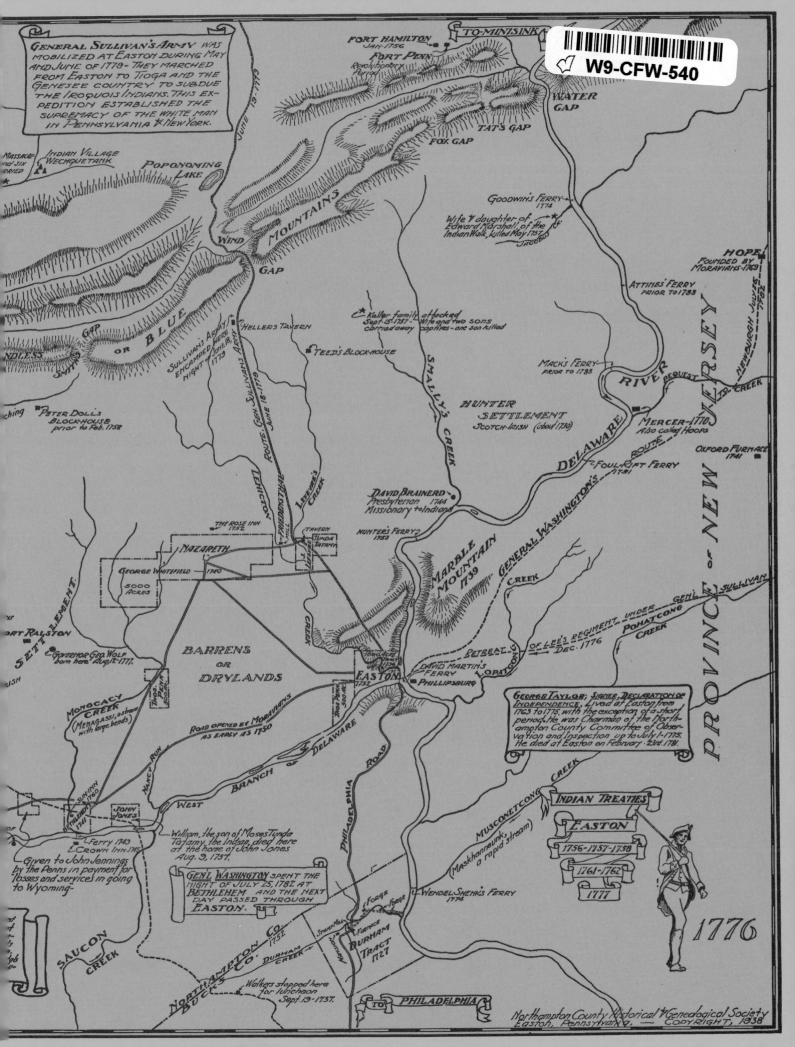

GENERAL SULLIVAN'S ARMY WAS MOBILIZED AT EASTON DURING MAY AND JUNE OF 1779 - THEY MARCHED FROM EASTON TO TIOGA AND THE GENESEE COUNTRY TO SUBDUE THE IROQUOIS INDIANS. THIS EXPEDITION ESTABLISHED THE SUPREMACY OF THE WHITE MAN IN PENNSYLVANIA & NEW YORK.

TO-MINISINK

FORT HAMILTON JAN. 1756
FORT PENN Revolutionary Period

WATER GAP
TAT'S GAP
FOX GAP

GOODWIN'S FERRY 1774

Wife & daughter of Edward Marshall, of the Indian Walk, killed May 1757 Jacobus

HOPE! FOUNDED BY MORAVIANS 1769

ATTINES' FERRY PRIOR TO 1783

MASSACRE AND SIX BURIED

INDIAN VILLAGE WECHQUETANK

POPONOMING LAKE

WIND GAP

Keller family attacked Sept. 15, 1757 - Wife and two sons carried away captives - one son killed

HELLERS TAVERN

TEED'S BLOCK-HOUSE

SMALLY'S CREEK

HUNTER SETTLEMENT Scotch-Irish (about 1730)

MACK'S FERRY PRIOR TO 1785

RIVER

MERCER-1770 Also called Hoops

OXFORD FURNACE 1741

DELAWARE

FOUL RIFT FERRY 1731

PROVINCE OF NEW JERSEY

SMITH'S GAP
OR BLUE MOUNTAINS

ENDLESS

PETER DOLL'S BLOCK-HOUSE prior to Feb. 1758

Sullivan's Army encamped here night of June 18, 1779

Gen. Sullivan's Army Route June 18, 1779

FRIEDENSTHAL ROUTE

LEHICTON

LEFEVRE'S CREEK

DAVID BRAINERD Presbyterian 1744 Missionary to Indians

HUNTER'S FERRY? 1753

THE ROSE INN 1752

TAVERN TUNDA TATAMY

NAZARETH

GEORGE WHITEFIELD 1740

5000 ACRES

MARBLE MOUNTAIN 1739

CREEK

GENERAL WASHINGTON'S ROUTE

NEWBURGH JCT 1783

REQUEST

Creek

SULLIVAN

GEN'L

OF LEE'S REGIMENT UNDER RETREAT DEC. 1776

POHATCONG CREEK

SETTLEMENT

FORT RALSTON

Governor Geo. Wolf born here Aug. 12, 1777

THOS. PENN 500 ACRES

BARRENS OR DRYLANDS

CREEK

1000 ACRE TRACT 1735

THOS. PENN 500 ACRES

EASTON 1752

DAVID MARTIN'S FERRY

PHILLIPSBURG

LOPATCONG

GEORGE TAYLOR; SIGNER, DECLARATION OF INDEPENDENCE. Lived at Easton from 1763 to 1775, with the exception of a short period. He was Chairman of the Northampton County Committee of Observation and Inspection up to July 1, 1775. He died at Easton on February 23rd, 1781.

MONOCACY CREEK (Menagassi; a stream with large bends)

ROAD OPENED BY MORAVIANS AS EARLY AS 1750

PHILADELPHIA ROAD

BRANCH OF DELAWARE

WEST

JOHN JONES

William, the son of Moses Tunda Tatamy, the Indian, died here at the home of John Jones Aug. 9, 1757.

GEN'L WASHINGTON SPENT THE NIGHT OF JULY 25, 1782 AT BETHLEHEM AND THE NEXT DAY PASSED THROUGH EASTON.

MUSCONETCONG CREEK

(Maskhanneunk, a rapid stream)

INDIAN TREATIES EASTON

1756-1757-1758

1761-1762

1777

FERRY 1743
L. CROWN INN 1745

Given to John Jennings by the Penns in payment for losses and services in going to Wyoming -

BETHLEHEM 1741

NANCY RUN

DUNTON 1760

SAUCON CREEK

NORTHAMPTON CO. 1752

DURHAM CREEK

STAMP MILL

FORGE

FORGE

FURNACE

DURHAM TRACT 1727

WENDEL SHENK'S FERRY 1774

1776

Walkers stopped here for luncheon Sept. 19, 1737.

TO PHILADELPHIA

Northampton County Historical & Genealogical Society Easton, Pennsylvania, — COPYRIGHT, 1938

The
LEHIGH VALLEY

AN ILLUSTRATED HISTORY

FOREST SCENE
ON THE LEHIGH
by Karl Bodmer.
Courtesy, The InterNorth
Art Foundation,
Joslyn Art Museum,
Omaha, Nebraska

The LEHIGH VALLEY

AN ILLUSTRATED HISTO

Illustration Research and Photography by
Adrienne Snelling

Produced in Cooperation with the
Northampton County Historical and
Geneological Society and the Lehigh County
Historical Society

Windsor Publications, Inc.
Woodland Hills, California

Windsor Publications
History Books Division

Publisher: John M. Phillips
Editorial Director: Lissa Sanders
Administrative Coordinator: Katherine Cooper
Senior Picture Editor: Teri Davis Greenberg
Senior Corporate History Editor: Karen Story
Production Manager: James Burke
Art Director: Alexander D'Anca
Art Production Manager: Dee Cooper
Composition Manager: E. Beryl Myers

Staff for *The Lehigh Valley: An Illustrated History*
Editor: Pamela Taylor
Designer: Alexander D'Anca
Layout Artist: Cheryl Mendenhall
Assistant Editor: Todd Ackerman
Picture Editors: Annette Igra, Jim Mather, Kevin Cavanaugh
Editorial Assistants: Susan Block, Patricia Dailey, Phyllis
    Gray, Greg Harris, Karen Holroyd, Mary Mohr, Susan Wells
Production Artists: Janet Bailey, Shannon Strull
Typographers: Shannon Mellies, Barbara Neiman

First Edition

Library of Congress Catalog Card Number 82-50187

ISBN 0-89781-044-9

CONTENTS

These early 19th century hand-lettered documents were given to Joseph and Maria Moser as a symbol of their marriage. Artist Connrad Daur, whose name appears below each surname, used ink and gouache on paper. The Latin inscription dedicated the union "to the glory of God alone." (LCHS)

FOREWORD

This book does not pretend to be a definitive history of the Lehigh Valley. No single volume could do justice to an area so large, rich, and basically under-researched. Nevertheless, we hope that this effort, in drawing together many scattered resources, published and unpublished, will not only give an adequate summary of the region's past, but will also encourage its residents to appreciate and look more deeply into the past that they share.

This task could not have been completed without the help of many people. We are especially indebted to the scholars and antiquarians who, over the past two centuries, have worked to preserve and record the region's history. Monica Bugbee of the Lehigh County Historical Society's library, Henry Drinkhouse of the Northampton County Historical Society, Donald Miller of the *Call-Chronicle* Newspapers, and Vernon Nelson of the Moravian Archives, were especially generous with their time. Lois A. Dancevic, librarian of the *Call-Chronicle* newspapers, provided us with invaluable access to the paper's microfilm holdings and clipping files. And the clerks of the courts of Lehigh and Northampton counties were invariably helpful and cooperative in helping us to find and use the public records of the area.

Karyl Lee Kibler Hall
Peter Dobkin Hall
Allentown,
June 1982

The Lenape Indians possessed
an intimate relationship with
their natural environment. They
revered nature and rarely
exploited it. Their numbers
were few compared to the white
invaders. Courtesy, Lehigh
County Historical Museum
(LCHM)

CHAPTER ONE

IN THE BEGINNING: THE PREHISTORY OF THE VALLEY

A billion years ago, there was no Lehigh Valley. Instead, a flat and empty continent stretched to the horizon. A great silence filled this plain. There were no animals, no trees, and very little vegetation. Only the primordial storms moving across the moss-covered land broke the stillness. About 600 million years ago, however, the antediluvian continent began to break apart. The western sections became North and South America. The eastern section became Europe and Africa. As this happened, sea waters advanced to form a shallow, warm body called the Appalachian Sea. This sea, which covered virtually all of what would become the Lehigh Valley, teemed with simple creatures, algae and trilobites. Their remains, combined with minerals precipitating out of the seawater, formed the clays, slates, and limestones that characterize the Lehigh Valley's geology. In certain places iron and zinc ores were concentrated on the sea bed.

The movements of the huge plates of the earth's crust that broke the continents apart and formed the new seas took millions of years but the change did not occur peacefully. The motion of these enormous areas against one another caused the earth's surface to buckle. The land on which the Lehigh Valley now lies was forced upward. A new mountain range, the Appalachians, began to form. The waters of the Appalachian Sea flowed away, leaving shallow swamps trapped in the folds of the land. Magma, superheated molten rock from the earth's core, oozed out of the cracks in the bedrock. Earthquakes and volcanos shook the almost barren land.

These dramatic changes in the landscape encouraged the development of new life forms capable of coping with and thriving under the new conditions of climate and geography. By 400 million years ago, the crude mosses and algae had evolved into huge ferns and primitive trees. Fish and reptiles lived in the shallow swamps left by the sea's retreat and as the waters continued to recede, some proved able to live on the land. Dinosaurs evolved from these creatures. So did the early mammals and birds. About 200 million years ago, the huge reptiles died off. Without rivals for food, the mammals, which had been tiny mouse-like creatures, developed in size and variety. Where the Tyrannosaurus rex once preyed and the Brontosaurus had peacefully grazed, enormous elephant- and rhinoceros-like mammals roamed the tropical forest of the Lehigh Valley.

But the earth was still changing and evolving. About 150 million years ago, the climate began to grow colder. The arctic ice advanced across North America, marking the first of a series of ice ages that would last for 100 million years. The forests and swamps and their inhabitants disappeared. The plant life died, decomposed, and over the centuries was transformed into the coal beds which lie to the north of the valley. Ice 1,000 feet thick covered the region. Only the peaks of the Blue and South mountains poked up through the frozen mass.

The Coming of Man

During the last ice age, the level of the seas was lowered because so much of our planet's water had turned into snow and ice. As the level of the seas declined, the area of land connecting Alaska and Siberia was exposed. Across this land bridge wandered the animals, particularly caribou, bison, and the woolly mammoth, who thrived on the plant life at the glacier's edge. Following them were bands of hunters whose food and clothing came from the hides and flesh of the mammoth and other big game.

There was nothing dramatic about the arrival of this new species on the North American continent. Its members did not come in a single group but straggled across in small hunting bands over several millennia, beginning perhaps 40,000 years ago. They did not even know that they had come upon a new world, for they had neither maps nor recorded history. Some went southward into Central and South America. Others followed the game along the line of the glaciers. The first men are believed to have reached the Atlantic Coast about 20,000 years ago.

We know very little about the Paleo-Indians, as the earliest human inhabitants of the Lehigh Valley are called. Some scholars believe they entered the area about 10,000 years ago when the last ice age was ending. The remains of a mastodon, one of

pieces of raw jasper

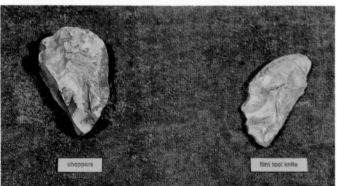

choppers

flint tool knife

TOP
Jasper is a kind of fine-grained quartz that is common in the Lehigh Valley. The stone was found in veins, cavities, and streambeds. (LCHM)

ABOVE
Jasper was favored by the Indians because it would hold a sharp, if ragged, edge. These choppers were held in the palm of the hand and swung with great force because they lacked handles to multiply the striking force. (LCHM)

the animals hunted by the Paleo-Indians, has been found at Marshall's Creek, near the Delaware Water Gap. It is estimated to have been there since 10,210 B.C. Recent excavations at Vera Cruz in southern Lehigh County suggest that men were mining the jasper there and making tools as early as 12,000 years ago. If so, it is likely that the Paleo-Indians were living right on the edge of the great Wisconsin Glacier, which terminated just south of Allentown.

Physically, the Paleo-Indians were modern men. Culturally, however, they were very primitive. Living along the line of glaciation in a tundra-like environment that could not support human settlements of any great size, this people hunted big game with stone-pointed spears. They supplemented their diet with nuts, roots, and berries, gathering whatever bounty the cold land had to offer. Because they were hunters whose survival was closely bound to the movement of particular animal herds, they made no permanent settlements. Their monuments—the bones of the animals they killed, scattered tools, and the ashes of their campfires—still lie hidden and unexplored under the earth of the Lehigh Valley.

About 10,000 years ago, the climate began to warm dramatically. The Wisconsin Glacier, which had covered most of the Northeast for 60,000 years, began to recede. The mass of ice turned into rivers and streams that ate into the newly exposed land. As the climate warmed, the environment altered radically. The cold-weather plant life on which the mammoth and mastodon had subsisted was replaced by conifer and deciduous forests. The large animals, unable to survive under these conditions, died off or were hunted to extinction. The Paleo-Indians also had to change or perish.

Evidence suggests that they chose to change and that the Paleo-Indians were becoming, from 8000 to 5000 B.C., the Archaic ancestors of the Delaware (Lenni Lenape) Indians. The retreat of the ice and the alteration of the Indian way of life seems to be described in the historical chronicle *Walam Olam*, the one surviving piece of Lenni Lenape literature:

After the rushing waters [had subsided] the Lenape of the turtle were close together, in hollow houses, living together there.

It freezes where they abode, it snows where they abode, it storms where they abode, it is cold where they abode.

At this northern place they speak favorably of mild, cool lands, with many deer and buffaloes.

As they journeyed, some being strong, some rich, they separated into house-builders and hunters. . . .

Those from the north being free, without care, went forth from the land of snow, in different directions.

The fathers of the Bald Eagle and the White Wolf remain along the sea, rich in fish and mussels.

Floating up the streams in their canoes, our fathers were rich, they were in the light. . . .

The ancestors of the Lenni Lenape eventually ended their wanderings. While they still hunted, their game was the deer, rabbit, and squirrel. They learned to fish, taking food not only from the fresh waters of the Jordan, Lehigh, and Delaware rivers, but also, in patterns of seasonal migration, from the waters of the sea. While not yet farmers, these Archaic Indians had begun gathering certain grains and grinding them in stone mills. Tools became more sophisticated. Living in the forests, they needed axes, adzes, and gouges for shaping the abundant wood. Polished bone and stone ornamental pieces were produced by Indian craftsmen.

From our perspective, the Indian life of 5,000—or even 500—years ago seems remarkably simple and unchanging. But this apparent simplicity is largely a product of our ignorance of the valley's earliest inhabitants. While the details of Indian history are forever lost to us, the artifacts that they left behind suggest a notable complexity and adaptability to changing conditions. The appearance of polished stone tools and weapons suggests that the Indians of the area were, 1,000 years before the birth of Christ, in contact with the highly developed civilizations of Central America, which excelled in the creation of polished stone implements. Indeed, recent discoveries at the Vera Cruz jasper mines seem to indicate that Indians came from all over the East Coast to obtain fine-quality stone for tool-making.

By 1000 B.C., the Indians of the Lehigh Valley were doing more than merely imitating the tool forms of their highly sophisticated cousins in Mexico. They were also profoundly influenced by Meso-American religion, engaging in a series of localized adaptations of burial and temple mound-building practices that were a woodland variant of the great stone temples of the Central American Indians. Certainly the most important contribution of this southern contact was the introduction of maize (corn) as an agricultural crop and the introduction of technologies related to maize agriculture, most notably the use of pottery vessels for cooking and storage. By the beginning of the first millennium, the Indians of this region had broken distinctly with their hunting and gathering past and were evolving

This 1980 watercolor by William Sauts Netamuxe Bock shows a Lenape girl with an owl. The light outlines on her arm are tattoos. The close kinship between the Lenape and the natural world was destroyed by the widespread slaughter of wildlife by the whites. (LCHM)

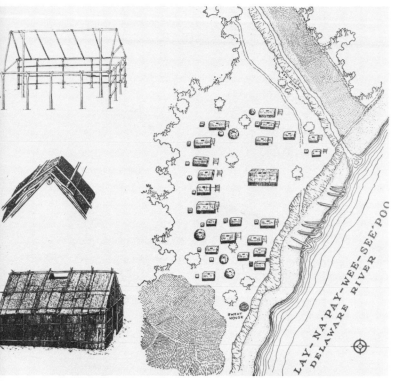

LAY·NA·PAY·WEE·SEE·POO
DELAWARE RIVER

SWEAT HOUSE

ABOVE
A map of a typical Lenape village is shown here with other illustrations demonstrating the construction of a Delaware bark house. (LCHM)

BELOW
Numerous stone tools and weapons of the Lenni Lenape have been found in the Lehigh Valley. The axe, spear points, a mortar and pestle, a soapstone bowl, a hammerstone, and a drill date from the Archaic Period, 10,000-7,000 BC. (LCHM)

relatively stable patterns of life. They still hunted and fished, moving between inland areas and the shore with the seasons. But their movements were governed by their need to sow and harvest the maize, beans, sunflowers, and other crops that had become essential parts of their pattern of survival. They no longer lived hand to mouth. They planned and planted, knowing that living comfortably through the winter depended on their summer's labors.

As Indian life stabilized in the Northeast, particular groups, usually defined by language and kinship, came to occupy or have rights to certain geographical areas. For example, the Delaware, or Lenni Lenape, Indians were a part of a large language group which spoke Algonquian. The Algonquians occupied an area from Virginia through Nova Scotia on the East Coast and large sections of the Midwest including what is now Michigan, Illinois, Indiana, and Wisconsin. To the north, in New York and northern Ohio, were those who spoke Iroquoian languages; to the south, speakers of Siouan and Muskogean. Originally the Indian languages were probably very similar. But as each group settled into particular locations and developed life-styles appropriate to different settings, the languages diverged. By the year of Christopher Columbus' arrival, it is estimated that Native Americans spoke some 2,000 mutually unintelligible languages.

Within the broad language groups were other divisions. Curiously, the tribe was not one of these divisions. While it is true that all Lenape recognized one another as members of the same people, there was no tribal government. Instead, the Lenape were organized into village communities based on common descent through a female ancestor. There were 30 or more of these communities. Authority within the communities was administered not by a powerful chief (sachem), but, according to historian C.A. Weslager, by a council of "older and spiritually powerful men." Decisions were arrived at through discussion and debate among these older men. The Lenape people were further organized into three units called "sibs." A "sib" was another grouping based on the descent of individuals through the female line. Sib membership affected not only patterns of loyalty and obligation, but also determined whom one could marry. Individuals were not permitted to marry members of their own sib. The sib system ensured regular communication between communities and lineage groups within communities as the young sought mates outside their own sibs.

Perhaps the best description of the decentralized character of Lenape society has been written by C.A. Weslager, author of a definitive work on the Delaware. He wrote that one might compare their society

to a number of small rural towns in modern America, scattered across the landscape, but lacking county, state, or federal affiliation, each responsible for its own government and the welfare of its citizens. The main difference was that in the Delaware Indian towns there was a high percentage of persons related to one another, and the frequent movements of the people and the perambulations of their communities gave the population a group mobility generally lacking in modern American towns. The inhabitants of Delaware Indian towns spoke dialects of the common language and had a sufficient feeling of common identity to call themselves Lenni Lenape, just as modern dwellers in small towns refer to themselves as Americans.

These loosely organized people normally spent their summers either inland, sowing and harvesting crops, or, if they were fishermen or shell-gatherers, near the shore. In the winter, the communities broke up, the family bands going up the rivers to their hunting territories in the interior. These hunting territories, some as large as 200 square miles, were owned collectively by members of lineage groups.

The loose organization of Lenape society would cause the Indians many problems, both with other Indian groups and ultimately in their dealings with European settlers. Scattered over a wide area—including portions of the present states of New York, Pennsylvania, New Jersey, and Delaware—and lacking any clearly defined system of political leadership, it was difficult for the Lenape to act as a unified group even in war. Thus, when the Iroquois tribes of western New York federated themselves in the early 17th century and began to expand their influence over other Indian groups, the Delaware were easily conquered. From the 1660s on, they had to pay annual tribute to their Iroquois conquerors and, in their later dealings with the Europeans, were required to have Iroquois approval for their actions.

This political fragmentation would later lead to confusion and bitterness between the Lenape and the Europeans. For the whites assumed that Indian societies were organized like European ones, with recognized leaders who could speak for their subjects. Thus they mistakenly thought that when they purchased a particular piece of land from a particular chief, that chief was acting with the consent of all of his people. Europeans frequently purchased land, only to find other Indian groups claiming that the land sale had no validity. By the late 17th cen-

Philadelphia was built at the crossroads of two long Indian trails. The Minsi Path led through the Lehigh Valley and across the future location of Bethlehem. From Ray Thompson, *Walking Purchase Hoax of 1737*, The Bicentennial Press

tury, a migrant Indian band might arrive on the shore at the end of a trek from the Forks of the Delaware only to find that their cousins at Brandywine or Tulpehoken had sold their land rights to the Swedes, the Dutch, or the English.

The problem of social and political organization was only one source of misunderstanding between the Lenape and the Europeans. More fundamental were radically different concepts of property ownership. For the Indians, property ownership meant the right to use the fruits of the land—to hunt, to plant, to fish. It did not imply absolute and exclusive possession. Thus, while the Indians amicably signed treaties granting tracts of thousands of acres to the Europeans, they were shocked to discover that they could no longer hunt, fish, or even traverse lands that they had used for thousands of years. To them, the European gifts of cloth, beads, tools, and liquor were merely tokens of hospitality and friendship, not purchase prices for pieces of real estate. But these conflicts between concepts of political authority and property were only symptomatic of a far more significant clash between Indian and European cultures.

The Coming of the Europeans

The Indians of the Lehigh Valley came into contact with European settlers long before the permanent settlements of the Swedes and English in the vicinity of Philadelphia. Explorers of various nationalities had encountered members of the Delaware peoples in the 1500s, a fact which is mentioned in passing in the *Walam Olam*. Following the explorers came traders, representatives of European merchants interested in furs, which were in great demand among the nobility and prosperous middle classes of the Old World. Preeminent among these were the Dutch, who were establishing forts and trading posts on the Delaware as early as the 1590s. By the time Penn arrived to establish permanent settlements in "Sylvania" in the 1680s, traditional Lenape life had been largely destroyed.

Because the Europeans were technologically superior to the Lenape, contact between the two cultures entirely unbalanced the more primitive group. The Europeans overwhelmed the Indian less by treaties or force of arms than by such minor things as the shovel, the needle, and the iron cooking pot. It is impossible to envision how important a simple item like an iron pot is to a people accustomed to laboriously manufacturing fragile pottery vessels. Similarly, the gun was more important as a weapon used by Indians in hunting than as a weapon used by Europeans against the Indians. The technological superiority of

European tools rendered insignificant thousands of years of Indian cultural evolution. The Indians were quick to recognize the value of European implements and quick to become dependent upon them. Within a generation, native skills of toolmaking and woodcraft were disappearing. The more dependent they became on European merchandise, the more intensively and efficiently they hunted and trapped. The result was a wholesale destruction of wildlife, which rendered the Indians yet more dependent upon European goodwill, for, by the end of the 17th century, nature could no longer supply their needs. Added to this undermining of their economy was a collapse of social stability. Dissolute Indian youth, faced with a choice between the rigors of life in the woods and the temptations of the trading post, often abandoned their families, becoming drunkards and beggars. According to A.F.C. Wallace in his account of Teedyuscung, king of the Delaware, prostitution by Indian women was so common that the Lenape village at Lewes, Delaware was known to the Dutch as Hoeren Kill (Whore's Creek) "from the liberality of the Indians in generously volunteering their wives or daughters to our Netherlanders at that place."

The first Europeans were sometimes peaceful and friendly. They were generous with their gifts to the natives. But their "great things" (as mentioned in the *Walam Olam*), even when given in the most amicable spirit, proved more destructive than war or pestilence. The people who had traversed continents and survived the rigors of the ice age, could not withstand the mixed blessings of the iron pot, woolen cloth, or European musketry. The Delaware might linger in Pennsylvania into the 19th century, but their Indian identity would be more a memory than a reality. The *Walam Olam* ends on a poignant note. After a long and uneventful narration of the succession of chiefs over many generations, it describes the coming of the Europeans:

> *White-Crab was chief; a friend of the shore.*
> *Watcher was chief; he looked toward the sea.*
> *At this time, from north and south, the whites came.*
> *They are peaceful; they have great things; who are they?*

The Lenape suffered deception and persecution at the hands of the white settlers. This oppression drove the Lenape from their ancestral lands. This poignant portrait of two of the survivors was painted by William Sauts Netamuxe Bock in 1980. (LCHM)

Johan Bjornsson Printz was
governor of the early 17th-
century Swedish settlements
along the Delaware before the
Dutch and the English arrived.
Courtesy, Historical Society of
Pennsylvania

THE PEOPLING OF THE LEHIGH VALLEY: 1700-1790

Through most of the 17th century, the Lehigh Valley was almost uninhabited. Its quiet woodlands were disturbed only by the seasonal movements of Lenape bands as they moved upriver to their hunting grounds in the mountains or downriver to the plains around present-day Allentown and Bethlehem where they annually burned off brush and scrub to clear land for planting maize, beans, and pumpkins. Even though their plantations were large enough to produce thousands of bushels of grain, their largest hardly intruded on the primordial forests and streams. For the Lenape numbered no more than 8,000 to 10,000 people scattered across four states.

Neither the settlement of the Scandinavian colony of New Sweden on the lower Delaware in the 1640s nor the incursions of New York-based Dutch traders affected the Lehigh Valley. Rich as its soil, timberlands, and mineral deposits might be, it was remote and isolated, protected by steep hills that rose west of the Delaware and by its distance from the coast. In any case, the Swedes and the Dutch were busy subduing the wilderness close to their settlements and with quarreling among themselves. All they wanted from the lands upriver were the animal skins brought by trappers and hunters. But events taking place in Europe would, within 100 years, fill the quiet and almost empty valley with the sound of falling trees and the haze of woodsmoke from the pioneers' hearths.

The 17th century was a troubled time in the Old World. In England, France, and Germany, changes were taking place in every aspect of peoples' lives. Politically, the rise of powerful monarchies, especially in France and England, put traditional aristocracies under tremendous financial pressures. The aristocrats had lived for hundreds of years off the products of farmers' and peasants' labors, usually taking their rents in the form of grain and cattle. As political power became centralized, the aristocrats, in order to maintain their influence at royal courts, moved to the great cities of Paris and London. The cost of city life, with its constant gambling and revelry and the expenses of buying offices and favors from the kings and their officials, forced the aristocrats to reconsider traditional ways of earning income. They introduced new kinds of agriculture, most notably sheep raising, which required the consolidation of their holdings. They also began exploiting their woodlands and their mineral resources. These innovations displaced thousands of small farmers, most of whom were forced to move to the cities in search of work. Although some benefited from this displacement, becoming prosperous as craftsmen and merchants, many others found urban life unpleasant and yearned to farm their own lands in the New World.

It was also a time of religious turmoil. Dissatisfaction with the Roman Catholic Church had been brewing in Europe since the 1400s. But not until 1517 did the Protestant Reformation crystalize with Martin Luther's eloquent condemnations of the Papacy. Luther made many converts among the German princes; and his translation of the Bible into German made it accessible to thousands of merchants, artisans, and peasants. Luther had a host of followers, among them John Calvin of Geneva, whose harsh doctrines won many converts in France. The English Reformation began with Henry VIII's break with the Papacy in 1534. In the vanguard were the powerful Calvinist-influenced Puritans, who commenced a struggle with the English monarchy that would erupt into a civil war in the 1640s. Germany, not yet a united nation, was sharply divided between Catholics and Protestants. The Catholics looked to France for help, especially after the ascension to the throne of Louis XIII in 1610. The Protestants looked to England, Sweden, and Holland for support. In 1618, war broke out, sweeping across Germany and resulting in the deaths of millions over the course of the Thirty Years' War. By the 1640s, as the war was ending, the Protestants were threatened with extermination in France and were frantically searching for religious asylum. In the provinces of Germany which had come under French control, particularly in the Palatinate section of southwestern Germany, thousands of Protestants began an exodus to Holland, where they boarded ships for the New World.

America was not necessarily a safe haven for these exiles. Neither the Southern colonies (Virginia and the Carolinas) nor New England were particularly tolerant of religious dissent. Of all the regions of the New World only Pennsylvania offered both the economic and religious freedoms for which these

Following the Thirty Years' War of 1618-1648, the German states were plagued with unemployment and unrest. Soldiers turned to highway robbery, as this etching shows. Such strife drove many to emigrate to the New World. From *The Age of Expansion*, published by McGraw-Hill; Copyright Thames and Hudson, 1968, London

refugees yearned. The fact that Pennsylvania was a land of genuine freedom was due entirely to a remarkable man named William Penn.

William Penn was the son of a prosperous merchant who, having survived the difficulties of the English Civil War, emerged after the Restoration as a distinguished admiral in the English wars with the Dutch in the 1660s. In the course of his naval career, King Charles II had become deeply indebted to Admiral Penn. When Penn died in 1670, his son, who had become a dissenter from the Church of England, offered to settle the debt in exchange for a grant of land in the New World. The king, who had come into possession of the Dutch colonies in the New World through England's victory over the Dutch in 1664, was willing to sign over the lands between New York and Maryland to young Penn. Not only was he grateful to be able to settle a large debt without having to raise cash, but he favored any scheme that would rid England of troublemakers. In September of 1682, William Penn, royal charter in hand, set sail for the Delaware to examine his new land and to make plans for its settlement.

Had William Penn been a different sort of man, Pennsylvania would not have been settled so rapidly and its settlers would not have been so willing to penetrate remote regions like the Lehigh Valley. Had he, for example, made his land a haven for Quakers and no one else, the Germans, Huguenots, and Scotch-Irish would have settled elsewhere and Pennsylvania would have been a stagnant backwater in spite of its resources. But Penn had learned much from the troubled times in which he lived. He had come to believe in religious tolerance as a matter of conviction. As a Quaker he believed that God revealed himself to men not through the pronouncements of bishops or the edicts of kings, but through intense personal experience. Because of this, he and the other Quakers opposed the intrusion of the state or of powerful religious organizations into the private relationship between man and God. He thus envisioned Pennsylvania as a commonwealth open to all, whatever their way of worshiping their Creator.

Penn was also a practical man. His family had raised itself to eminence by cleverly navigating the treacherous tides of religion, politics, and trade. And to stay afloat, he had to do the same. He recognized that the immense land grant given to him by the king was only valuable if it was inhabited by people willing to purchase or rent portions of this vast estate. And, because he was a merchant, he recognized that settlers meant markets for imported goods, sources of valuable raw materials, as well as tenants for his property. To open Pennsylvania to the thousands of Europeans displaced by war, intolerance, and economic disorder would serve both his religious convictions and his pocketbook.

When William Penn and his party arrived on the site of Philadelphia in 1683 the colony consisted of over 2,000 people, mostly Swedes and Englishmen. They were hardly enough to begin to populate the 35 million acres that had been granted to Penn, the Proprietor. Even with the colonists' remarkable fertility and high rates of immigration in later years, it would be decades before the first European settlements appeared in the Lehigh Valley. Another obstacle to the entry of Europeans into the Lehigh Valley was the fact that the Indians, King Charles notwithstanding, regarded the lands granted in Penn's charter as their own. Penn, motivated by his Quaker pacifism and profiting from the mistakes made by the English settlers of New England, who had waged bloody warfare with the natives for decades, decided that the Lenape should be paid for their lands and their mutual rights established by written treaties. Finally, as a merchant with an eye for profit, Penn wished his lands to be settled in an orderly fashion. His model of order was a feudal one: the grant would be divided into manors, the basic English unit of rural government. The "lords" of these manors would not only possess basic responsibilities for the administration of justice, but also for collecting "quitrents," annual sums of money or goods paid to themselves and to the Proprietor. He also established a general government with an executive (the governor), to be appointed by the Proprietor, and a legislature (the assembly), to which representatives would be elected from the various civil divisions, townships, and boroughs of the colony. Pennsylvania may have been an early model of political democracy and religious tolerance, but it was also, first and foremost, a private land speculation.

Early Settlement and the Walking Purchase

Few Europeans ventured into the Lehigh Valley before the 1720s. Not only was the area still regarded as Indian territory, but migration also was impeded by the formidable barrier of the South Mountain. In any case, far more accessible and fertile lands lay to the south and west of Philadelphia, in Chester, Lancaster, Berks, and York counties. By the third decade of the 18th century, however, William Penn was dead, and the entire white population of Pennsylvania could be estimated at under 10,000. But as the younger Penns struggled to pay off their father's debts and as immigrants, particularly from Germany and Ireland, began to arrive in the colony in ever-increasing numbers, attention turned to the lands at the Forks of the Delaware and beyond.

By the 1730s, much of the Lehigh Valley had been granted by the Penns to an assortment of friends, relatives, and creditors. These included such colonial notables as Caspar Wistar, James Bingham, James Hamilton, and William Allen. Allen, for example, acquired his lands at Allentown from his business partner, Joseph Turner, who, in turn, had received them from the Penns in settlement of a debt. These land speculators were anxious to earn profits from their Lehigh properties. And their anxieties increased as they watched a growing number of squatters moving onto their lands. Added to pressures on these Philadelphia gentlemen were the protests of the Indians, who resented the squatters' unauthorized incursions into their territories. It was clearly time to open the area to orderly development and to the blessings of civil government. The first step would have to be the negotiation of a treaty with the Lenape. And this would be no easy task.

Although Penn's pacific and legalistic approach to Indian affairs had spared Pennsylvania colonists the murderous struggles that had typified New England's relations with the natives, European incursions into the Lehigh Valley presented a host of difficulties. For, as the Lenape had ceded their lands on the coast and the lower Delaware, they had moved in large numbers to Tulpehoken, the region along the Lehigh between the South and Kittatinny Mountains. In this isolated valley, they struggled to retain the remnants of their traditional way of life. They resented their dependence on the whites for guns, tools, cloth, and food; and many lamented the loss of their once vast domain. Decimated by rum, disease, and cultural upheaval, they were especially reluctant to permit further cessions of their possessions to the English.

But the Penns and their friends were insistent. They spoke of a treaty made by William Penn in 1686 which granted to the Proprietor lands north of the Lehigh Hills, as far north as a man could walk in a day and a half. Although the document itself was never produced, the Lenape, after three years of tortuous negotiations, agreed to grant the English a tract of land whose boundaries would be established by a day and a half's walk. The Indians no doubt expected that this "walking purchase" would follow the pattern established by an earlier purchase of that sort. When William Penn had originally obtained his lands at Philadelphia from the Lenape, he had been granted as much as a man could walk in three days. Penn had proceeded Indian fashion, taking several chiefs with him and moving along at a leisurely pace, stopping frequently to smoke, rest, and take refreshments. In three days, the group had covered less than 30 miles.

But the younger Penns and their representatives were more hardheaded. They not only wanted clear title to as much salable land as possible but also wanted to begin exploiting the valuable resources of the area. James Logan, their chief negotiator with the Lenape, had been the leading partner in an ironworks which had been operating at Durham Furnace, a few miles south of the Forks, since 1727. Promising tracts of timber and ore were known to lie in the Lehigh Valley. Accordingly, while negotiations went on, English surveyors were measuring out the route that would bring the Proprietor's heirs and their clients the most territory. "Walkers" were selected and trained; plans were made for feeding and refreshing them. The Walking Purchase of 1737 would be very different from its predecessor.

At sunrise on September 19, 1737, the three "walkers," Solomon Jennings, James Yeates, and Edward Marshall, set out from Wrightstown in Bucks County. They were accompanied by colonial officials on horseback, an assortment of curious onlookers, and a party of Indian observers. They followed a straight surveyed course toward the northwest, paralleling the Delaware overland, and converging with the Lehigh near the site of Allentown. The walkers continued along the Lehigh River until they reached the Indian village of Hokendauqua, where they stopped for the night.

Had the walkers proceeded in a leisurely fashion, as the Indians had expected, the whites would have stayed to the south of the Kittatinny Mountains. This would have preserved intact the Lenape's ancestral hunting grounds. It would have also erected a formidable natural barrier to further white expansion. Indeed, there was disagreement as to where the northern limit of the purchase should lie. The Indians maintained that it should follow a line directly eastward from the terminus of the walk to the Delaware River, which would have kept the Europeans south of the mountains. The Europeans insisted that the northern boundary should follow a line at right angles to the line of the walk, which would have roughly doubled the amount of land claimed and given them almost the entire west bank of the Delaware. Had the walkers moved more slowly, this disagreement about the northern boundary would have been a moot point. Either way the boundary would have satisfied the Lenape. But the walkers' rapid progress on the first

William Penn received his lands in the New World from the King of England in payment for debts owed to his father, Admiral Penn. William Penn set out from England for the Delaware in 1682. Drawing by Francis Place; Courtesy, Historical Society of Pennsylvania

William Allen acquired land in the Lehigh Valley in 1735 from his business partner, Joseph Turner. In 1762 Allen surveyed the area, laid out streets, and became the founder of Allentown. (LCHM)

Lappawinsoe of the Lenni Lenape tribe was one of the tribal chiefs who was induced to sign the Philadelphia Treaty of 1737, also known as the notorious "Walking Purchase." Lappawinsoe's portrait was painted in 1735 for John Penn by Gustavus Hesselius. Courtesy, Historical Society of Pennsylvania

day made it clear to the Lenape that the Europeans were going to be able to claim not only all the land south of the Kittatinnys, but a considerable tract to the north as well. The Lenape realized that they were being cheated. The Indian observers quit the party in disgust, their leader, Lappawinsoe, angrily declaring that they had already "got all the best of the land, and they might go to the Devil for the bad, and that he would send no Indians with them."

As they camped for the night outside of Lappawinsoe's village, the walkers and those who accompanied them were kept awake by the shouting and singing of the Indians. Some accounts state that the Lenape were conducting a noisy religious ceremony. Others suggest they were organizing to resist further progress by the walkers. The next morning at dawn, Edward Marshall, the only walker who still had the strength to continue, and the white observers, set out on their marked course up the Lehigh and through the Kittatinny Mountains at the Lehigh Water Gap. They struggled on until noon, terminating the walk at the junction of the Lehigh and Tobihanna Creek in what is now Carbon County. In the course of the 18-hour walk, the whites had covered a distance of 55 miles, giving them a claim to over 1,200 square miles of territory. This included not only the Indians' best farmlands, but also a significant portion of their hunting grounds to the north of the mountains. The claim embraced many Indian villages which, of course, would have to be evacuated.

The Lenape were enraged, a fact that became increasingly evident as the whites retraced their steps along the course of the walk. At the village of Pocopoco, near the Lehigh Gap, Old Captain Harris, a respected Lenape chief, expressed his stern disapproval of the way in which the walk had been conducted, claiming that the whites had run rather than walked. Thomas Furniss, a young saddler of Newtown who had accompanied the walkers with his friend Timothy Smith, sheriff of Bucks County, later recollected the return trip:

In our return we came through this Indian town or plantation— Timothy Smith and myself riding some forty yards, more or less, before the company—and as we approached within about one hundred and fifty paces of the town, the woods being open, we saw an Indian take a gun in his hand and advance towards us some distance, placed himself behind a log that laid in our way.

Timothy observed his motions and being somewhat surprised, as I apprehended, looked at me and asked what I supposed the Indian meant. I said I hoped no harm, and that I thought it best to keep on;

which the Indian seeing he arose and walked before us into the settlement. I think Smith was surprised, as I well remember I was through a consciousness that the Indians were dissatisfied with the walk, a thing the whole company seemed to be sensible of, and upon the way in our return home frequently expressed themselves to that purpose.

And indeed, the unfairness practiced in the walk, both in regard to the way where, and the manner how it was performed, and the dissatisfaction of the Indians concerning it were the common subjects of conversation in our neighborhood for some considerable time after it was done.

Edward Marshall, one of the walkers, visited Hokendauqua eight weeks later. Lappawinsoe, the Lenape chief, was still angry. He declared that the whites "should have walkt along by the river Delaware or the next Indian path to it. . . . The walkers should have walkt for a few miles and then have sat down and smoakt a pipe, and now and then have shot a squirrel, and not have kept upon the run, run all day." The chief threatened to bring his entire tribe to Philadelphia the following spring, each with a buckskin, to buy the land back from the Penns.

Realizing that they had perhaps gone too far and that the resulting Lenape resentment might impair the value of their properties, James Logan, the Penns' representative, made some significant concessions to the Indians. He relinquished all claims to lands north of the Kittatinny Mountains and granted to the Lenape a 10-square-mile tract south of the mountains, which included the major Lenape villages. This calmed the hotter heads among the Indians and, in the short run, preserved the peace. But the Lenape, among the least belligerent of all the Eastern Indians, would continue to resent the unfairness of the Walking Purchase. And their resentment would increase as their former lands in the Lehigh Valley began to fill with white settlers, reminding them of the full extent of their dispossession. The events of 1737 marked the end of the friendly and trusting relations between the Indians and the English. What had begun in 1683 with the declaration in Penn's 1683 treaty with the Delaware, that the two peoples should live together "in love as long as the sun and moon endure," was, by the 1760s, characterized by Lord Jeffrey Amherst's request that his officers contrive "to send the Small Pox among these disaffected tribes of Indians." Within 20 years of the Walking Purchase, the blood of settlers and Indians would stain the soil of the Lehigh Valley.

Although a few European families had been living in the Lehigh Valley since the 1720s, they represented only scattered settlements until the next decade when groups of Germans, Scotch-Irish, and Huguenots began to build churches and set out farms on the frontier. Most of these early settlements lay below South Mountain, in the vicinity of Milford and Saucon townships. Some brave souls like Jeremiah Trexler had settled as far north as the outskirts of Hokendauqua as early as 1733. But the largest groups of settlers did not begin to arrive in the region until after 1737, when the Walking Purchase had settled the ownership of the valley.

The 18th-century settlers of the Lehigh Valley belonged to four large groups. The first consisted of individual German Protestants, members of the Reformed and Lutheran churches, who purchased land in various parts of the county, and considerable numbers of French and Swiss farmers who made common cause with German members of the Calvinist Reformed Church. They clustered in groups, largely for the convenience of being near grist and sawmills, near their churches, and for their mutual defense. They did not, however, proceed with any common plan of settlement.

The second group was also largely German, but unlike the rugged individualists of the Reformed and Lutheran churches, these settlers (Moravians, Mennonites, Dunkers, Amish, and Schwenkfelders) were communitarians. Religious radicals, they combined to varying degrees intense piety with doctrines of civic and family organization which set them apart not only from the English, but from their fellow Germans. The most radical, the Moravians, held much of their property in common, coordinating all of their energies for collective pious purposes. Their motto was "We pray together, we labor together, we suffer together, we rejoice together."

The third group, the Scotch-Irish, was composed of Protestant families from the north of Ireland. Their ancestors had been brought to northern Ireland by a succession of English monarchs beginning with Elizabeth I in order to dilute the power of the native Irish Catholics. By the 1720s, however, a series of poor harvests in Ulster, combined with severe land scarcity, motivated several hundred families to look for opportunities in the New World. Some, like the group that ultimately settled Portland in Northampton County, originally emigrated to Massachusetts, where they were refused asylum by colonial authorities. They were invited by Governor Hunter of New York to settle in the western part of that province. By accident, they wandered into the Lehigh Valley in the 1730s. Others, like the group led by Thomas Craig, a relative of William Allen, purchased a large tract of land, "Craig's Settle-

ment," in what is now Allen township, and subdivided it among themselves. Still others, men like one known only as "Mr. Smalley," settled as individuals, setting up a grist mill in 1728 at Martin's Creek. Although not communitarians, the Scotch-Irish tended to cluster together for religious and social reasons. Most were Presbyterians and were anxious to cooperate in building churches. Many were friends and relatives who had grown up together in the Old World and wished to remain together in the New. The areas of the valley where they settled with particular density lay along the eastern bank of the Lehigh between Hokendauqua and Catasauqua and eastward to the town of Bath.

The fourth group, the English, never settled in great numbers in the Lehigh Valley during the 18th century. Nevertheless, they were particularly important because they were the largest landowners in the region. While they sometimes worked through German-born agents like Conrad Weiser, more frequently they chose other Englishmen to represent their interests, to survey and divide their properties, and to collect their quitrents. The English concentrated in towns like Easton which, in 1752, became the shire town of the new county of Northampton. Here sat the courts of the frontier region. Here the wills and deeds were recorded. Since these transactions were conducted, by law, in the English language under the jurisdiction of justices appointed by the government at Philadelphia, it is hardly surprising that Englishmen clustered together in the new town. Of the 12 families listed as inhabiting Easton in 1752, nine had English names. The early lawyers of the town were all English or Scotch-Irish. And even where the English were numerically insignificant, their influence was pronounced, for they decided where the major townships would be, they laid out the house lots of Easton in the 1750s, and those in Allentown in 1762. They were responsible for attracting settlers to those places as part of their plan to develop the region and profit from their investments. They exercised considerable social influence as well. The country seats of Philadelphia gentlemen like William Allen and Lynford Lardner, Keeper of the Proprietary Seal, set the tone of luxury and ease in a frontier setting.

Hard Times, 1755-1763

The orderly settlement of the Lehigh Valley was interrupted between 1755 and 1763 by a series of bloody Indian uprisings. These were part of the larger struggle between the French and

TOP
This small house of square-hewn logs is the oldest Moravian building in the United States. Originally built in 1740 as a school, the structure is used today by a Moravian missionary. Artist Mary Alice Frack painted the cottage in 1926. Courtesy, Northampton County Historical and Geneological Society (NCHGS)

ABOVE
This log structure in Emmaus, called the Shelter House, was built in 1734. The building was used as a stopover for travelers on a trail that connected the Great Swamp with Macungie. The building is currently maintained by the Shelter House Society. Courtesy, Shelter House Society; photo by Adrienne Snelling

the English for control of the New World. The English were allied with the Iroquois tribes of New York, who had held the Lenape in subjection for nearly a century and who had consented to the bargaining away of their rights in the infamous Walking Purchase. The Lenape saw in the French-English conflict an opportunity to regain their ancient domain and to settle old scores with their Iroquois enemies. In addition, they were inspired by an Indian religious movement which had begun in the West through which the culturally broken natives hoped to revive their morale and resume their former dominance of the continent. Finally, there were very concrete economic and political grievances underlying the uprisings. In 1749, the Iroquois sold all the remaining Delaware lands to the Penns, including those to the north of the Kittatinny Mountains. They claimed a right to do so by virtue of their 17th century conquest of the Lenape and other tribes in the area. As the Indian leader Teedyuscung would assert regarding this transaction:

Then one King has land beyond the River, and another King has Land on this Side, both bounded by Rivers, Mountains, and Springs, which cannot be moved, and the Proprietaries, greedy to purchase Lands, buy of one King, what belohgs to the other—this likewise. . . . I have been served so in this Province: All the land, extending from Tohiccon, over the Great Mountain, to Wioming, has been taken from me by Fraud; for when I had agreed to sell the Land to the old Proprietary by the Course of the River, the young Proprietaries came and got it run by a straight Course by the Compass, and by that Means took in double the Quantity intended to be sold.

Cheated by the Penns in 1737 and sold out by their fellow Indians in 1749, the Lenape were desperate. To these humiliations were added a more immediate and pressing concern: a shortage of the trade goods, particularly liquor and gunpowder, on which the Indians had come to depend for survival. Although this shortage had begun when certain Indians and their Quaker allies in the assembly attempted to stem the demoralization of the natives by alcohol, it had been intensified by the early 1760s, when the British military assumed control of Indian affairs. Knowing the sympathy of certain tribes for the French and wishing to nip any uprisings in the bud, Lord Jeffrey Amherst, governor-general of British North America, effectively blocked the sale of trade goods to the Indians. The Indians, having no market for their furs and no means of obtaining the tools, firearms, and clothing on which their lives depended, were faced with starvation. From Pennsylvania into New York and as far west as Ohio, desperate Indians began to arm for war. Having as their ally the mighty French nation, their hopes of regaining what they had lost were not entirely unreasonable.

Complicating the deterioration of relations between the English and the Indians were conflicts among the Europeans themselves which rendered the situation of settlers in the Lehigh Valley very uncertain. The first involved land claims made by the colony of Connecticut on the northern part of the Province of Pennsylvania.

In 1662, when Charles II granted Connecticut its charter, he designated its lands as running "from sea to sea" (encompassing an area to the present-day California coast) and its southern boundary as 41 degrees north latitude. Nineteen years later, when William Penn received his charter, King Charles granted him lands whose northern boundary lay along 43 degrees north latitude. The Connecticut grant included all lands north of the Delaware Water Gap—a considerable chunk of Pennsylvania and New York. This overlap was an insignificant issue in the 17th century when European settlements still clustered on the seacoast and contained a mere handful of inhabitants. But as the colonies' populations swelled and as land speculators in Connecticut and Pennsylvania sought new sources of profits, King Charles' vagueness about North American geography developed into a major crisis, the Pennamite War.

The major antagonists in this war were the Province of Pennsylvania and two Connecticut-chartered private corporations, the Susquehanna Company and the Delaware Company. These companies were granted lands in the disputed territory by the Connecticut General Assembly. The Connecticut people, regarding the land as their own, did not feel bound by an arrangement made by the Penns with the Lenape, who, by the 1750s, had retreated into the Wyoming Valley north and west of the Lehigh. The representatives of the Susquehanna Company met with the Iroquois chiefs at Albany in 1754 and purchased what they regarded as legitimate title to these lands. Shortly afterwards, the company sent a party of surveyors to the region to locate sites for the projected colonization of the area. Within the year, families from Connecticut began to arrive. By 1760 the sheriff of Northampton County reported to the governor of Pennsylvania that the Yankees had set up three townships containing three log houses, 30 cabins, a sawmill, and a grist mill. More parties of settlers were expected daily.

While Pennsylvania authorities were disturbed in principle by the Connecticut incursions into their territory, they had far more concrete reasons for alarm. The legal issues of land claims could always be worked out in the courts of Great Britain. But the complaints of the Indians about the marauders could not be ignored. By 1760, Teedyuscung, the Lenape leader, was warning the governor of Pennsylvania that if he would do nothing about "those intruding people" that "the Indians will put a stop to it," which would, he threatened, "certainly bring on another Indian war." In addition to the danger of an Indian uprising, the Connecticut incursion was stirring up political discontent among the European settlers on the frontier. Many of them, unhappy with the Penns' feudal system of land tenure through which they were only permitted to lease land rather than buy it outright, were attracted by the possibilities of fee-simple ownership offered by the Connecticut companies. They also looked to the opportunities offered by the opening of the Wyoming to white settlement, a move which had been forbidden by the Penns' treaties with the Lenape and Iroquois.

The conflict between Pennsylvania and Connecticut, the anger of the Indians, and the dissatisfaction of the frontiersmen was further aggravated by the development of a fundamental split in Pennsylvania politics between those who supported the Proprietaries (the Penns and their friends) and those who supported the Quaker merchants of Philadelphia. This cleavage anticipated the conflict between Tories and Whigs that would emerge in the 1760s and would bear fruit in resistance to the Stamp Act and culminate in the American Revolution.

The Proprietaries' interests were closely tied to those of the British government. They favored enforcement of the Navigation Acts, which limited where and in what commodities Americans could trade and which curtailed manufacturing activities in many areas, including iron, glass, and hats. Their Indian policies, in line with the Walking Purchase of 1737, were geared to the maximum expansion of European settlement along the feudal lines originally projected by William Penn. The Quakers, on the other hand, favored free trade, avoided British efforts to enforce trading laws whenever possible, and favored the enforcement of Lenape claims on disputed lands, especially in the Wyoming Valley.

This conflict had serious consequences, for it rendered the governor of Pennsylvania virtually powerless to deal with either the Connecticut incursion on the Susquehanna or Teedyuscung's threat to call his braves to arms. As the governor tried to negotiate with the Indians, as he did at Easton in 1756 in an effort to calm them, he found the Indians being advised by major Quaker political leaders. The Indians, recognizing that the whites no longer spoke with one voice, were quick to attempt to play off one party against the other. More important-ly, because the Provincial Assembly was controlled by the Quakers, the governor of Pennsylvania could do no more than write angry letters to the governor of Connecticut protesting the settlement in the Wyoming Valley. And he could not obtain authorization to send an armed force to the area to deal with the invaders or to protect frontiersmen from Indian attack because the Quakers, as pacifists, opposed the use of force and violence.

On July 9, 1755, 400 miles west of the Lehigh Valley, a band of several hundred Indians, including many refugee Lenape, joined battle against British Regulars under General Edward Braddock near Fort Duquesne, the present site of Pitts-burgh. The brightly uniformed and highly trained professional soldiers, unfamiliar with the guerilla techniques of frontier war-fare, were routed. British authority collapsed in the Ohio Valley and the French began to move in, taking over British trading posts and military strongholds.

The news of the British defeat traveled fast, as the French overtures to the pro-English Iroquois and to disaffected lesser tribes like the Lenape gained in urgency. By October, the Lenape were on the warpath. On the sixteenth of that month, they descended on a settlement on the Susquehanna near Selinsgrove, killing or capturing 25 people. By November, set-tlers in the Lehigh Valley were gripped by fear. Moravian mis-sionaries at Gnadenhuetten, near the Lehigh Gap, wrote to their Bishop in Bethlehem begging that their Indian converts be escorted to safety and that guards be sent to protect the village against imminent attack. On November 24, 1755, the Indians attacked Gnadenhuetten, killing 11 of the 15 inhabitants and burning their barns and houses. The Indian attacks continued into December, moving ever closer to the centers of settlement along the Lehigh and Delaware rivers. Among those killed were the wife and two children of Edward Marshall, the only man to have completed the Walking Purchase. The residents of the frontier counties repeatedly asked Governor Morris for aid in defending themselves, but he could do nothing, for the Quakers controlled the assembly and refused to grant him funds for such a purpose.

Finally, in January of 1756, Benjamin Franklin, agent of Governor Morris, was sent to the Lehigh Valley to see to its defense. He arrived in Bethlehem on January 7 to find the town crowded with terrified refugees from the surrounding countryside, including the remnants of the Northampton County militia, who had been soundly defeated by the Indians

ABOVE
Powderhorns served two purposes: first, a powderhorn kept the powder dry; second, it provided a sure way to transfer the powder into the musket barrel. This powderhorn, dated 1746, is inscribed "calling in two part." Courtesy, Lehigh County Historical Society, (LCHS)

TOP
In 1756 Benjamin Franklin, on orders from Pennsylvania's Governor Morris, designed a defensive strategy for the Lehigh Valley. Relations between whites and Indians were strained, and Franklin chose a network of blockhouses and forts as the best method of defense. Courtesy, Historical Society of Pennsylvania

TOP
The oldest drugstore in America was built in Northampton County in 1752. Set back from Main Street in Bethlehem, the "apotheke" became Simon Rau and Company. (LCHS)

ABOVE
The oldest extant stone structure in Lehigh County was built by Peter Troxell in 1744. Early stone construction inhibited the use of windows because of stress problems. The house is now in South White Hall Township. Courtesy, Jeres Corporation; photo by Adrienne Snelling

on the road to Gnadenhuetten on New Year's Day. Franklin, a notable organizer, took command of the confused situation. Rallying 500 troops, he left on January 15 for Gnadenhuetten, where he began construction of Fort Allen. It was completed 10 days later, establishing a major military stronghold at the strategically important Lehigh Water Gap. Within the next few weeks, Franklin and his men constructed half a dozen other forts and blockhouses along the frontier in Schuylkill, Monroe, and Carbon counties.

These measures, while not ensuring complete security from Indian depredations, were sufficient to convince the settlers that Philadelphia had not entirely abandoned them. By April of 1756, Governor Morris, although still opposed by the Quakers, declared war on the Lenape, offering cash rewards of $130 for the scalp of every male Indian over 10 years of age and $50 for the scalp of every Indian woman or girl. At the same time, he opened negotiations with the Indians in a series of conferences at Easton which would meet intermittently between 1756 and 1762.

These conferences were the Lenape's last stand. Caught up in an international power struggle between two great world empires, the English and the French, their rights overlooked in the boundary dispute between Connecticut and Pennsylvania, and outrun in the jockeying for imperial favor among other Indian tribes, they could do little more than vacillate between impotent threats and pathetic appeals. The Lenape's situation was summed up by Teedyuscung when he declared:

I sit here as a Bird on a Bow—I look about, and do not know where to go; let me therefore come down upon the Ground, and make that my own by a good Deed, and I shall have a Home for ever.

Landless, demoralized, and scattered, the Lenape stood little chance of recovering what they had lost. The failure of the French to hold the Ohio Valley deprived them of their strongest ally. Continuing raids on isolated white settlers not only alienated their Quaker friends in the Pennsylvania Assembly, but also aroused such hostility among frontiersmen that no Indian, whether Christian or pagan, was safe even in broad daylight. The last Easton conference, in the summer of 1762, left the status of the Lenape unresolved. They were free to live in the Wyoming Valley as far as Pennsylvania authorities were concerned. But the Wyoming was occupied by Connecticut settlers whom the government at Philadelphia was powerless to displace. Teedyuscung, watching the continuing expansion of the New Englanders' settlements, kept up his protests to English authorities, but to no avail.

In the summer and fall of 1763, the long struggle of the Lenape finally ended. On April 19, Teedyuscung, who had remained with his people in the Wyoming Valley, was burned to death as he slept in his cabin. The fire had been set by agents of the Susquehanna Company who, at the same time, put the entire Indian village to the torch, burning more than 20 houses and chasing their inhabitants into the woods. The destruction of Wyoming was accompanied by other outrages against the Lenape. During July, a group of Indians returning from Philadelphia, where they had sold some pelts, stayed at an inn in Bethlehem. The landlord's wife, who had an intense hatred of Indians, urged her white patrons to violence, stating that she "would freely give a gallon of rum to any one of them that would kill one of those black devils." Before the night was over, the Indians had been robbed of their money and goods by drunken whites and ejected from the inn. Although they sought legal redress through the local magistrate, the whites told them they would be murdered if they lingered in Bethlehem or attempted to bring charges against their attackers. Prudently, they fled. In August of 1763, Zachery, his wife, Zippora, and his infant son (Christian Indians from the northern part of Northampton County) were set upon by a company of soldiers. Zachery and his child were murdered while the terrified Indian woman begged on her knees for their lives. Later, she too was killed. Once again, the authorities did nothing.

By fall, the Lenape were ready for revenge. Early in October, Captain Bull, Teedyuscung's son, descended with a war party on Northhampton County, killing 54 persons. Shortly after, they struck the Connecticut settlement at Wyoming, where between 30 and 40 persons remained, in spite of the likelihood of Indian attack. The A.F.C. Wallace account, *Teedyuscung: King of the Delawares*, relates:

> On them, Captain Bull took his revenge. Nine men and one woman were tortured to death on the spot. The woman was roasted over a fire; red hot hinges were inserted into the joints of her hands. "Several of the men had awls thrust into their Eyes, and Spears, arrows, Pitchforks, &c sticking in their Bodies." The dead were scalped, and some of the houses burned ... About twenty persons were led off into captivity. Only three of four of the population escaped death or capture.

These attacks sealed the fate of the Indians. The government could not protect them, as groups like the Paxton Boys at Lancaster were killing every Indian they could find—man, woman, and child. Nor were they sufficiently numerous or well-armed to protect themselves. Those who could escape the wrath of the frontiersmen fled into the wilderness, first to Wyalusing on the Susquehanna and, after 1768, west of the Alleghenies. By the 19th century, the remnants of the tribe were scattered throughout Oklahoma, Indiana, and Canada.

The Pennamite War between Connecticut and Pennsylvania was not finally settled until the 1770s. Although no actual fighting took place between the two colonies, it was a struggle of major consequence. First, the aggressiveness of the Connecticut settlers sparked a conflict between the whites and Indians which not only caused enormous bloodshed, but also, by its conclusion, had eradicated the Indian presence in the colony. Secondly, the impotence of the British government and its agents in dealing with the Connecticut invaders and the Indians permanently discredited English officialdom in the eyes of the settlers. This alienation would have much to do with the enthusiasm with which the inhabitants of the Lehigh Valley would greet the outbreak of the American Revolution. Finally, the Yankee invasion, while confined to regions north of the Lehigh Valley, had much to do with the hostility and suspicion with which Yankees would be henceforth regarded among the predominantly German inhabitants of the area. Alienated from Philadelphia to the south and the Yankee cities to the north, the Germans of the Lehigh Valley would be forced to develop their own cultural and economic resources.

War and Peace in the Lehigh Valley

With the eradication of the Lenape in the early 1760s, the people of the Lehigh Valley passed beyond the frontier stage and began to build their own distinctive version of the American Dream. Virtually every corner of Lehigh and Northampton counties was dotted with farms, taverns, and mills by the last quarter of the 18th century. The towns grew rapidly. In 1752 Easton, at the confluence of the Lehigh and Delaware rivers, had only 12 families. By 1763, 63 houses had been built, including 8 taverns. And the entire spectrum of civilized skills and professions was represented among its 250 inhabitants, from attorneys, blacksmiths, and carpenters, through hatters, physicians, tailors, and weavers. Similarly, Allentown, which was laid out in 1762, grew from 15 families in the first year of settlement to 56 by 1773. Bethlehem, the largest and oldest town in the valley, contained a population of nearly 500 by the 1780s.

Bethlehem was the metropolis of the Lehigh Valley during this period. Unlike Easton—which owed its growth to the Penns' promotional activities, its strategic location at the juncture of the Delaware and Lehigh rivers, and its establishment as Northampton County's shire town—or Allentown—which was the result of land speculation pure and simple—the size and character of Bethlehem were products of the radical Protestants who had first settled it in 1741. The Moravians, or Unity of Brethren (*Unitas Fratrum*) were descended from a reformation movement that antedated the preachings of Martin Luther by almost a century. Many members became influential in the Pietist movement within the German Lutheran Church during the closing decades of the 17th century. Persecuted by the authorities, they came under the protection of Count Nicholas Ludwig von Zinzendorf. On his estate in Saxony, they built the first of the religious communities that would soon spread to North America.

The Moravian settlement in Pennsylvania occurred accidentally. The sect had originally hoped to colonize Georgia, a party of 10 arriving at Savannah in 1735. The non-Moravians, however, proved unfriendly—especially after the Moravians refused to bear arms against Spanish marauders from neighboring Florida. In Georgia, however, the Moravians encountered George Whitefield, the Presbyterian evangelist. Whitefield, who owned a large tract of land which included the present sites of Bethlehem and Nazareth, had hoped to establish in the Pennsylvania wilderness a school for Negroes and a sanctuary for English debtors. He proposed that the Moravians come to his "Barony of Nazareth" to begin building houses for his beneficiaries. The Moravians, under the leadership of Peter Boehler, arrived on the site of Nazareth in May of 1741, and immediately set to the task of building a commodious log house. By fall, Whitefield had joined them—and began a theological debate that resulted in their expulsion from the barony. Fortunately, the Moravians had made friends among the other settlers, including Nathanial Irish, land agent for William Allen. After debating whether to move to Philadelphia or New York, the Moravians cast their lot for a tract of Allen's land at the junction of the Lehigh and the Monocacy rivers. By the next year, when Whitefield found himself in financial distress, they were able to purchase his holdings in the Lehigh Valley.

The Moravian settlement grew rapidly from that point on. The pioneers were soon joined by some of their brethren from

Peter Boehler established a Moravian settlement at Nazareth in May 1741. The Moravians intended to settle in Georgia, but a hostile reception there drove them north into the Pennsylvania wilderness. Courtesy, Moravian Museum of Bethlehem

Count Nicholaus Ludwig von Zinzendorf provided religious freedom to the pietists on his estate in Saxony. Zinzendorf later visited the Moravian settlement of Bethlehem in December 1741. Courtesy, Moravian Museum of Bethlehem

The radical Protestant Moravians settled Bethlehem in 1741, and the first log structure was built in the same year. The steep roof shed snow while the deep eaves kept water out of the house. Courtesy, Moravian Museum of Bethlehem

ABOVE
The Northampton County Courthouse was built in Bethlehem in 1754. Structures such as this symbolized the new power of government in the land. The establishment of counties bound regions together with a common name and identity. (NCHGS)

LEFT
This steeple on the Central Moravian Church of Bethlehem served as the public address platform for the Moravian community. The weather vane atop the steeple is dated 1803, the year the construction of the church began. Photo by Adrienne Snelling

Germany. It became a center for missionary activities among the Indians. Moravian evangelists on their holy errand into the wilderness were responsible not only for the settlement of much of Northampton County, but also points to the westward in Pennsylvania and Ohio.

The Moravians regarded religion as the organizing principle of their lives. Accordingly, they devoted their property and their labor to the collective purpose of doing God's work. Their everyday life was governed by the community's religious leaders, who separated its members by age, sex, and spiritual seniority. They bent their every effort to protecting their followers from temptation by worldly outsiders. Although the more overtly communistic regulations of the community were abandoned by 1762, the ownership of real estate in the towns that they controlled—Bethlehem, Emmaus, and Nazareth—remained restricted to the Moravian Church until the 1840s. The social institutions of the church, including separate dormitories for single men and women, remained options for members of the sect until well into the 19th century. The pooling of their resources and the coordination of their activities enabled the Moravians to mount educational, cultural, and missionary ventures that belied their location on the frontier. Within months of their first settlement, the strains of fugues and cantatas could be heard on the banks of the Lehigh. And they encouraged musical originality among their members, one of whom, David Moritz Michael, wrote a composition entitled "The Lehigh Valley Water Music," in imitation of Handel's elegant composition for King George II. At the first performance of this piece, the musicians, according to Bethlehem historian W. Ross Yates, "rode on a flatboat propelled up the Lehigh while the audience strolled along the bank."

The Moravians also encouraged the visual arts. John Valentine Haidt, who arrived in Bethlehem in 1754, was one of the most skilled portraitists in colonial America. He had received his training in Berlin, Venice, and London. He was employed by the church to paint its leading members and to produce religious scenes. He and his successors created a visual record of life in an early American community that is unrivalled, even by major cities like New York and Boston. The Moravians did not confine their interests to aesthetic and religious matters. They were accomplished engineers and architects. Their pumped water system at Bethlehem, the first in North America, began operation in 1754. Moravian architects built large structures of stone and brick that still stand today, unimpaired by almost two and a half centuries of use. And Moravian engineers laid out

George Taylor, one of the first men to manufacture iron near Easton and Catasauqua, was the 30th man to sign the Declaration of Independence on August 2, 1776. (NCHGS)

During the American Revolution the Liberty Bell was hidden in the basement of Zion's Reformed Church in Allentown to prevent its capture by the Tories. The efforts of the British to acquire the bell added to its mystique. From John Grafton, *The American Revolution*, Dover

the roads that made Bethlehem the hub of the region.

The American Revolution left tiny Allentown, busy Easton, and cosmopolitan Bethlehem physically untouched; for the centers of fighting lay to the north in New England, New York, and New Jersey, and to the south in Virginia and the Carolinas. While most of the Moravians were pacifists and did not fight in the war, they maintained a stance of friendly neutrality towards the patriots. Among the non-Moravians, however, support for the cause of independence was almost universal. When the people of the county (which included the present counties of Lehigh and Northampton) were called upon to swear oaths of allegiance to the Continental Congress in 1777, 4,821 subscribed to the declarations. Only 59 refused. By May of 1775, over 2,000 volunteers stood ready for military service. George Taylor, the pioneer iron manufacturer of Easton and Catasauqua, was one of those who stepped forward to sign the Declaration of Independence.

The Lehigh Valley had much to gain from the revolution. An unusually fertile and productive agricultural region, it was a major supplier of provisions to the Continental armies. The struggling government set up military hospitals at Easton, Bethlehem, and Allentown. Among the disabled soldiers who recuperated in the valley was the young Marquis de LaFayette, who had been wounded at the Battle of Brandywine in 1777. As Philadelphia fell to the British in the autumn of that year, the Lehigh Valley became a place of refuge for the patriots. The Liberty Bell, symbol of the new nation's aspirations, was transported to Allentown and hidden in the basement of Zion's Reformed Church to prevent it from falling into the hands of the Tories. Bethlehem became an important meeting place for patriot leaders. The Founding Fathers—Washington, Adams, Jefferson, and Hancock—and such military notables as Casimir Pulaski, Baron von Steuben, Henry Knox, Nathanael Greene, and John Paul Jones, all spent time in Bethlehem during the war. But the most important effect of the war on the Lehigh Valley involved the development of manufacturing, particularly of desperately needed armaments. Many of the German craftsmen of the area were descendants of ancient arms-making families in central Europe. Bringing their skills and tools to the wilderness, they had been quick to adapt the European rifle to frontier uses, producing the remarkably accurate and dependable Pennsylvania rifle. As the patriotic armies mustered, the armorers of the Lehigh Valley set to work, producing thousands of swords and guns. Just south of Easton, the Durham ironworks of George Taylor and Richard Backhouse made larger ordnance (cannons and cannonballs) out of native iron ore. The stimulus of war lay the basis for the subsequent industrial development of the region, which would be largely devoted to the mining and manufacturing of ferrous metals.

With the end of the war, the artisans and farmers of the Lehigh Valley returned to their normal pursuits. In spite of a promising start, the area did not continue along the path of industrial development. Progress along this line would have to wait for the further development of the young nation's economy. The Lehigh Valley remained largely rural. Of the 25,000 inhabitants of the region in 1800, less than 2,000 lived in its three largest towns. And it was even more Germanic than it had been before the war, for many of the Scotch-Irish of Northampton County, unwilling to support the struggle for independence, had departed for places where King George was more favorably regarded.

As the farms in the countryside grew more prosperous, producing surpluses of grain, dairy products, and cattle, the towns grew larger. Not only were they entrepôts for farm products bound for the coastal cities, they also became trading centers where the farmers went to sell their goods and purchase what they could not make or grow themselves. The general stores of the valley sold tools, gunpowder, English china, and West Indian goods—coffee, spices, rum, and tobacco. Craftsmen in the towns made the farmers' clocks, guns, shoes, and saddlery. The towns were also centers of information. In the taverns the farmers, artisans, and merchants wrangled over state and national politics, exchanged gossip, and renewed old friendships. Their arguments as well as their sense of identity were no doubt fueled by German-language newspapers, which had been published in Philadelphia as early as the 1750s and which, by 1810, were being printed in Easton and Allentown.

After almost three-quarters of a century of being alternately flattered and neglected by the English-speaking politicians of Philadelphia, the Pennsylvania-Germans were beginning to recognize where their political interests lay. Profoundly conservative, tied by choice to the land, and intensely suspicious of officialdom of any kind, the Germans were quick to oppose efforts to increase the power of both state and national governments. In 1789, they stood fast against the ratification of the Constitution, which proposed to unite the former colonies. In 1790, they voted against the efforts of the mercantile interests to create a state government with a stronger executive branch and less representative legislative body. With the rise of national political parties in the mid-1790s, they became ardent supporters of Thomas Jefferson who, like themselves, was a farmer and a champion of individual and states' rights.

The Pennsylvania-Germans' devotion to self-government was so great that, in 1798, when Federalist President John Adams attempted to levy a direct federal tax on real estate in order to finance the unpopular undeclared war with France, they rose in rebellion. Liberty poles were erected throughout the Lehigh Valley and the old revolutionary slogans about taxation without representation were heard in the taverns and other meeting places. When federal marshals arrested those who had refused to pay the tax, John Fries, a former Revolutionary War officer, led two companies of riflemen and a company of calvary (140 armed men) to Bethlehem to effect their release. The rebellion was finally suppressed in the spring of 1799, but only after the President mobilized a militia from the Philadelphia area, who arrested Fries and the movement's other leaders. The suppression of the rebellion gave the Pennsylvania Germans yet another reason for distrusting the English-speaking politicians and merchants of Philadelphia.

This localism and cultural insularity did not, for the most part, cause the inhabitants of the Lehigh Valley to turn away from the greater world. While it is true that the Moravians became increasingly withdrawn and isolated, outcasts even among their fellow Germans for their neutrality during the revolution and their acquiescence to federal authority during Fries Rebellion, the majority of Pennsylvania Germans were actively interested in commerce and politics. Indeed, with Jefferson's election to the presidency in 1800 and the subsequent relaxing of suffrage laws, they became major participants in state politics, promoting the movement of Pennsylvania's capital to Harrisburg and, after 1820, electing a series of Pennsylvania Germans to the governorship. The Lehigh Valley stood ready to do its part in building the state and nation. But it would do so on its own terms.

View of Bethlehem was painted in 1840 by Carl Bodmer. This tranquil scene, painted before industrialization had seriously begun, conveys the peaceful atmosphere that Bethlehem was able to preserve for many years. Courtesy, Amon Carter Museum, Fort Worth, Texas

CHAPTER THREE

BEFORE THE COMING OF INDUSTRY: 1760-1830

Not much is known about the early settlers of the Lehigh Valley. Their names can be traced from passenger lists filed with the provincial government, through land and court records, militia lists, and the colonial and federal censuses of the late 18th and early 19th centuries. But these sources reveal little about how the early inhabitants lived, and they reveal almost nothing about how they came to create the distinctive way of life that survives, even today, in the Lehigh Valley.

Europeans would begin establishing permanent settlements in the Lehigh Valley by the late 1720s. Before coming, some had been skilled craftsmen; many had been farmers. Even though they sought to settle on land that was similar to what they had been familiar with in Germany, Switzerland, and southwestern France—gently rolling, well-watered, limestone-based soils—they could not simply recreate their old lives in the new world. In Europe, the land had been tamed. It had been carefully farmed for thousands of years; and it was valuable and scarce. Living in their farmhouses clustered in manorial villages, the German peasants who would eventually settle the Lehigh Valley tended narrow strips of land in outlying fields. They planted the crops that their forefathers had planted, shared their labor and tools at sowing and harvesting time, and pastured their livestock in common fields.

While the Lehigh Valley would be familiar in its soil and topography, it would still be a strange new land. It was an untamed wilderness. The first task was to survive. The forests had to be felled, basic shelters built, and the ground broken for crops. Having no machines, few animals, and only the crudest hand tools, everything had to be done by muscle power. Not surprisingly, life in the Lehigh Valley up through the 1780s was very primitive. The solid stone barns and farmhouses, the abundant fields of grain, the orchards, and the pastures of fat cattle that we associate with the Pennsylvania-German farm country lay far in the future. At first the settlers huddled together in crude log huts of one or two rooms while their scrawny hogs, cows, and horses ran at large, foraging for sustenance among the stumps in half-cleared fields or in the swamps and forests.

Only later did the familiar image of stolid prosperity begin to emerge, and when it did, the culture of the Pennsylvania-Germans, while bearing some resemblance to its Old World origins, had evolved into something quite different. In their years of struggle, the people had been compelled to adapt what they had brought with them to the conditions of a new and unfamiliar world. Their diet, clothing, social customs, methods of farming, and patterns of settlement owed much to the unaccustomed abundance of the valley. Every married man had his own farm, his own tools, and his own livestock. He strove with each passing year to improve what he had. It was not easy to give up old ways of life, but survival was a stern instructor. If buckskin was what was most available, it was what people wore; if maize, pumpkins, and beans—which were unknown in Europe—grew best, that was what people ate. Habits learned in times of necessity were not given up with the passing of the frontier. The Pennsylvania-German farmers continued to work on their improved lands as hard as they had when they were wresting them from the wilderness. Even when artisan skills from the Old World were preserved and passed on to sons, the artisans were, first and foremost, farmers.

Farm life was relentless in its demands, for the hardy yeomen produced virtually everything that they consumed and consumed very little that they did not produce. Even the few necessities that they could not make or grow themselves—gunpowder, salt, spices, metal tools and weapons, and the services of millers, shoemakers, gunsmiths, wheelwrights, and other artisans—they obtained not with money, but by trading the products of their labor or, at times, their labor itself.

No one was idle, except perhaps the very young and the very old. Childhood was not a carefree time. It was the beginning of a long apprenticeship in the skills of self-sufficiency that would not end until a boy or girl married and went off to become masters or mistresses of their own little commonwealths. Toddlers began their working lives picking stones and weeds from their mothers' flower and vegetable gardens. As they grew older, girls learned from their mothers the skills that would make them assets to their hardworking husbands. They learned to grow and prepare food. This involved more than cooking: they helped in the sowing and harvesting, the slaughtering and the butchering. They transformed these raw products into a year's store-drying, smoking, salting, pickling, and baking. (Canning would be unknown in the region until after the Civil War.) Learning how to clothe a family similarly encompassed a whole range of productive processes. Flax—the fibrous plant from which linen was made—had to be planted, harvested, soaked, beaten, and made into thread. Sheep had to be sheared, their wool cleaned, carded, and spun into yarn. These yarns and threads had to be woven or knitted into cloth that could, in turn, be made into garments. Hauling water from the streams and wells was also women's work, as was cooking over the great hearth that also provided the only heat in the early farm house. And the almost unending task of bearing and raising children punctuated the heavy tasks of the farm woman's year.

Boys, by the age of five or six, were driving cattle to pasture, cleaning barns, milking, and pitching hay and straw as well as learning to plant, plow, and harvest, and to doctor and butcher animals. Hunting and fishing were important survival skills, as was the woodcraft that made it possible for a farmer with only a knife and an axe to build or make almost anything, from a delicately carved toy to a commodious barn.

Farm life involved an unvarying and unending cycle of activity, since the struggle to stay fed, clothed, and sheltered was a full-time job. There was no retirement, no vacation, and no season of idleness. The year began in spring as the snows melted off the fields. As the sap rose in the maple trees, it was gathered and cooked down to make maple sugar and syrup, the only sweetener besides honey available to the Lehigh farmers. As the ground began to dry, root crops—potatoes, carrots, beets, and turnips—had to be planted, fields had to be plowed, and summer wheat had to be sown. The winter's accumulations of manure had to be moved away from the barn and spread on the fields. Sheep had to be shorn of their wool. When the weather was warm enough, in late April and early May, it was time to plant corn, squash, beans, and pumpkins, and to harvest winter wheat and rye. The grain had to be laboriously separated from the chaff, and the straw set aside for making baskets, hats, and beehives, and for animal feed.

The heat of summer brought no rest, for the high sun and the fertile soil sprouted weeds that had to be hoed. Summer wheat had to be harvested and the ground readied for the planting of winter wheat. The orchards and berry patches would begin to bear, starting with strawberries and—as the weather began to cool—apples, peaches, pears, and nuts. Hemp and flax was harvested and processed. Throughout the season,

ABOVE
Listed on the Lehigh County tax rolls in 1798 as a 25-foot by 20-foot log structure, Philip Bennighof's house was assessed at $150. The Bennighof family was among the original settlers of Lowhill Township. (LCHS)

LEFT
This hand-carved and hand-painted toy is called a whirligig. Farmers were adept at woodcraft and made most of their families' toys and furniture. Courtesy, collection of Mr. & Mrs. David Mest; photo by Adrienne Snelling

Early farmhouse kitchens in Lehigh Valley typically had walk-in fireplaces that provided heat for cooking and also warmed the rest of the house. The hearth served as the focus of house activities, especially in winter months. Photo by Adrienne Snelling (LCHS)

milk was made into butter and cheese; hay was cut, raked, and stored; and corn, the cattle's major food, was harvested and put in cribs. After the first frost, it was time to slaughter the animals for winter's consumption, utilizing not only their meat, but their viscera for sausage casings, and their hides for shoes and clothing; and the frost marked the time to begin the greatest of winter tasks—the endless cutting, hauling, and splitting of firewood for the voracious hearths.

In many ways the struggles of the Pennsylvania-German pioneers in the 18th century were the same as those of any group settling on the American frontier before the Revolution, but there were important differences. The horrors of religious warfare in Europe, in which the possession of a single piece of territory might pass, within 30 years, between half a dozen governments, had made the Pennsylvania-Germans intensely suspicious of all authority. This suspicion was intensified by their experiences with the English colonial government and their encounters with aggressive New Englanders in the northern part of the valley.

Even though they had become prosperous by the beginning of the 19th century, they remained wary of the English-speaking social and economic mainstream. Unlike the Yankee farmers, who borrowed money to finance improvements and altered their agriculture to suit commercial demands, the Pennsylvania-German farmer did not eagerly embrace the opportunities of the marketplace. Even though the Revolution had demonstrated the marketability of nonagricultural resources of the region—iron, timber, and manufactured goods—they did not rush to open mines in their fields, or cut down their woodlands to supply the wood dealers and sawmills of Philadelphia. Their English-speaking neighbors, while admiring their industriousness, considered them hopelessly unenterprising and backward. They did not realize that the Pennsylvania-Germans knew that the price of pursuing wealth as an end in itself could lead to the erosion of family life—as sons spurned their fathers to go off and seek their fortunes—and a loss of independence as the inevitable consequence of indebtedness, along with a loss of language and religious traditions.

Thus, while the Yankees were quick to extract from their land what they could before moving on to the West or into commerce and manufacturing, the Pennsylvania-Germans single-mindedly kept at the task of improving the land, manuring and liming their soil to maintain its productivity, replacing makeshift wooden structures with stout fieldstone farmhouses and the famous "Swisser" barns built into the sides of hills.

TOP
Die Gawidder Miel, or "The Thunderstorm Mill," was located just beyond Emmaus. The mill, nearly 150 years old, could only operate when a hard rainstorm provided enough water to turn the wheel, hence the name by which such mills were popularly known. (LCHS)

ABOVE
William Parsons, surveyor general of Pennsylvania, built this home for George Taylor in 1757. Taylor signed the Declaration of Independence. The house has been maintained by the George Taylor Chapter of the Daughters of the American Revolution since 1906. (Windsor)

They avoided such speculative fevers as the "merino mania" of the years 1810-1816 in which some farmers paid as much as $1,500 for a single ram, only to see the price for the animal fall, by 1817, to a mere five or ten dollars; and the "fat cattle craze" of the 1820s, in which steers and oxen were bred for size and force-fed until they weighed thousands of pounds. While the farmers of New England were mortgaging their farms to invest in agricultural fads and in turnpike and canal speculations, the Pennsylvania-Germans of the Lehigh Valley doggedly went their own way.

The fundamentally agrarian nature of the people of the Lehigh Valley gave the towns a unique character. Unlike towns situated in the heart of other agricultural regions, the Lehigh Valley towns of Easton, Allentown, and Bethlehem did not drain off the wealth of the surrounding countryside. Although the population of urban areas in the nation increased at almost double the rate of rural areas between 1790 and 1830, the towns of the Lehigh Valley grew no faster than the rural townships around them. The earliest paintings of Easton, Allentown, and Bethlehem show them, in the 1820s and 1830s, to be small clusters of buildings set amid pastures and fields.

Allentown, although it was the fastest growing town in the area (having become the seat of Lehigh County, which had been set off from Northampton County in 1811), was remarkably pastoral. In 1814, nearly all of its 160 households kept cows; and their inhabitants undoubtedly grew most of their produce in gardens on the generous house lots laid out by William Allen in his "Town Plan" of 1762. At the town's center was a marketplace where farmers came to sell their surplus produce. Several prominent citizens operated farms of considerable size within the town limits. Nearly all of Allentown's residents were artisans, taverners, or storekeepers whose livelihoods were closely tied to the activities of nearby farmers. With a population too small to constitute a market for the services it offered, Allentown could be no more than an adjunct of the countryside.

The strong ties between town and countryside were not coincidental. They were a product of the Pennsylvania-German's profoundly traditional attitudes which regarded land as the only real source of security and the family and the Scriptures as the only true sources of authority. Because the rural Pennsylvania-Germans felt so strongly about the land and the family, they endeavored, through their inheritance practices, to keep family farms intact. They did this by leaving farms to their eldest sons. The younger sons were not neglected, however, for

their older brothers were usually required to pay them the cash value of their shares in the paternal estate. For example, when Peter Meyer of Upper Saucon died in 1813, he left the bulk of his estate to his eldest son, Jacob; to his younger son, Peter, he gave the use of 12 acres of woodland and an additional 40 acres. Jacob, as head of the family, bore heavy and continuing responsibilities toward his mother and his younger siblings. He had to pay his younger brother £375 in annual installments of £25. He had to care for his mother, giving her use of her bedroom and kitchen in the family farmhouse; he had to plow and sow a quarter of an acre of potatoes and flax annually; help his mother with the kitchen garden, provide her with a pasture and stable for her cow, and give her three bushels of wheat, seven and half bushels of rye, six bushels of corn, 250 pounds of pork, 50 pounds of beef, one barrel of cider, five pounds of clear wool, and, as Meyer noted in the will, "as many apples as she wants." Jacob also had financial responsibilities toward his married sisters. Thus, while the eldest son inherited the family farm (which was kept intact rather than divided between the children in the New England fashion) his patrimony carried with it continuing responsibilities that kept him closely tied to his brothers and sisters and they to him.

The younger brothers most often used the monies left them to buy farms in other places. Those who didn't often went into Allentown and Easton and set themselves up as storekeepers or craftsmen. They carried their rural sensibilities and their family loyalties with them into the towns. If they did well, they invested their savings in farms or in city real estate in preference to the more risky but more lucrative investments in banks, canals, turnpikes, and manufactures that were so attractive to Yankees; and they not infrequently returned to farming. Even if they remained in town, they maintained close ties to their brothers and sisters in the country, helping them to find markets for their goods and assisting their sons and daughters in finding mates and careers.

Typical of this pattern is the Eckert family of Allentown. In 1838, when William Eckert left his family's farm in Salisbury Township, he moved with his wife and four children to Allentown. There he went into the tobacco business with his cousin, John Eckert. John and William trained their sons as tobacconists and, when they came of age, set them up as partners in business. This business relationship was cemented by the marriage of William's son, William H. Eckert, to John's daughter, Lydia. Interestingly, of William H. Eckert's 12 children, most of them went back to farming, on Nebraska lands in which their father

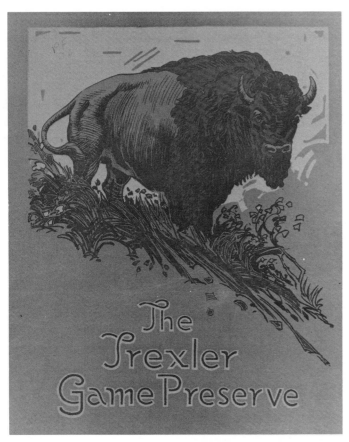

This is the cover of a promotional brochure describing the Trexler Game Preserve. A herd of non-native buffalo roamed the preserve. (LCHS)

had invested.

A similar pattern can be seen in the Trexler family, pioneer Lehigh Valley farmers. Although the three sons of Reuben Trexler (1804-1840) all went into commerce as partners in a lumber business, all bought farms. Reuben's grandson, Harry Clay Trexler, became one of the most successful industrialists in the area. But he was fascinated with farms, bought hundreds of them, and, by the early 20th century, was the major agricultural innovator in the region.

As one writer in Allentown in the 1880s noted:

It is not therefore, to be wondered at that nearly two hundred years' intermarriage among the Pennsylvania Dutch has produced the curious human mosaic that is to be met with hereabouts today. Family ramifications extend in every direction. The people of every village, town, and township, seem to be more or less inextricably interwoven in marriage relationship. Almost every man you meet can consume a half-day telling you the various branches of his family that run throughout the county. This kinship, within certain limits, produces the relationship known as freundschaft, *a term of widest business and political significance. The word is German and literally means friendship, but is substituted for the proper word* verwandtschaft, *or relationship. Its potency, however, is far-reaching and subtle. It is responsible for numerous traits and conditions for whose existence ethnology fails to account. While it is often powerless to impose the moral obligation of materially helping your neighbor, or of attending his funeral unless within a narrow circle, it is of towering importance if you nurse political aspirations. It is here it exercises its widest field and is productive of a condition that places the freundschaftless candidate for office, for instance, in about the same position as the gentleman occupied, who once promenaded between the devil and the deep sea.*

Unlike the sons of Yankees who went to the cities in the early 19th century to seek their fortunes with nothing but their wits and the clothes on their backs, landless Pennsylvania-German younger sons could, when they came into Allentown or Easton, find kinsmen on whom they could depend for guidance and support. And they could reasonably expect, if they so desired, to return to the land—as many of them ultimately did.

This ongoing relationship between country and town led to a perpetuation of rural conservatism. The towns, rather than becoming outposts for the spread of economic, political, and religious activities inimical to the preservation of Pennsylvania-German culture were, rather, citadels of resistance to the English-speaking mainstream. When the Pennsylvania legislature attempted, in 1809, 1824, and 1834, to force the towns to set up tax-supported public schools, the Pennsylvania-Germans in both town and country stoutly resisted, claiming that the term "free schools" mandated by the statutes was inappropriate to institutions that they were forced to support. As educator Henry Muhlenberg would later write,

The Germans of our state are not opposed to education as such but only to any system that seems to them to trench on their parental and natural rights. They still retain the German theory of education—that the child belongs first to God, then to the parents, then to the state. The chief responsibility for their education, therefore, rests on church and parents. Their educational system is preeminently a religious one ... . An additional reason, of course, is their attachment to their own dialect.

In the view of the Pennsylvania-German parents, the public schools—which were nonsectarian and English-speaking— would have undermined both morality and parental authority. They were not entirely mistaken in their suspicions, for the English-speaking political leaders of Pennsylvania had, since the 1750s, feared the power of the Germans as a group and encouraged efforts, especially educational ones, that might dilute their power.

A conservative cultural stand on education did not result, however, in a lack of educational opportunity in the Lehigh Valley. Private academies in Easton, Bethlehem, and Allentown, as well as in a number of the rural townships, were established in the early years of the 19th century and were modestly successful in educating the children of the well-to-do. Certain institutions, like the Moravian Seminary, had been going concerns since the mid-18th century. Nor were the Pennsylvania-Germans uniformly opposed to all public education. The father of public education in the state is generally considered to be George Wolfe, a Pennsylvania-German farmer's son from Northampton County. Nevertheless, public education made halting progress in the region. Allentown had no public school until 1837. In the countryside, illiteracy remained common until after the Civil War. It was only through the strenuous efforts of such educational reformers as A.R. Horne in the 1870s and 1880s that the prejudices against formal learning were finally overcome.

The solid alliance of town and country can also be seen in the religious controversies of the early 19th century. America as a nation was, from the late 1790s through the 1840s, shaken by a series of religious revivals known as the Second Great Awakening. Although the Presbyterian and Episcopal churches had been profoundly shaken by this movement, which began within them, but soon broke off into a variety of evangelical sects, the Lutheran and Reformed churches to which most of the Pennsylvania-Germans belonged were largely unaffected. In 1792, however, Jacob Albright, a German farmer of Lancaster County, became a convert to the Methodists, an evangelical offshoot of the Episcopal church. In 1796, he became a lay preacher, touring Lebanon, Bucks, Schuylkill, and Northampton counties and devoting his energies to the conversion of the Germans. By 1803, he had recruited enough followers to form his own German-Methodist church, the Evangelical Association, which sent young men into the villages, farms, and towns of the Lehigh Valley in search of converts. These evangelists were met with stout opposition, not only from the established ministers, who saw Albright's followers as rivals and who resented the Evangelicals' attacks on their preaching and doctrines, but also from conscientious parents, who saw the new sect as another threat to their authority over their children. Evangelical ministers were met by mobs. A. Stapleton, in his history of evangelism, states that when the Reverend J.G. Zinzer attempted to preach at the house of John Hittle in Upper Milford Township in 1831,

the house was surrounded by a mob who howled and yelled like so many demons, so that it was impossible to conduct the services.

Some miscreant, bolder than the rest, hurled a stone into the window, which was the signal for a general attack. The windows were quickly demolished and some of the inmates were hit by flying missiles. By crouching in a corner beyond the line of the windows, most of the people escaped bodily harm. The pandemonium continued several hours. Eventually, after many of the rowdies had withdrawn, David Shubert, with his daughters, and a few others, ventured out to escape to their homes. They were, however, discovered, and were stoned and clubbed in a terrible manner. A daughter of Mr. Shubert almost lost her life by being ridden down by a fiend on horseback, who made three attempts to kill her in this way.

Similar scenes were enacted throughout the Lehigh Valley between the beginning of the century and the mid-1830s. But, just as with the establishment of public schools, tradition began to give way to the new religious fervor. The turning point came in 1831, when Francis Gabel of Upper Milford came down to Cedar Creek, near Allentown, to work in the woolen mill of

Wm Oberly

William Oberly brewed the first beer in Allentown in 1850 at the Old Brewery on Sixth and Union streets. Patriotic fervor extended to inking in an American flag on the pole behind the brewery. William Oberly appears at upper left. (LCHS)

General Henry Mertz and his son, David. Gabel was a steady and reliable workman. He was also an enthusiastic Evangelical. As he bore witness to his beliefs in his work and conversation, he soon won the confidence of his employer and his employer's family. David Mertz and his wife became converts and were soon followed by General Mertz and others in the vicinity, who had been members of the Lutheran congregation. The Mertz's defection to the Evangelicals caused great agitation in the community. The pastor of the Lutheran Church to which the Mertzes had belonged preached a sermon on Sunday against the "Albrights" and those who supported them. The showdown between the Mertzes and the religious establishment is described by A. Stapleton in his *Flashlights on Evangelical History:*

The pastor, in his discourse, most bitterly assailed the Evangelical preachers as heretics and deceivers, and also denounced, without naming, a high official of his church for permitting the Evangelicals to preach in his house. This everyone understood to be General Mertz.

After the close of the service, the battle opened in earnest by the pastor, who turned on General Mertz. He accused him of being the chief cause of the inroads of the Evangelicals because he permitted them to preach at his son David's house. As an official of his Church, he forbade the General to any longer permit the meetings on his estate.

Upon this peremptory order, General Mertz asserted his rights as a citizen to do as he pleased in the matter, and turning the tables on his pastor, told him that since his son's connection with the Evangelicals he was a better man. He told him that drunkenness, profanity, and disorders were prevalent in the community and the pastor had never lifted up his voice against it. He said that Evangelical preachers were necessary, because they did what he failed to do. For this reason he declared that he would not change his course, and that the matter rested with his son David. . . . The Mertz family left the church without being harmed, but they returned no more.

The conversion of a family as wealthy, prominent, and energetic as the Mertzes soon had its effect. By 1838, the first Evangelical congregation was organized in Allentown. It built a church on a lot given to it by General Mertz, his son David, his son-in-law, Solomon Butz, and two others. The Mertz children and grandchildren became active in the mercantile and social life of Allentown, spreading their religious convictions, which were to influence a significant number of Pennsylvania-Germans, as they went.

Thus, ironically, it was the countryside rather than the city that took the lead in altering the Pennsylvania-German Old

World heritage and adapting it to the conditions of the young republic. In coming to evangelical Protestantism in this way, the Pennsylvania-Germans, rather than merely resisting change, accommodated themselves to it and made it their own. The Evangelicals conducted their services in German, thus preserving the German language. At the same time, by giving greater emphasis to the role of the individual and his own conscience, the Evangelicals prepared the young people of the Lehigh Valley for the temptations and challenges of the capitalist marketplace. This pattern of creative response to challenges—through which tradition accommodated itself to the new without losing its essential character—was a testament to the vitality of Pennsylvania-German culture and to the fact that it was not merely a transplantation of European customs to America, but was a unique interaction of a European heritage with wilderness conditioning and, later, commercial and industrial development. The close ties between city and town, based on the ties that bound families together, were the foundations of this remarkable adaptability.

Perhaps the best-known product of Pennsylvania-German culture is its folk art—the *frakturs* (illuminated manuscripts), quilts and other needlework, carved and painted chests, metalwork, slip-decorated pottery and ornamented barns. Interestingly, these products were not the result of carefully preserved European traditions. They were, rather, the outcome of the process of challenge and accommodation that characterized the German immigrants' religious and commercial activities. While the immigrants were certainly familiar with Old World traditions of decoration, there is little evidence that they brought them into play until the 1750s, when the Lehigh Valley began to interact extensively with the English-speaking world during the Revolution. The early clothing chests, for example, were relatively simple pieces of cabinet work and had little painted or carved ornamentation; but by the 1750s and 1760s, they not only began to reflect ornate late-Georgian forms in their construction, they also—as if in defense against the intrusion of the new and alien Georgian style—exhibited decorative painting and carving of extraordinary power and beauty. The botanical, faunal, and geometrical motifs—rather than being mere reproductions of traditional motifs brought from the Old World—were in most instances native creations, often based on primitive craftmen's interpretations of printed fabrics originating in Philadelphia and London. The result of the encounter of German and English cultures was not the eradication of German design, but the transformation of German styles into forms that accommodated the English influence but maintained, intensified, and transformed the German motifs into something distinctly American—or, to put it more accurately, something distinctly Pennsylvania-German.

A similar transformation occurred in the evolution of Pennsylvania-German pottery. Individualized eating utensils were unknown to the German settlers of the early 18th century, who, like their medieval ancestors, ate out of common, usually wooden, vessels called trenchers that were placed in the middle of the table. The idea that each person should have his own dish was derived from English culture, in which ideas of individuality were far more developed. While adopting the idea, the Pennsylvania-Germans once again made it their own, eschewing imported English Staffordshire and using, in preference, their own beautifully decorated native redware.

By the 1820s and 1830s, the Lehigh Valley presented rich possibilities to the enterprising. The entrepreneurs of Philadelphia, New York, and Boston looked to its untapped iron, coal, timber, and agricultural resources with eagerness. The Pennsylvania-Germans, however, having created and perpetuated their own distinctive way of life, were not about to permit the Lehigh Valley to be transformed into a colony of avaricious outsiders. Nor were they, like the Amish of Lancaster or the Moravians of Bethlehem, willing to turn their backs on the new. In the end, commerce and industry would develop in the Lehigh Valley along lines quite different from the way it did elsewhere.

The social gulf between owners and laborers characteristic of many industrial cities would be largely absent in the Lehigh Valley of the 19th century, for employers would be reluctant to exploit those who were part of their *freundschaft*; and the laborers, for the same reason, trusted their employers to act in their common interest. Because the Pennsylvania-German community was so powerful and cohesive, industry would come to serve the community; the community would not merely exist for the convenience of industry.

An 1886 history of Allentown by the city's Board of Trade sums up the unique character of Pennsylvania-Dutch society:

You might search every nook and corner of this great country, from Maine to the Gulf, and not find a community so socially untrammelled. The word society has a broader and wider meaning than it has elsewhere. There is an absence of all real or quixotic claims to superiority of birth or lineage that emphasizes Pennsylvania Dutchdom as the paradise of democracy. Wealth is as incapable as it is indisposed to create a distinct social circle. To clothe oneself with zephyrs in Allentown has always been unhealthy. As long as your character is not fly-blown you maintain your social position with becoming indifference to either your wealth or your poverty. This pleasant social condition is a triumph of the unity of ethnical origin, which, taken in connection with the dialect in the past, effectively shut out Anglo Saxon influences elsewhere so potent in molding views, giving color to thought and drawing rigid lines of caste distinction.

FACING PAGE
This strongly-built three drawer chest was constructed for Henrich Schmidt in 1792. Craftsmen often made such objects for a specific buyer. (LCHS)

ABOVE
To some, marriage certificates were more than legal papers. These ornately decorated documents were affirmations of commitment to be displayed prominently in the couples' home. (LCHS)

Mauch Chunk, situated on the Lehigh River, prospered from the anthracite coal mining operations in the Mauch Chunk Mountains. The business activities of the town connected with the mining operations included the manufacture of the machinery required for the mining, transporting, and shipping of coal. From M.S. Henry, *History of the Lehigh Valley*, Easton, 1860

THE TURNING POINT: 1820-1880

The Pennsylvania-Germans of the Lehigh Valley were not alone in their desire to remain simple, honest, independent farmers. Thousands of other Americans shared a belief with their hero and chief spokesman, Thomas Jefferson, that a nation of wage-earners, dependent on the good will of others for their livelihoods, could not long remain a republic. America in 1776 was, overwhelmingly, a nation of family farmers, and the party of Jefferson wanted to keep it that way. But this Arcadian dream could not last.

The basic condition for maintaining independence from Great Britain was not a brave paper declaration or years of bloody fighting. It was economic independence—the ability of the new nation to produce rather than import essential commodities. To continue importing metal goods, tools, textiles, glass, and other essentials from Europe drained America of its wealth and placed it in a bondage more onerous than the chains of colonization it had just thrown off. Moreover, the Revolutionary War had left the states deeply in debt both to domestic creditors (including the farmers and craftsmen of the Lehigh Valley) and to foreign governments and bankers.

As significant as the Constitution itself, which forged the political union of the former colonies, was the financial settlement of the Revolutionary War debt through which the federal government assumed the debts of the states in exchange for their claims on lands west of the Appalachian Mountains. Having taken on this enormous responsibility, which in 1789 amounted to over $77 million, the new government was faced with the task of generating revenue to pay off this debt. Sale of public lands in the West would help. But Alexander Hamilton, chief architect of the new monetary system, recognized that the industrialization of the United States was also essential. Not only would domestic manufactures reduce the republic's dependence on Europe and curtail the flow of funds abroad, it would also, by increasing the amount of taxable property, create revenues that the government could use to retire the national debt.

As it happened, the development of American industry could not take place without the discovery of an abundant new source of fuel. The building of houses and ships—and the voracious fireplaces and forges—had, by the last decade of the 18th century, eradicated the woodlands near the cities. Timber and cordwood began to command prices so high that the search for alternative fuels and construction materials became not only prudent, but essential. Aggravating this scarcity was the effort to promote industrial development, particularly in the metal trades. The early iron industry was dependent on charcoal for fuel; and the production of adequate amounts of charcoal, even for a small iron foundry that used an acre of timber per day when in full blast, resulted in the deforestation of enormous areas. Although abundant woodlands existed inland from the coastal cities, the timber and firewood had to be transported ever-greater distances over bad roads and down barely navigable rivers. The more complicated journey resulted in a higher market price. Thus, demand spread for a fuel that could compensate for increased costs with greater efficiency. Coal was such a fuel. The English had been using it since the 17th century, and many urban Americans, by Revolutionary War times, were burning it as well. The only ready source of American coal, however, lay in Virginia, far from Philadelphia, New York, and Boston. The great expense of mining coal, transporting it to tidewater, and loading it onto ships bound for the city made it a luxury fuel.

The existence of coal on the upper Lehigh River, beyond the Kittatinny Mountains, had been known since the 1760s, when a frontier blacksmith near Wilkes-Barre began using it in his forge as a substitute for charcoal. A few Pennsylvania arms makers used coal during the Revolution, but little was known about it, save the difficulties of getting it to burn in conventional grates and hearths and the fact that the sources of the new fuel lay in areas remote from civilization. Not until the 1790s, with the increasing scarcity of wood and the outburst of entrepreneurial enthusiasm sparked by Alexander Hamilton's economic measures, would anyone attempt to exploit the Lehigh's "black stones" for profit.

In 1792, Philip Ginter, a pioneer who had settled with his family on the wilderness slopes of Mauch Chunk, discovered by accident a large outcropping of anthracite. According to I.D. Rupp's *History of Northampton, Lehigh, Monroe, Carbon, and*

The *Alfred Thomas* exploded in a tragic accident on March 6, 1860. This lithograph provides a broad view of Easton behind the explosion. The two tall spires are part of (left to right) the German Reformed Church and the Brainerd Presbyterian Church, and Lafayette College's first building is on the side of the hill at the right. Courtesy, New York Public Library

TOP
The Lehigh Valley was originally covered by abundant forests. As the fuel needs of industry consumed increasing amounts of wood, timber became more expensive. Industry began using coal as an alternate source of fuel, and wood was restricted to house and ship construction. This logging camp uses a steam-powered sawmill to convert trees to lumber. (LCHS)

ABOVE
In 1792 a hunter named Philip Ginter discovered anthracite coal under the roots of a fallen tree in the Mauch Chunk area. Anthracite soon replaced the softer bituminous coal as the most widely used fuel throughout Pennsylvania. (Windsor)

Schuylkill Counties:

After being out all day with his gun in quest of food, he was returning, towards evening, over the Mauch Chunk mountain, entirely unsuccessful and dispirited; a drizzling rain beginning to fall, and night approaching, he bent his course homeward, considering himself one of the most forsaken of human beings. As he trod slowly over the ground, his foot stumbled against something which, by the stroke, was driven before him; observing it to be black, to distinguish which there was just enough light remaining, he took it up, and as he had often listened to the traditions of the country of the existence of coal in the vicinity, it occurred to him that this might be a portion of that "stone coal" of which he had heard. He accordingly carefully took it with him to his cabin, and the next day carried it to Col. Jacob Weiss, residing at what was then known by the name of Fort Allen.

Jacob Weiss lost no time in bringing the stones to Philadelphia, where he managed to persuade Michael Hillegas, first treasurer of the United States, and Charles Cist, a successful printer, of the commercial possibilities of the fuel. In 1793, they organized the Lehigh Coal Mine Company and obtained from the Commonwealth deeds to 10,000 acres of land in the vicinity of Ginter's discovery. (Ginter had been paid off by the gift of a small tract of land on which he built a mill and a tavern. He lost both when they proved to be standing on property claimed by another owner.) The coal company's owners faced two monumental tasks: first, to create a market for their fuel and then, to provide for its safe and cheap transportation to market. While a demand for an alternative to wood existed, it was by no means clear that anthracite would gain public acceptance. Eighteenth-century Americans were resistant to innovation, and since the fuel would not burn without specially constructed grates, they thought it a nuisance rather than a blessing. Further, transporting large quantities of coal overland to the riverside and then on barges down the tumultuous rapids of the Lehigh and Delaware rivers presented almost insurmountable difficulties. While Weiss, Hillegas, Cist and others expended thousands of dollars in trying to improve the navigation of the river, their efforts proved unsuccessful. When two Philadelphians visited the mines in 1804, all they found were "three or four small pits, which had much the appearance of the commencement of rude wells."

In 1806, shipping was interrupted due to the Napoleonic wars, and the supply of Virginia coal to Philadelphia became uncertain. William Turnbull, an enterprising Philadelphian hoping to revive the fortunes of the promoters of the Lehigh Coal Mine Company, commissioned the construction of a wooden barge (or ark) at Lausanne. Turnbull loaded the barge with anthracite and hired men who successfully navigated the bulky craft downriver to Philadelphia. A portion of cargo was sold to the Philadelphia Water Works for fueling its steam pump engine, an experiment that was conspicuously unsuccessful because the boilers were not equipped with proper grates. The remainder of the shipment was broken up into gravel and spread around the paths of Philadelphia's Center Square.

The promoters were not, however, entirely discouraged, for the value of anthracite was slowly being discovered as blacksmiths and other ironworkers experimented to discover the best way of using it. During the War of 1812, several thousand tons were floated downstream to Philadelphia by Charles Cist and his associate, Charles Miner, a Connecticut Yankee from Wilkes-Barre. One of Cist and Miner's customers was a young manufacturer named Josiah White. He had heard that anthracite had been successfully used at a rolling mill at the falls of the Schuylkill River and, since he could purchase "stone coal" at the bargain price of a dollar a bushel, he decided to attempt to use it in his wire factory. White and his partner, Erskine Hazard, labored mightily to make the fuel burn, using an entire wagonload in their first attempt. They obtained another cartful and continued with the experiment. After several days of fruitless labor, they gave up, closed their mill for the night and went home. One of their laborers, however, had left his coat in the factory. When he returned to retrieve it, he found the furnace door to be red hot and the supposedly unburnable stones burning with a white heat. He excitedly summoned White, Hazard, and his fellow workers who, although it was the middle of the night, proceeded to heat and roll four parcels of iron by a single fire. Hazard and White became converts to anthracite. They sold their iron mill and henceforth devoted their energies to the problems of mining and transporting Lehigh coal.

Late in December of 1817, Josiah White, George F.A. Hauto (an adventurer who claimed to have access to Philadelphia capital), and William Briggs (a stonemason in White's employ) set forth from Philadelphia to inspect the coal fields on the Lehigh River and to determine the best means of transporting Lehigh coal to Philadelphia. They arrived in Bethlehem on Christmas Eve, and proceeded the next day to Lausanne and Lehighton. White was pleased with what he saw. As he noted in his autobiography,

On returning home it was concluded that myself, G.F.A. Hauto & Erskine Hazard would join in the enterprise. I was to find plan, & Hauto the money through his friends & Erskine the Skribe & a good mechanic & excellent councellor. Hoto assured us the larger the plan the easier it would be for him to raise the money, through his rich friends.

The scheme looked good on paper. But White underestimated the difficulties of raising capital among suspicious Philadelphians, many of whom had already lost a good deal of money in earlier navigation improvements, and the obstacles posed by the Lehigh River were greater than he imagined. It would be almost three backbreaking years before the first coal ark descended from Mauch Chunk to Philadelphia.

White and Hazard had no difficulty in buying out the interests of the older dormant coal and navigation companies. The surviving owners of the Lehigh Coal Mine Company were willing to lease their holdings for one ear of corn a year. While the legislature was reluctant to provide financial aid, it quickly gave White and Hazard clear title to river navigation, one member stating that the body was happy to give White and his friends "the privilege of ruining themselves." Having settled these legal matters, White and Hazard, in April of 1818, set off with borrowed instruments to survey the Lehigh River from Mauch Chunk to Easton. Having completed this task, they drew up a prospectus and began calling on potential investors. They were not greeted with enthusiasm: Joseph Bonaparte, son of the Emperor, who had taken up residence outside of Philadelphia, refused to see them; Stephen Girard was not interested in any venture that he did not wholly control; Joshua Longstreth, having agreed to meet with them, was not home when they called but, according to Josiah White, " . . . was gone to a party next door to have some fun"; Charles Roberts admitted the merits of their proposal but said that Girard's enormous fortune would be inadequate to the task and advised them to abandon it before they ruined themselves. Finally, after days of closed doors and cold shoulders, they persuaded John Stoddart, a merchant "esteemed lucky and to never miss with his actions," to invest. His commitment turned the tide, and within a short time White and Hazard managed to pull together $100,000 in capital.

If gathering capital was difficult, the actual work of building the necessary dams on the Lehigh River was even more arduous. Technical problems aside, no one had ever attempted to maintain a work force of several hundred men in the middle

Martha Best helms barge number 219 of the Lehigh Coal and Navigation Company away from a dock. This unloaded barge was returning to the

Lehigh Canal after a trip down the Delaware River. Courtesy, Pennsylvania Canal Society Collection, Canal Museum, Easton

Josiah White was born and raised in the Society of Friends. A man of great mechanical aptitude, White played a major role in the growth and development of the Lehigh Coal and Navigation Company. From M.S. Henry, *History of the Lehigh Valley*, Easton

Erskine Hazard was Josiah White's lifelong partner and friend. Hazard pioneered the Mauch Chunk coal industry, but his major contribution to the partnership with White was his financial wizardry. Courtesy, Pennsylvania Canal Society Collection, Canal Museum, Easton

of a remote wilderness. Dressed in buckskins and accompanied by whatever hands he could recruit, White began work at the mouth of the Nesquehoning Creek. He and his men lived on four 30-foot scows, which they jokingly called "Whitestown on the Lehigh." They worked for three years, from early spring through the freezing up of the river in the fall, cutting timber as they went and moving stones and earth by hand and oxen. White and the other managers, working side by side with their men, often in chest-deep water, went armed, for fear that members of their disorderly crew might rob them.

To finance the work, which quickly outran the capital they had gathered, White sold his interests in the falls of the Schuylkill River to the city of Philadelphia, and used the money to buy timberlands along the Lehigh River. The timber was cut and sold to cover his expenses. Late in the fall of 1819, White was able to send scows down the river to prove the success of his "bear trap" dams and the system of artificial freshets. Finally, by the end of 1820, the first arks loaded with Lehigh anthracite were floated down to Philadelphia. But as White noted in his autobiography, it was five years before the success of the venture was assured:

Stove makers & grate sellers now, for the first began to boast of having preferable patterns of grates and stoves for burning anthracite coal. Some patriotic ladies also began their sample fires of anthracite coal: among them the Widow Guest in Sansom St. stood the most conspicuous, and of the grate sellers Jacob F. Walters took quite a leading part & several others not recollected . . .

This Winter 1824 & 25, may be considered the turning point in the use of anthracite coal, & made the company begin to think the coal business would grow fast enough to require making an ascending navigation . . .

In its earliest day the Lehigh navigation had been a crude matter of knocking together wooden scows, loading them with coal, floating them downstream to Philadelphia, and, after unloading the coal, breaking up the boats and selling them as lumber. By 1827, however, the enterprise began to take on a far greater sophistication. First, as White noted, it began to be worth investing in the construction of an ascending or "slack-water" system of locks that would permit traffic to move both up- and downriver. Implicit in this suggestion was diversification of the proposed canal's cargoes beyond coal to include other products: lumber, slate, and the Lehigh Valley's agricultural bounty.

Two-way traffic would also facilitate the movement of imported and domestic goods upriver from Philadelphia, linking the towns and villages of the valley to the markets of the nation and the world; and it would open the region to "auslanders," settlers and speculators seeking their fortunes in the hitherto isolated region. Work was already underway on two other major canals, the Delaware from Easton to Bristol and the Morris from Phillipsburg to the Hudson River. The completion of slackwater navigation of the Lehigh River in the early 1830s would link the Lehigh Valley to the two largest cities in America and set in motion forces that would, within a few years, transform the area from a sparsely settled wilderness into an industrial heartland for the growing nation.

The Changing Valley

For almost a hundred years the citizens of Lehigh and Northampton counties had lived quietly and peacefully, going their own way in a nation that seemed to be spacious and bounteous enough to permit people almost total control of their lives. No one, not even those inhabitants who had invested in the Lehigh Coal and Navigation Company or those who had profited from selling land, timber, provisions, or labor, could have envisioned the ultimate results of the completed canal. In tying the economy of the valley into that of the nation—and its residents into international markets as buyers, sellers, and consumers of agricultural commodities, manufactured goods, and minerals— the canals and the enterprises associated with them introduced into the region a force that was entirely alien. Industry was alien not only in the sense that it was largely built and owned by outsiders, but also, more significantly, it was really beyond anyone's comprehension or control. The rhythms of nature, of seasonal sowing and harvesting, would be replaced by the business cycles of boom and bust; the manipulations of speculators in London and Paris, as well as in New York and Philadelphia, would come to be as threatening to the Lehigh Valley and its residents as the Indian raids of the 1750s and 1760s.

The accounts of early industrialization along the Lehigh River give a sense of the inexorable and irresistible quality of these changes. Moravian bishop Joseph L. Levering's 1903 history of Bethlehem tells how at the first dawning of the "modern carboniferous age," few in Bethlehem paid much attention to the crews of laborers and boatloads of tools and hardware heading up the Lehigh. The few who cast a vigilant

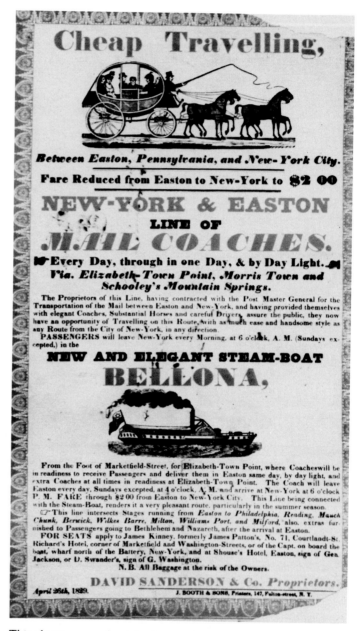

This advertisement, dated April 26, 1829, announced reduced traveling rates between New York and Easton. The last line of the ad reveals that baggage problems are nothing new. (NCHGS)

eye—Moravians like John Schropp, Charles Cist, and Jacob Weiss—had been among the first promoters of Lehigh anthracite, and undoubtedly, they viewed the new developments with some skepticism. Apparently the administrators of the Moravian church did not take the threat very seriously, for as work began on the ascending navigation in the late 1820s, excavation for the canal, which encroached on church-owned properties, proceeded without interruption. Soon, according to Levering, there were fleets of arks

... passing Bethlehem with hundreds of tons of the valuable fuel which men were now learning how to burn; and then they became a familiar sight. They were significant, in that transition time, of a transition also in the associations of the beautiful Lehigh at Bethlehem from the sentimental to the utilitarian.

Where only a few years before barges had been towed downriver while musicians aboard played David Moritz Michael's "Lehigh Valley Water Music" for delighted spectators strolling along the river's wooded banks—beside fields that had been tilled for almost a century—extraordinary changes were now taking place. As Levering noted:

The first effect at Bethlehem was local encroachment and necessary changes where the cut for the canal was made. ... one building that had to be removed was the laundry of the Young Ladies Seminary. The new one was finished early in September of 1829, just before the large force of diggers invaded the locality. Havoc was also wrought with the fertile acres between the Monocacy and the Lehigh which had been under tillage as the "boarding school fields." ... many a fine tree and familiar path, with embowered nooks here and there, had to be sacrificed at the foot of Bethlehem's hill; and the pitiless ravages of industry upon the picturesque, which have never ceased along the course of the Lehigh River, had fairly set in. The canal itself added some pretty landscape features, after it became old, which partly compensated for those which it destroyed, but at first the new ditch must have been a sight far from attractive.

The changes wrought at Bethlehem were more pronounced—and more to be lamented—than at Allentown, Easton, or any of the villages along the river, for Bethlehem was a settled community that was consciously striving to protect its citizenry from the corruptions of the outside world. It had self-consciously developed a distinctive and highly sophisticated culture, but it was becoming harder and harder to resist the temptations of the marketplace and its promises of speculative wealth. The system under which the property of the Bethlehem Moravians was collectively held and administered came under extraordinary pressure both from within and without. The pressures from within the community stemmed from two sources. First, certain commercially-oriented groups in the community, seeing fortunes to be made from creating new industries directly or indirectly related to the canal and the coal trade, were agitating for an abandonment of the lease system, under which the Moravian church owned all the land in the community. They wanted to be able to sell their property to whoever would pay the highest price. Second, the building of the canal and the development of new enterprises brought large numbers of non-Moravians into the community, diluting the tranquil and disciplined religious settlement that the Moravian proprietors had been striving so hard to preserve. Politically, the non-Moravians were a force that could not be ignored.

Among the external forces encroaching on the community was the indebtedness of certain Bethlehem entrepreneurs to merchants and manufacturers outside the area. These creditors had the Northampton County sheriff seize local properties. Such properties were to be sold to the highest bidder. In order to prevent them from falling into the hands of non-Moravians, however, the church felt compelled to bid against outsiders. Within a short time, the church itself was under heavy financial pressure. It was forced to sell several properties in fee-simple to developers for mill sites, hotels, and other commercial purposes. By the early 1830s, the administrators of the Moravian estates were beginning to seriously discuss necessary steps to alter or abandon the lease system.

The Panic of 1837, which heralded the first great national depression—a financial catastrophe that lasted over five years—dealt the final blow to the old Moravian communal order. In the fall of 1842, Owen Rice, whose trading and manufacturing ventures had been the most extensive in town, proved unable to meet his obligations. His failure affected all of Bethlehem, for he not only acted as a private banker, investing large sums for individuals, but also as trustee and treasurer for many organizations, including the Moravians' Society for the Propagating of the Gospel. When Rice failed, he carried many others along with him. As Levering noted:

... all the merchants and shop-keepers felt it in varying degrees. While many not engaged in business found their little hoard swept away. In consequence of these experiences, the conviction rapidly

ABOVE

The locomotive *Champion* was built in 1882 at the Lehigh Valley Railroad's shop in Weatherly. The wheel arrangement of 4-8-0 was unusual for the time. This type of locomotive was called, logically, a "twelve wheeler." This engraving appeared first in *Recent Locomotives*, 1883. From John White, Jr., *Early American Locomotives*, Dover, 1972

E.A. Douglass,the chief engineer and superintendent of the Lehigh Coal and Navigation Company, was responsible for overseeing the upper grand section, the most specialized canal in the United States. He also played a key role in the development of the American Iron Wire Rope Industry. From M.S. Henry, *History of the Lehigh Valley*, Easton, 1860

matured that, without further delay, steps toward the complete reconstruction of property control and financial management must be taken by the authorities, and that everything in the existing system of Bethlehem which, in order to maintain it, compelled the further purchase of houses that men were driven to sell, must be set aside, for it had now become impracticable to continue this burdensome method.

The elders of the church conferred. Letters were dispatched to the General Wardens of the Moravian Church in Europe, warning that, without financial assistance, the community would have to dissolve itself. In November of 1844, the General Wardens replied that the Moravians of Bethlehem could expect no further advances of money for the purpose of buying houses to maintain the exclusive system. In January, having no other choice, the Congregational Council reluctantly voted to abolish the lease system and began discussing how to go about dismantling the century-old church-village. In 1845, Bethlehem was incorporated as a borough, and, within a few months, the congregation began selling off its real estate to whomever wished to buy it.

By the 1850s, the industrialization of Bethlehem began in earnest. The picturesque village so lovingly depicted by such Moravian artists as Gustavus Grunewald would disappear, obscured by the belching smokestacks of the new iron mills; and the leadership of the town would pass from the educated and dignified German-speaking church elders to a coterie of Yankees with close ties to the coal industry. As Levering, himself a Moravian bishop, pointed out, this transformation did not occur suddenly:

It has been customary to lay so much stress upon one detail of the reorganization—the action of January, 1844, when the Congregation Council confirmed the action of the two village boards, sustained by the Provincial Board and the Unity Elders' Conference, in favor of terminating the lease-system, as a step in the process of reconstruction, and to speak of the town having then been "thrown open" that many who are not acquainted with the facts fancy the beginning and the end of the change to have lain in that vote. Moravians themselves have been partly responsible for this impression, in their manner of speaking and writing about that epoch in later years.

The development of Bethlehem after 1844 was a remarkably orderly process, carried out under the control of the Liquidation Committee, which disposed of the church's excess property holdings, and several village boards, which acted to lay out streets and alleys and regulate land use in accordance with the needs of the borough. Gradual as the change might have been, it was nevertheless inexorable. Its pace began to accelerate with the completion of the Lehigh Valley Railroad in April of 1855 and the establishment of the Bethlehem Rolling Mills and Iron Company in March of 1857. These enterprises would grow mightily with the coming of the Civil War and the rage for railroad building that followed.

The impact of the transportation revolution on the early phases of industrialization was both less pronounced and less traumatic in Easton than in either Bethlehem or Allentown. From its founding in the mid-18th century, Easton had been dominated by its English-speaking lawyers, merchants, artisans, and shopkeepers, most of whom had come there in expectation of the kinds of opportunities that the completion of the canals and the subsequent growth of industries brought about. Easton had always been in the avant-garde of modernization. It had been incorporated as a borough in 1789, 22 years before Allentown attained that status and more than a half-century before Bethlehem. In addition to being a river port of considerable significance as early as the 1770s (when Revolutionary War quartermasters were building warehouses on the banks of the Delaware River to store supplies for Continental troops), it was a center of overland transportation. Stagecoaches began making regular runs from Easton to Philadelphia in 1796, a service which would not come to Allentown or Bethlehem until a decade later.

The first newspaper in the Lehigh Valley, Jacob Weygandt's German-language *Eastoner Bothe and Northampton Kundschafter* commenced publication in Easton in September of 1793, whereas Allentown would not have its own newspaper until 1810, when Christian Jacob Hutter began *Der Unabhängige Republikaner* (The Independent Republican); and Bethlehem, although an early center for the printing of religious and educational books, would not see the publication of such a secular sheet until 1846, when Julius Held and his brother, William, began publishing *Die Biene* (The Bee).

Not surprisingly, the first bank in the region was established at Easton when the Philadelphia-controlled Bank of the United States opened a branch office in the town in 1800. In 1814, when the legislature passed a bill liberalizing the granting of bank charters, enterprising Eastonians, under the leadership of attorney-politician Samuel Sitgraves, were quick to establish the Easton Bank; in its early years, it was the only bank between Philadelphia and Wilkes-Barre.

The first turnpike in the Lehigh Valley, the 68-mile-long Easton-Wilkes-Barre Turnpike, which took 10 years to build, was organized under the leadership of Easton residents Samuel Sitgraves and Henry Drinker. Thus, the little town, which had only 709 residents in 1790, grew rapidly, along with the economy of the state and nation. By 1810, it had more than doubled its population to 1,657, and by 1850, it could boast 7,250—as against Bethlehem's 1,516 and Allentown's 3,703.

With its rapidly growing population, the connections of its leading citizens to urban centers beyond the Lehigh Valley, and its strategic location as a river port and hub of the region's canals and turnpikes, it is hardly surprising that Easton should have been the seedbed of corporate development in the region. Most notably, it was the birthplace of the iron industry in the Lehigh Valley. This industry had its origins at Durham Furnace, just south of Easton, where the smelting of native ores with charcoal had begun in 1727. During the Revolution, under the direction of Easton resident George Taylor, the Durham Furnace had been a major producer of iron ore for military purposes. In 1812, iron mining operations began on the Old Philadelphia Road, just three and a half miles outside Easton.

South Easton early became a center of iron manufacturing. In the 1820s, the firm of Stewart and Company began manufacturing iron nails there. It was joined in 1835 by the Franklin Iron Works, manufacturers of engines, pumps, and agricultural machinery, and, in 1839, by Barnet Swift and Company, which erected a charcoal-fueled blast furnace. In the early 1840s, after the development of anthracite-fueled blast furnaces, ironmaster William Firmstone built two furnaces in adjoining Glendon. (Both South Easton and Glendon had originally been part of Williams Township.) In 1853, the Glendon Iron Works, which had bought out several earlier concerns in the area, began operations. This company was founded by Charles Jackson, Jr. of Boston, nephew of the father of the American factory system, Patrick Tracy Jackson. By the mid-1850s, the Glendon Works boasted the largest anthracite blast furnace in the United States, employing, according to William J. Heller, 150 men and producing annually almost 22,000 tons of pig iron.

Easton also led the valley in other kinds of corporate activity, most notably in the field of higher education. In 1824, 39 years before the transformation of the Moravian Theological Seminary into a liberal arts college and 43 years before the founding of Muhlenberg College in Allentown, a group of leading Easton citizens met to discuss the desirability of founding a college in

ABOVE
In 1860 the manufacturing town of Easton on the Delaware and Lehigh rivers was a transportation crossroad where a great double bridge connected the New Jersey Central and the Lehigh Valley railroads. The Lehigh, Belvidere, and Delaware canals were nearby. From M.S. Henry, *History of the Lehigh Valley*, Easton, 1860

RIGHT
After they received a charter in 1826 to open a college, the residents of Easton needed six years to raise the necessary funds and organize a faculty. In 1832 they were able to convince the Reverend George Junkin to bring his Manual Labor Academy students from Germantown to form the basis of Lafayette College. (NCHGS)

the town. Their motives were doubtless economic, for urban leaders in the early 19th century were acutely aware of the value of "charitable and literary institutions" to a town's prestige as well as to its economic well-being. Although they succeeded in obtaining a charter from the legislature in March of 1826, it would be another six years before the trustees could raise the necessary funds, hire a president, and organize a faculty.

In 1832, they invited the Reverend George Junkin, a Presbyterian minister in charge of the Manual Labor Academy in Germantown, to bring his students to Easton as the basis for the new college, which was to be named Lafayette in honor of the Revolutionary War hero who had recently completed a tour of the United States. Junkin was part of a movement in the early years of American higher education that believed that it was possible for colleges to both fulfill their mission of character formation and support themselves by the manual labor of their students. As Junkin's system promised to bring Easton the prestige of a college at a bargain price, his academy seemed to the town fathers a most worthy enterprise.

Encouraged by the college's early success in attracting students, the trustees purchased land for a campus on a hill overlooking the junction of the Lehigh and Delaware rivers and began the construction of the college's first buildings, the first of which was the central portion of South College, completed in May of 1834. The school's prosperous condition did not last, however. Like so many other promising ventures it fell victim to the Panic of 1837, and to the fact that, as a non-sectarian institution, it was unlikely to attract much support from the intensely religious Lutherans, Moravians, and Calvinists of the Lehigh Valley. It barely limped through the 1840s and would have closed its doors had not the Philadelphia Synod of the Presbyterian Church, with major financial support from a New Yorker, James Lenox, taken over the government of the college.

Not until after the Civil War, under the dynamic leadership of the Reverend William Cattell and with the support of the college's alumni, did Lafayette find itself on a firm financial foundation. By 1883, when Reverend Cattell resigned as president, the school's assets had grown from $88,666 to $1.1 million—and the number of students from 39 to over 400.

Easton's industrial activities, though they began auspiciously, did not maintain their preeminence. Its iron industry was, by the 1860s, outstripped in size and productivity by plants in Allentown, Bethlehem, and Catasaqua. By the last quarter of the 19th century, the growth of its population failed to keep pace with that of the other cities of the valley. The reasons for the slowing of Easton's development are complex. One factor was the town's proximity to Philadelphia, which was situated only 50 miles down the Delaware River. Because of this, Easton tended to be subservient to the larger city's economic interests, serving as a shipping point for goods to Philadelphia and a market for goods distributed from Philadelphia.

Another factor was Easton's relative remoteness from the richest iron ore deposits in the Lehigh Valley, which lay closer to Bethlehem, at Hellertown, and in Lehigh County. In the intensely competitive iron industry of the Civil War era, a seemingly small matter of distance from fuel, water power, ore deposits, or transportation could, by adding a few cents to the cost of producing a ton of pig iron, mean the difference between the success or failure of an enterprise. Certainly the predominance of outside investors like Charles Jackson of Boston, who were proprietors of Easton's industries, weakened the town's economy; for, having no connection to the community, such individuals had no qualms about withdrawing their capital and deploying it elsewhere if it proved advantageous to do so—as many of them did after the Panic of 1873.

Finally, the relative isolation of Easton's entrepreneurial leadership from the Pennsylvania-German majority in the region deprived the town of the talent, capital, and patronage of the countryside which, instead, tended to gravitate to Allentown. Ironically, the very factors that gave Easton its head start—the large population of commercially-oriented non-Germans, its proximity to Philadelphia, and its connections to the world beyond the Lehigh Valley—may have proved to be its undoing in industrial development.

For Allentown, the years up to 1850 were inauspicious, hardly foretelling the remarkable "take-off" that would occur after the Civil War. While the completion of the Lehigh Canal in 1829 stimulated local business, Allentown remained basically a trading center for farmers. Its somnolences persisted in spite of the efforts of an aggressive group of entrepreneurs to promote industrial development. Led by John Rice, president of the Northampton Bank, the institution and its officers were involved in a series of speculative ventures in real estate, mining, and coal delivery contracts that would, in the wake of the Panic of 1837, bring about a financial disaster.

This circle of boosters did not content themselves with promoting commercial and industrial ventures. They were instrumental in organizing the North American Academy of Homeopathic Healing Art. This venture had a particular appeal to its

Situated on the Lehigh River at the junction of the East Pennsylvania and Lehigh Valley railroads, Allentown's skyline in 1860 reveals the proximity of the agrarian and business communities. From M.S. Henry, *History of the Lehigh Valley*, Easton, 1860

adherents since it promised to publicize Allentown as the site of the world's first homeopathic medical school. Courses were to be taught in German by such homeopathic notables as Dr. Constantine Hering, a student of Hahnemann (homeopathy's founder) and a prominent immigrant from Germany. It is worth noting that this institution's endowment, gathered from contributors in Philadelphia and New York as well as from local residents, constituted a handsome block of capital—which was to be managed by Solomon Keck, a director of the Northampton Bank. The bank's avarice for capital accumulation did not stop there. In a seemingly altruistic gesture designed to protect the property interests of children, John Rice, the bank's president, persuaded a number of widows to draw up prenuptial contracts with their second husbands that named Rice as trustee and guardian of their property. This gave him control of their capital, which he could invest in schemes in which he was interested.

The Northampton Bank did quite well during the period of moderate economic growth of the 1830s. It did even better when, after the suspension of specie payments in May of 1837, it could issue paper currency without concern for its ability to back its notes with hard cash. But, in the spring of 1842, when specie payments were ordered resumed, the bank collapsed. As one commentator, Rueben Holben, later remarked:

Over a generation ago a shrewd, oily Herrnhuter [Moravian] by the name of John Rice who was more notorious than famous, ingratiated himself into the good graces of the stockholders of a certain bank. He possessed many bewitchments of popularity and was brimful of machinations with lots of pure native ambition to rule or ruin, and was minded not to take stock in a balloon unless it would go up. He was made president, and he soon became the autocrat of the institution. He hypnotized the directors and they all vied to do his bidding. He directed and the directors didn't. When the gold reserve was questioned he procured a number of nail kegs filled with nails and covered them with layers of gold with a view of deception. But at last the bubble bursted and the creditors of the bank learned that Rice had too much sand in his sugar for table use and not enough for building purposes.

56

banks, corporate speculation, and Yankees that would take many years to get over. Indeed, although it was a growing city, Allentown would not have another credit institution until the establishment of the Allentown Bank (now the First National Bank of Allentown) in 1855.

The great bank debacle was not Allentown's only misfortune during the disastrous decade of the 1840s. In January of 1841, the Lehigh River experienced the greatest flood since the settlement of the town. The waters rose 35 feet above the low water mark, sweeping away the bridge over the river, destroying houses and businesses in the lower part of town, washing away over 2,000 tons of coal, thousands of dollars worth of lumber, and a large number of canal boats. The destruction of uninsured property in this flood was an important factor in the failure of the Northampton Bank, as it was in the insolvency of Owen Rice in Bethlehem.

The end of the decade was marked by the Fire of 1848, which destroyed most of the dwellings and business establishments in the center of town. The fire was started in the barn of tobacconist John Eckert. Two of his apprentices, angered at having to work on Ascension Day, set fire to the structure. A strong northwesterly wind fanned the flames, spreading them from wooden structure to wooden structure. Allentown's volunteer firemen, manning their two hand pumps and carrying fire buckets, were powerless to stop it. The town experienced over a quarter of a million dollars in uninsured losses.

As Charles Roberts noted in his *History of Lehigh County,* the fire may have been a blessing in disguise, for it coincided with the rapid development of the iron industry in the area, the earnings of which soon replenished the fortunes of the town's merchants and put wages in the hands of its workingmen. The rebuilding of the city permitted a concentration of commercial development in a relatively compact location, and the process of rebuilding not only created employment but led to the establishment of new industries, most notably the manufacture of brick. A special census of Allentown taken in 1855 showed that in spite of the fire, the town possessed 35 more houses and 1,550 more people than it had before the fire.

The failure of the Northampton Bank, like the bankrupty of Owen Rice in Bethlehem in the same year, was a catastrophe for the whole community. Not only did the institution's debts amount to over half-a-million dollars (the equivalent of three years of its total circulation), it carried along with it to ruin a number of important local firms and charities. The homeopathic medical school went into bankruptcy and was sold at auction by the sheriff in 1843. The Presbyterian Church, of which John Rice was treasurer, found itself encumbered with debt and was also seized and sold by authorities. The tidal wave of lawsuits against the bank and its officers took on the character of legal warfare between the Yankee and Pennsylvania-German elements of the community. Feeling against Rice ran so high that he was forced to flee to New York. Trials against him and the directors were shifted to Lancaster County, for no jury in the Lehigh region could be counted on to render a dispassionate judgment. Indeed, Allentown's entire legal community was so enmeshed in the bank's affairs that no lawyer or judge could be considered free from questionable associations with Rice and his associates. The affair left a legacy of bitterness and distrust of

The Iron Age in the Lehigh Valley

While the completion of the Lehigh Canal in 1829 initiated the process of industrialization in the valley, large-scale development did not begin to occur until the 1850s, with the building

ABOVE
The Lehigh Coal and Navigation Company played an important role in the industrial development of the Lehigh Valley, and the company is often referred to as one of the catalysts of the American industrial revolution. Courtesy, Pennsylvania Canal Society Collection, Canal Museum, Easton

RIGHT
Asa Packer, a man with integrity and an ability to recognize opportunity, made the railroad an important part of Lehigh Valley industry. His businesses included a boat yard, a general store, and mining interests. (NCHGS)

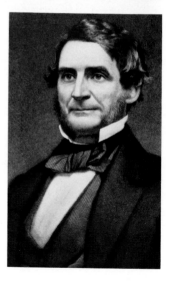

of the Lehigh Valley Railroad. Growth up to the 1850s was really no more than a by-product of the coal trade, the profits of which tended to go into the pockets of the Lehigh Coal and Navigation Company's stockholders in Philadelphia. The Company played a crucial role in the origins of the iron industry by bringing to the area David Thomas, a Welsh ironmaster, who was commissioned to develop methods of smelting local iron ores using anthracite as a fuel. He was successful, and, by the early 1840s, blast furnaces and foundries were being erected not only along the river at Allentown, Easton, and Catasauqua, but also in more remote areas of the countryside, such as Alburtis. Still, the full-scale development of the iron industry was retarded by the difficulty and expense of bringing together the necessary raw materials—iron ore, limestone, coal, and water. The ore supply was a particular problem, for major deposits generally lay some distance from the Lehigh River and had to be hauled by wagon over increasingly impassable roads. Albert Ohl in his *History of Upper Saucon* gives a fairly accurate description of the difficulties involved:

The hauling was paid by the ton, therefore overloading was often the rule. Nobody not having lived in this era can half imagine the commotion. Wagons often stuck in the mud up to the axle: drivers cracking the long snake whips, with a report of revolver shots: drivers cursing to high heaven. This was certainly a hard life, but they helped each other. But it cost a lot of horses and many broken down wagons and broken harnesses. The saddler trade was in good in those days. Each teamster liked to boast of how many loads he could haul, but it did not pay. Bridges were broken down, roads got into terrible condition, etc.

With the supply of ore and limestone flux so dependent on the vagaries of weather and on the expense of man and animal power, the prospects for the iron industry remained uncertain. The fact that the transportation of coal to factories and finished iron products to their markets beyond the Lehigh Valley was interrupted in the winter when the canal froze over, and in the spring when sections of it were frequently destroyed by floods, also slowed the industry's rate of growth. But the railroad industry would soon change everything. Its need for iron created a tremendous market for the products of Lehigh furnaces. Even more important, the railroad's dependability and low cost finally brought together the basic factors necessary for industrial growth: cheap transportation, proximate raw materials, and a willing work force.

The father of railroading in the Lehigh Valley, Asa Packer, was a heroic figure. A tough, daring man, he struggled upward from humble beginnings in Mystic, Connecticut, where he was born in 1805. As a youth, he, like so many individuals in impoverished parts of New England, went west. According to William J. Heller's *History of Northampton County:*

At the age of seventeen he packed all his worldly possessions, consisting of a few simple articles of clothing, shouldered his humble pack, and set out afoot to make his own way in the great world which was altogether unknown to him. Trudging along the rugged roads of that almost primitive time, the plucky lad walked the entire distance between his birthplace in the land of the blue laws and wooden nutmegs [Connecticut] to Brooklyn, Susquehanna County, Pennsylvania. . . . After many days of weary walking, of climbing his way up rocky hills and toiling through dusty alleys, in sunshine and in rain, the lad arrived, footsore, weary, and hungry, at the home of his cousin, Mr. Edward Packer, in Brooklyn. Mr. Packer was a house carpenter, and young Asa determined to learn the trade under his tutelage. He applied himself to his work with genuine enthusiasm and characteristic thoroughness, and became an accomplished mechanic. No master of the trade could push a plane truer or more rapidly, or send a nail home with greater precision.

Packer's ability to recognize opportunities, his capacity for hard work, and his willingness to take risks served him well. Within two years of his footsore arrival in Mauch Chunk, he retired from the canal boat business (while retaining an interest in the enterprise) to turn his energies in other directions. He bought a general store, which he placed under the management of his brother-in-law, James Blakeslee. He established a boat yard in which vessels were constructed for operation not only on the Lehigh, but on canals in New York and New Jersey. By the 1840s, he was mining and shipping coal on his own—a situation which enabled him to examine critically the transportation monopoly enjoyed by the Lehigh Coal and Navigation Company. By this time the railroad was beginning to evolve from an experimental novelty to a revolutionary and successful innovation in the field of transportation. He decided that the time had come to free the industries of the Lehigh Valley from the grip of the seasons.

Packer was not the first entrepreneur to contemplate the value of railroads to the Lehigh Valley. The Lehigh Coal and Navigation Company itself had been using a gravity-powered "switchback" railroad from Summit Hill to Mauch Chunk since

1827, but, with so much invested in the canal, the stockholders were reluctant to expand the company's operations into building and operating a railroad over some of the roughest terrain in the Northeast. In the mid-1840s, a group of investors, led by Edward R. Biddle of Philadelphia, obtained a charter from the legislature for a railroad through the Lehigh Valley; but the financial risks and the physical obstacles discouraged timid urban investors just as the proposal for the Lehigh Canal had a generation earlier.

Like Josiah White, Asa Packer was not easily discouraged. In 1852, a group comprised of Packer, his family, and some associates bought up the outstanding stock of Biddle's dormant company and began work on the 46-mile line from Mauch Chunk to Easton. During the three years that it took to complete the route, Packer, like his predecessor, White, sunk his entire personal fortune into the enterprise. At various points the newspapers and credit agencies reported that he was "very much in debt," "laboring under great financial difficulty," and on the brink of failure; but, by the force of his personality, his political insight, and his intimate knowledge of the economic and topographic features of the region, he managed, in 1855, to complete the road. He—and the communities through which the line passed—would soon reap the rewards of his years of hard work. When Packer died in 1879, he was one of the wealthiest men in Pennsylvania.

Sir Isaac Newton, when asked about his discoveries in the field of physics, is said to have replied that his achievements were due to the fact that he stood on the shoulders of giants. The same thing could be said for early industrialists like Josiah White, Asa Packer, and the Welsh immigrant David Thomas. Their enterprises certainly depended on their own courage and genius, but they also depended on what others had done. We cannot understand the success of the Lehigh Valley Railroad and the industrial take-off of the Lehigh Valley unless we appreciate the extent to which the success of one type of industrial venture rested on the success of earlier ones. The success of coal mining, for example, depended on the ability to transport the mineral to where it was needed. In the case of anthracite, it was necessary to encourage demand for the product, not only by promoting the invention of coal grates and stoves capable of burning the fuel, but also by supporting the invention of devices capable of harnessing the "black stones" for industrial uses.

Had the management of the Lehigh Coal and Navigation Company been less foresighted, the iron industry in the Lehigh

Valley never would have developed; but Josiah White, recognizing the industrial possibilities of the Lehigh Valley, was willing to provide major incentives to anyone who could successfully employ anthracite coal in the smelting of iron. There is considerable debate about who can be credited with the development of this process. Jesse Quinby of Harford Furnace in Maryland claimed that he had been smelting iron with anthracite since 1815. Throughout the 1820s, unsuccessful experiments with the fuel were carried on at Mauch Chunk, in Rhode Island, in Massachusetts, and in France. In 1828, James B. Neilson of Scotland obtained a patent for the use of blown hot air in smelting ore—a patent, in other words, for a blast furnace. In 1833, Dr. F.W. Geissenheimer of New York obtained an American patent for a similar process and made some successful, though uneconomical, experiments at the Valley Furnace near Pottsville in Schuylkill County. Between 1837 and 1839, William Lyman of Boston engaged in a series of ultimately satisfactory trials at the Pioneer Furnace, also in Schuylkill County. Anthracite iron smelting was an idea whose time had come.

As Craig Bartholemew has noted in his definitive study of anthracite iron making in the Lehigh Valley, "despite their persistent efforts, none of the American iron masters were to achieve the distinction of being the first to use anthracite successfully for commercial iron production." That honor would go to a Welsh immigrant, David Thomas. Thomas was born at Tyllwyd, South Wales, in 1794. At the age of 17, he went to work at the Neath Abby Iron Works, where he learned the elements of iron making. In his early twenties, Thomas was appointed general superintendent of the iron furnaces at Yniscedwin, which were owned by George Crane, a hardware merchant who was just beginning a new career as a manufacturer. As it happened, the Yniscedwin works were located on the only deposit of anthracite coal in Wales; but, because no one knew how to use the fuel, the foundry had to use coke, transported from mines and coke ovens nearly 14 miles distant. With Crane's encouragement, Thomas began experimenting with anthracite smelting in 1820, but nothing came of his efforts until the mid-1830s, when he heard of Neilson's patent. Neilson's blast furnace was not, it should be pointed out, specifically designed for burning anthracite. Its purpose was to improve the efficiency of the fuel by blowing hot air over coke or charcoal. The blast of preheated air reduced the amount of fuel needed to produce the requisite heat for smelting and working iron. When Thomas learned of the Neilson "stove,"

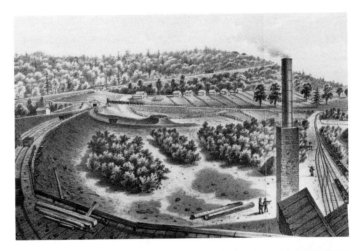

ABOVE
Ore barges, such as these at Mauch Chunk, received the coal from hoppers that poured the black fuel into the barges' open holds. This development saved shoveling time and costs and permitted many boats to be loaded at once. Courtesy, Pennsylvania Canal Society Collection, Canal Museum, Easton

TOP RIGHT AND ABOVE
The rail system that connected Mauch Chunk to Summit Hill went through two phases. In 1827 a horse-powered switchback design was built. This was converted to a steam-powered incline plane in 1840. After the Civil War the railway became a tourist attraction until it closed in the 1930s. From M.S. Henry, *History of the Lehigh Valley*, Easton, 1860

he was quick to see its possibilities. He persuaded Crane to send him to Glasgow to visit Neilson and view his invention. Late in 1836, he returned to Yniscedwin and began construction of an anthracite blast furnace. It began operation in February of 1837 and was immediately successful.

Solomon W. Roberts, a nephew of Josiah White's and an employee of the Lehigh Coal and Navigation Company, happened to be in Wales when word of Crane and Thomas' success became known. Roberts went to Yniscedwin to see the furnace for himself and quickly reported back to his employers in Philadelphia. After several efforts to duplicate the Crane-Thomas achievement failed, Erskine Hazard, acting for the Lehigh Coal and Navigation Company, was sent to Wales to try to induce George Crane to come to Pennsylvania. Instead, Crane suggested that the company hire David Thomas. In January of 1839, a new corporation, the Lehigh Crane Iron Company, was formed. Five of its eight directors were also officers of Lehigh Coal and Navigation. In July of 1839, David Thomas arrived at Biery's Bridge, three miles north of Allentown, and began construction of an anthracite furnace on the Lehigh River. The furnace was "blown in" in January of 1840 and ran continuously until the following year, when its fires were extinguished by the rising floodwaters of the Great Flood of 1841.

Because the Lehigh Crane Iron Company was, for all practical purposes, a subsidiary of the Lehigh Coal and Navigation Company, Thomas' employers were quick to spread the news of their success and even to lend Thomas himself to other companies such as that of William Lyman near Pottsville. The Lehigh Coal and Navigation Company really had more to gain from encouraging rivals than from discouraging them since new iron companies would undoubtedly locate their plants adjacent to the canal, paying the Lehigh Coal and Navigation Company for water rights, purchasing its real estate and its coal, and transporting finished products to market by canal. Not surprisingly, the iron industry along the Lehigh River began to develop rapidly. By 1850, there were five companies operating 13 anthracite-fired blast furnaces along the Lehigh at Glendon, South Easton, Allentown, Catasauqua, and Coplay. By 1860, with the economies resulting from the building of the Lehigh Valley Railroad and smaller lines that connected the iron mines to the mills by the river, there were six companies operating 33 furnaces. The building of the smaller railroads, such as the Ironton and the Catasauqua and Bath, permitted ironworks to locate away from the river and closer to ore deposits. Thus, by the late

1860s, large factories were being constructed amid the cornfields at Macungie, Hellertown, Alburtis, Williams Township, and Emmaus—and iron mines were sinking their shafts throughout the two counties.

The iron industry and the railroads provided stimulus for the growth of other productive activities. Blast furnaces required firebrick in their construction, a demand which Allentonians Samuel McHose and O.A. Ritter were quick to meet. With extensive deposits of clay within the city limits, brickmakers in Allentown supplied the basic materials for workers' houses and for constructing the factories in which they worked. Lumberyards and planing mills, as well as individual craftsmen—carpenters, cabinetmakers, painters, paperhangers, wood-carvers, and masons—flourished in the rush to provide for the laborers who flooded the cities of the valley.

New industries were developed. One of the most important, especially by the end of the century, was the manufacture of cement. Cement is made by subjecting mixtures of limestone and clay to high temperatures. When this product is mixed with sand and water it produces an efficient bonding agent between brick and stone. When hardened, it is impervious to water and fire. Not surprisingly, the builders of the Lehigh Canal were delighted when they found large deposits of minerals suitable for making cement near the Lehigh Gap in the mid-1820s. The system of locks that they were building required enormous quantities of sealed masonry to contain the waters on which the canal boats moved. Samuel Glace, a canal supervisor, built cement kilns at Lehigh Gap, and later at Siegfried's Bridge in the 1830s and 1840s, producing about 10 barrels of cement a day.

But it was the housing boom of the 1860s that really gave impetus to the cement industry. In 1866, David O. Saylor, Esaias Rehrig, and Adam Woolover organized the Coplay Cement Company to exploit a deposit of "cement rock" that had been uncovered a few years earlier by the builders of the Lehigh Valley Railroad. They built two small kilns and, by 1869, were producing 250 barrels of cement a day. In the early 1870s, Saylor patented a new process for making Portland cement. Demand for the product proved so great that within 10 years the company had built 17 kilns and was producing almost 200,000 barrels a year. By the end of the century, the Saylor company had been joined by others, most notably Lehigh Portland Cement, and production had jumped to tens of millions of barrels a year, the majority of which was shipped to the great cities of the Northeast and Midwest where reinforced concrete

TOP
The Lehigh Crane Iron
Company operated five
furnaces in 1860, the most
extensive iron works in the
U.S. at that time. The ore
from the company's mines
was transported to the
furnaces by the Catasauqua
and Fogelsville Railroad.
From M.S. Henry, *History of
the Lehigh Valley*, Easton,
1860

ABOVE LEFT
David Thomas, a Welsh
immigrant, was elemental to
the success of the iron
industry in the Lehigh Valley.
He built the first anthracite
furnace in the area and later
founded the Thomas Iron
Company in Hokendauqua.
From M.S. Henry, *History of
the Lehigh Valley*, Easton,
1860

ABOVE RIGHT
This anthracite-burning iron
furnace at Catasauqua, on the
Lehigh Canal, was erected by
David Thomas in 1839-1840.
It was the first Lehigh Crane
iron furnace. Courtesy,
American Iron and Steel
Institute

TOP

Slatington was a picturesque village of 450 inhabitants in 1860. The slate quarries in and around Slatington developed by the Lehigh Slate Company were among the largest in the U.S. and furnished the finest quality slate in the country. From M.S. Henry, *History of the Lehigh Valley*, Easton, 1860

ABOVE

Zinc ores from the mines in the Saucon Valley were manufactured into white oxide of zinc at the Pennsylvania and Lehigh Zinc Company's works. In the 1850s and 1860s the company product was considered to be of unsurpassed quality. From M.S. Henry, *History of the Lehigh Valley*, Easton, 1860

building technology had revolutionized the kinds of structures that men could build.

Another building-related industry that flourished in the Lehigh Valley, beginning with the Civil War period, was the quarrying and finishing of slate. As with the coal, iron, and cement industries, slate mining drew on the Lehigh Valley's mineral resources, and, like them, development depended on low-cost transportation. Slate quarrying began as early as 1844, when two Welsh immigrants, William Roberts and Nelson Labar, were walking from Easton to Mauch Chunk on their way to seek work in the coal mines. While resting near the present site of Slatington, they noticed some pieces of stone resting against the barn of Peter Heimbach. They remarked on their similarity to the slate of their native country and wasted no time in finding out where Heimbach had obtained the pieces. Having little money, Roberts and Labar could neither buy the land nor pay high rent on it, but the owners proved agreeable to the idea of basing payment on the amount of slate produced—a royalty of 28 cents for every ton of slate shingles that Roberts and Labar made. By the spring of 1845, the quarry was operating profitably and others in the area moved quickly to discover and develop slate properties. The absence of railroads restricted the growth of the industry, but by the 1860s, as branch lines crisscrossed the hamlets of Lehigh and Northampton counties, the center of quarrying shifted from Slatington, which was fortuitously located on the banks of the Lehigh River and thus was served by the canal, to a variety of more isolated places, most notably Bangor and Pen Argyl. As quarrying and finishing techniques became more sophisticated, the number of products that were being made from slate was truly amazing. They included products as diverse as mantels, bathtubs, mangers, billiard tables, and tablets.

Slate and cement were not the only new extractive industries to develop in the Lehigh Valley in the wake of the canal and the railroads. The discovery of zinc in the Saucon Valley by Jacob Uberoth in the 1840s uncovered yet another source of mineral wealth. Uberoth apparently thought that the ore he had found was iron. He dug out a wagonload and hauled it to the Mary Ann Furnace in Berks County. An attempt to smelt it failed. The metal was not iron. But no one in the vicinity knew what it was or how to make it commercially valuable. Eventually a sample of the ore was brought to the attention of the noted Bethlehem geologist, William Theodore Roepper, who pronounced it to be zinc. After costly experimentation Samuel Wetherill perfected a process for transforming the ore into zinc oxide, the basic ingredient in white paint. Begun in 1853, Wetherill's little paint factory was hardly in a position to fully exploit so valuable a mineral, but in 1855, his operation was taken over by a new corporation, the Pennsylvania and Lehigh Zinc Company, which was capitalized at a million dollars and controlled by Philadelphia and New York interests. While the new company continued to make zinc oxide for paint, it recognized the value of zinc as an easily workable rust-proof metal. By the mid-1860s, the company was producing zinc in sheet form. Soon its market would expand further as the process of galvanizing iron and steel was perfected and applied to a wide range of industrial and household products.

As industrialization changed the face of the Lehigh Valley, the process itself changed and exhibited different characteristics. If the first phase of industrialization in the Lehigh Valley had involved extractive industries, the wealth of which was derived from the region's mineral resources, the second phase, which began in the late 1850s, was based on the finishing of raw mineral products. Surrounding the iron mills of Allentown, Easton, and Bethlehem—as well as the smaller cities up and down the river—were concerns that transformed iron into boilers, pumps, horseshoes, fencing, pipes, rails, structural members for bridges and buildings, railway car parts, tools, barbed wire, and a wide range of other products. The first phase of industrialization was largely dominated by outsiders like Josiah White and Asa Packer. The latter phase was largely the doing of Pennsylvania-German entrepreneurs.

Industrial growth necessarily stimulated commercial expansion. Banking, which had languished in the Lehigh Valley since the Northampton Bank debacle of the early 1840s, became a necessity as businessmen, needing capital to expand their operations, sought money for hire. In 1851, there were only two banks in the Lehigh Valley, the Easton Bank, which had begun operations in 1814, and the private banking house of W.H. Blumer and Company of Allentown. Within 10 years, three more had been founded, two in Allentown and one in Easton. By 1870, Allentown could boast nine banks, Easton four, and Bethlehem one. The valley became a center for building and loan societies, which enabled those of small means to pool their capital, usually for the purpose of financing housing construction. In 1875, Northampton County possessed 14 of these institutions; Lehigh County could boast more than a dozen. Thus, capital for local investment became increasingly available from local sources.

Complementing the area's burgeoning population and industrial take-off was a revolution in retailing. Before the 1850s, most residents of the Lehigh Valley, when they came to town to trade, dealt directly with local tradesmen. They went to a shoemaker for shoes, a tailor for clothing, or a miller for flour. But coincident with a rising volume of demand came shifts in public taste. As people subscribed more extensively to periodicals printed in New York and Philadelphia, a window was opened into a more cosmopolitan world. Likewise, new residents introduced new demands that the local merchants were quick to satisfy by offering a wider range of goods, from increasingly diverse origins, to a fast-growing population of buyers. Thus, the general dry goods store, the ancestor of the department store, was introduced. Allentown's early dry goods emporiums (which stocked nearly everything that anyone could desire) included H. Leh & Company, founded in 1850; Bittner, Hunsicker & Company (1857); and Zollinger-Harned (1865). Groceries brought to consumers included exotic tropical fruits and fresh vegetables out of season, as well as fragrant spices, coffees, and teas from the Orient and Latin America. Large industrial breweries were established that took over the old inns, establishing new ones and operating them as chains.

The variety of stores selling specialty and luxury items also grew until there was hardly an item made anywhere in the nation or in the world that could not be bought in the Lehigh Valley's retail stores. Assisting in the task of promoting these products was a host of new newspapers. In Easton, by 1870, there were five English-language and one German newspaper being published; in Bethlehem, four; and in Allentown, eight (only two of which were in English). In addition, city and county directories, which first began to appear in the 1860s, not only provided essential sources of information for manufacturers and retailers in their search for customers, but also, through their advertising, directed the attention of subscribers to the enormous assortment of goods and services available in the region. Finally, educator-publishers like A.R. Horne of Allentown, recognizing that language constituted a major barrier between merchants and the German-speaking farmers in the countryside, began publishing a series of "Pennsylvania-German manuals." These manuals were combinations of English-German dictionaries, grammar books, anthologies of dialect verse, Pennsylvania-German history sources, and, perhaps most important, shopping directories to Allentown stores.

The fortunes of farmers, who were the major occupational group in Lehigh and Northampton counties in the 1840s, were necessarily affected by the industrialization of the region. In the

Stores lining Hamilton Street in downtown Allentown included many of the dry goods stores that opened to meet the needs of the growing population. One of the ancestors of the department store was Leh and Company (on the right), which is still in business today. (LCHS)

19th century, its effect was most beneficial. Farmers profited handsomely by selling land, timber, and supplies to the canal and railroad builders, as well as by selling off portions of their farmsteads to miners and manufacturers. The expanding populations of the cities provided a market for their surpluses. Gradually, patterns of agriculture began to change as the needs of the marketplace encouraged the introduction of new crops, most notably the potato, and the phasing out of flax, hemp, and sheep. With the availability of manufactured cloth, there was little reason for farmers to continue investing in crops for making homespun. Similarly, crops like rye and buckwheat declined in importance, while wheat, oats, and corn, for which there was substantial demand outside the valley, took their place.

An important factor in the transformation of agriculture from a subsistence to a commercial orientation in the period 1840-1880 was the organization of agricultural societies in Allentown, Easton, and Bethlehem. These organizations were dominated by businessmen with agricultural interests. They recognized that fairs could play an important role in directing the attention of farmers to new kinds of crops; that they could promote the improvement of livestock and plant breeds through competition for prizes; and that they would enable salesmen of agricultural machinery, fertilizers, pesticides, and seeds to more easily reach potential purchasers. The fairs played important social roles as well. Not only did they provide opportunities for farmers throughout the region to meet and confer with one another, they also reaffirmed the long-standing solidarity between town and country. Amid an "old home week" atmosphere, countryfolk and their city cousins met together at the beer garden or rooted for their favorites at the trotting races, renewing old friendships and cementing old loyalties.

The Civil War Era

The Civil War era, from 1860 through 1873, was one of unparalleled prosperity for the Lehigh Valley. All occupational sectors grew spectacularly, stimulated not only by new manufacturing and transportation technologies in the valley, but also by the demand for the region's products in the great cities as well as by railroads and new population centers that were moving westward. Between 1850 and 1870, Northampton County's population grew from 40,996 to 61,432, a 50 percent increase; Lehigh County's grew from 32,479 to 56,796, a 65 percent increase. The population of Allentown alone jumped from

3,703 in 1850 to 19,936 in 1870, a 438 percent leap. While the rural population continued to grow, the greatest increases were in the cities and boroughs, which attracted both outsiders and farmers' sons in search of their fortunes.

Amid all this development, however, there were signs of disturbance. However profitable market farming might be, or whatever eminence a native-born merchant or manufacturer might attain, there was a price to be paid. It was less a financial price than a cultural one. Financially, the inhabitants of the Lehigh Valley had gained much, and, because of their innate conservatism, they had avoided the speculative excesses of other regions. They were, as a result, less vulnerable to cycles of boom and bust in the national economy. But the coming of the Civil War and the events that followed it—particularly the economic crises of the 1870s—demonstrated the extent to which participation in the economics of the nation also demanded shifts in cultural and political loyalties that the Pennsylvania-Germans were not sure they wanted to make.

The Civil War was a long, bitter, and desperately fought struggle, and often the most desperate battles were not fought by armies at the front, but between political factions in places like the Lehigh Valley. Only the war in Vietnam in the 1960s produced more conflict, dissension, and anger on the home front. The Lehigh Valley was not unique in this respect. In March of 1861 president-elect Lincoln was forced to pass secretly through the city of Baltimore on the way to his inauguration. A month later, federal troops rushing to the defense of Washington, D.C. had to fight their way through anti-war mobs. In New York City, in the summer of 1863, opposition to the draft resulted in a week of rioting, lynching, and looting. Reasons for opposition to the war varied from place to place. Many felt that the conflict could have been solved through peaceful means. Others believed that Southerners should be permitted to maintain their "peculiar institution" of slavery without federal interference.

There was widespread disagreement over Lincoln's conduct of the war. Among the Pennsylvania-Germans of the Lehigh Valley, grievances stemmed from feelings whose roots lay deep in the area's historical experience, with its traditions of resistance to central authority and its distrust of Yankee aggressiveness. Most of all, farmers who depended on the labor of their sons to help them sow, plough, and harvest found it hard to understand why a government that was supposed to represent them was now interfering in their private lives. One gets some sense of this opposition from the Reverend William Helffrich's

ABOVE
Unfamiliarity with the new-fangled gadget called a camera could account for the variety of expressions exhibited by this farm family in the 1860s. Each person seems to regard the photographer from a different attitude. (LCHS)

RIGHT
Located at Sixth and Liberty streets in Allentown, the main building of the Lehigh County Agricultural Society housed one of the organizations that, from 1840-1880, reoriented Lehigh Valley agriculture from subsistence farming to commercial enterprise. (LCHS)

account of wartime in Fogelsville. Reverend Helffrich was an ardent supporter of Lincoln and the Union, which somewhat colored his view of what he described:

A wonderful bit of evidence of the patriotism of our Democratic counties and townships was "Exemption Day" which was held in Fogelsville. The government decreed certain days for certain townships when those citizens who were scheduled for military service were examined by physicians and, if they had defects, were exempt from the draft. One such exemption day was set for the citizens of Lynn, Weisenberg, and Upper Macungie Townships at Fogelsville and Dr. Romig of Allentown with other doctors were the examining committee. Here one had a good opportunity to observe the good patriotism of our people. A larger crowd of men had hardly ever been in Fogelsville. Here one saw sick and crippled of all sorts; some came in here limping with canes in their hands who hardly had had a stick in their hands in twenty years; indeed who ever had a broken bone came to be examined for exemption. One had a heart complaint; another had liver trouble; others had dyspepsia; and a lesion was nurtured. . . . Others complained that they couldn't be away from home overnight and still others that they couldn't sleep in a strange bed.

In Lynn Township one fellow chopped off the thumb on his right hand. The doctor asked whether he was left handed. "No," was the reply. "Well, how then could you cut off your right thumb?" The poor fellow had not thought about that. Later he was drawn and paid, besides losing his thumb, $1,200 for a substitute. In short, the three townships, with little exception, were a total hospital; hardly one resident thereof had even a healthy skin. If Uncle Sam had no other means, the Union would have been in a bad way.

The Democratic Party was the majority in the Lehigh Valley, as it had been since the days of Thomas Jefferson. As Helffrich noted, the pro-Southern antiwar Copperhead movement recruited many members into the lodges of its "Knights of the Golden Circle":

Almost every Democrat of our neighborhood joined this society and all of them declared themselves against the War and manifested a certain hatred for every Republican because they blamed that party for the War in order to throw the blame from themselves. The Copperhead movement brought tension between neighbors. One of our rich Fogelsville farmers declared to me: If he would not have to go into the service, he would first begin at home to shoot people he didn't like.

Not even the ministry was exempt from political attack. As the Reverend Helffrich's pro-Union sympathies were well-known, he became a particular object of hostility. Democrats circulated vicious rumors about him in an effort to force his ouster from his Fogelsville pulpit. One opponent, James Lichtenwalner, was so outspoken and malicious in his statements about his pastor that Helffrich was finally compelled to bring a civil suit against him. As late as the fall of 1863, even after Southern armies had invaded Pennsylvania, feeling against Helffrich and the Republican cause ran so high that on election night, as the votes were being counted, crowds gathered outside his house screaming insults. During the day, these same crowds had loitered around the polling places, shouting insults to known Republicans.

If certain districts in the countryside were strongholds of opposition to the war, the cities tended to be rallying points for pro-Union sentiment. The day after the attack on Fort Sumter, which initiated open hostilities between North and South, hundreds attended a public meeting held in the public square at Easton. Within a week, five volunteer companies were organized, four at Easton and one at Bethlehem. Allentonians responded with particular enthusiasm and, the Allen Rifles, under the leadership of Colonel Tilghman Good, were among the "First Defenders" who rushed to Washington, D.C. to save the nation's capital from capture by the Confederate army. Ironically, their first battles took place not with Southerners, but with fellow Northerners who opposed the war. Thomas Yeager, commander of the first Allentown regiment, vividly described the adventures of his company as they travelled to Washington in late April of 1861:

Questions from the mob when we passed through; I had my men instructed to say nothing or look around, but stick to me; they did so: "Say, you traitors;" "Abolitionists;" "Abe Lincoln's Militia;" "Hurrah for South Carolina;" "Capital Success;" "Hit him;" "Stone him;" "Kill him;" "What muskets;" "No locks;" "No powder;" "Sponges to wipe cannons for Jeff Davis."

Right and left on us, their fists on our noses, you have no idea of the language, conduct, danger. The only reply I made was in one case: "Where are you going?" My remark was—"For my country."

Yeager, a successful Allentown merchant, would be killed by Confederate snipers at the Battle of Fair Oaks on June 1, 1862.

If the Civil War represented years of struggle and sacrifice, it also had moments of humanity. As in any modern army, the adage among Civil War soldiers might have been "hurry up and wait." While waiting, the soldiers devoted themselves to keeping warm, dry, and fed. They were aided in these efforts by friends and relatives who tried to keep them supplied with provisions from home. William J. Reichard, a private in Company G, 128th Pennsylvania Volunteers, happily thanked his father for "the bread, dried beef, 2 tin boxes of preserves & 2 of butter, apples and, the best of all, Sallie's wedding cake." When his father visited him at the front in December of 1862, he brought with him a turkey, fresh beef, and potatoes from the family farm. Even when they were strangers to one another, Lehigh Valley folks stuck together. As Reichard noted in one of his letters, "an old Allentown baker came to camp yesterday with sponge cakes which you can expect we fellows did relish. He lives in Alexandria, Virginia. His name I do not remember. He used to live in East Allentown."

Though the war engendered conflict on the home front, it did foster among those who served a powerful affirmation of fellowship. The war brought together city youth, farm boys, and newcomers, especially the valley's recent immigrants from England, Ireland, Wales, and Germany. This war generation would, at the conclusion of hostilities, become the leaders of the Lehigh Valley's economic and political life and would do so with a sense of community that would be inclusive and innovative rather than exclusive and conservative.

The role of these veterans in the area's political life is evident in Allentown, where 17 years after its incorporation as a city in 1867, five of its seven mayors had served in the Civil War. The organizer of the city's Board of Trade was veteran E.G. Martin. The father of the cement industry in the Lehigh Valley, David O. Saylor, was a veteran, as was his partner, Esaias Rehrig. James W. Fuller, who went on to found the Lehigh Car & Axle Works, the ancestor of Fuller Industries, was a veteran, as was William A. Roney, the man who introduced electricity to the Lehigh Valley. Success in the postwar world would go to those who knew how to apply the principles of responsibility and discipline that they had learned in the army to political, social, and economic activity.

It was a good thing that those who assumed political and economic leadership in the postwar period had undergone a "trial by fire" as preparation, for the bubble of wartime prosperity and postwar boom came to an end in 1873, with the collapse of the national economy. This collapse originated with the bankruptcy of the nation's leading investment bank, Jay Cooke and Company, whose failure was, in turn, linked to the insol-

These men were three Lehigh Valley residents who heeded the Union's call to arms for the Civil War. There was much opposition to the war in the rural areas of the valley, but the cities were full of pro-Union sentiment. (LCHS)

vency of the Philadelphia and Reading Railroad. Its impact on the Lehigh Valley consisted primarily of a drop in demand for iron and steel products, the major manufacture of the region's factories. The impact of this drop in demand was intensified by a change in the technology of iron manufacture, specifically the introduction of the Bessemer process which used soft coal. While some firms like the Bethlehem Iron Company were willing to accommodate themselves to this change, others—most notably the iron companies of Allentown, Easton and Catasauqua—were not. As a result, the valley's iron industry, which was once the greatest in the nation, would (Bethlehem excepted) shrink to insignificance.

The failure of the iron industry affected not only the cities and boroughs where the mills were located, but also the country towns where ore and flux were mined. There, the industrial crisis was matched by a crisis in agriculture. Farmers, by tying themselves to national commodity markets, had profited in the short run, since the canals and railroads had enabled them to sell their products in national and world markets. But, by the 1870s, as vast new agricultural domains were opened up in the American West and in Canada and Russia, Pennsylvania-German farmers found their products in competition with those of farmers throughout the world. Ironically, the more efficiently they produced crops—thanks to fertilizers, pesticides, new seed stocks, and machinery—the less they got for their products. Agricultural markets were becoming glutted with commodities.

Thus, the post-Civil War leaders of the Lehigh Valley faced broad tasks of economic reconstruction that encompassed both city and countryside. They also faced major social challenges. Economic development and crisis had brought to the Lehigh Valley all the problems of modern America: diverse populations in which the foreign-born were increasingly important; radical labor organizations such as the Knights of Labor and the Molly McGuires; an increasingly dislocated and disconnected rural population; and the difficulties of governing, educating, and overseeing the public health of rural crossroads and sleepy villages which had grown overnight into populous cities. Without committed and foresighted leadership, the valley could have easily become a forgotten economic backwater—as many regions of New England did after the Civil War. But in the Lehigh Valley, the peoples' special sense of cultural identity helped them to make a full transition into modern American nationality.

FACING PAGE
The importance of women in Pennsylvania-German farm families is clear in this photograph from the 1880s. Traveling photographers recorded these invaluable portraits of the uncommon folk of the day. (LCHS)

LEFT
Quilts were an important defense against the harsh Pennsylvania winters, and group quilting fulfilled a social function. In this 1884 photo Susan Lindenmuth continues a strong Lehigh Valley cultural tradition. (LCHS)

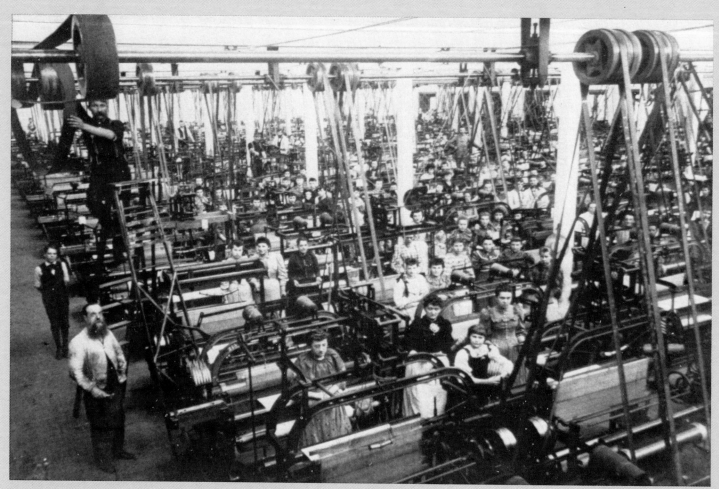

The industrial revolution of the 19th century brought women into factories. In this vast room at the Keystone Silk Mill in Emmaus, women cluster around machines powered by an overhead belt system. (LCHS)

CHAPTER FIVE

THE CRISIS OF ORDER: 1860 - 1920

In the early days before the Civil War, few residents could anticipate the impact industry would have on the entire character of life in the Lehigh Valley. Most people viewed the new mines, factories, canals, and railroads as improvements which enabled them to produce more and travel faster. Marvels, in short, which enlarged their world without really changing it. Hardly anyone saw them as forces capable of altering the network of human relationships that comprised family and community life.

Industrial growth came late to the Lehigh Valley. Then too, it was scattered over the countryside rather than concentrated in urban centers. But when it began to occur, it proceeded with incredible rapidity. Thus the people of the region remained innocent of the revolutionary possibilities of industrialism. As late as the 1850s, the towns and villages along the river were still places where everyone knew everyone else, where most people were still family farmers or merchants and artisans running family businesses, and where the traditional power of the churches and the leading families remained largely intact. Although shaken by the Panic of 1837 and the long depression that followed it, these events were viewed as affirmations of the strength and stability of the social order. They affected only speculators who, like John and Owen Rice, had striven too hard and aimed too high.

Only in the Moravian communities of Bethlehem, Nazareth, and Emmaus, where economic pressures had forced the aban-

donment of exclusivity, were the social dimensions of economic growth really evident. And even in Bethlehem, the extent of obvious change was limited, for outsiders like Asa Packer and his ambitious Yankee associates concentrated their activities in South Bethlehem, which lay across the Lehigh from the old religious settlement. Similarly, industrial growth in the Easton area occurred downriver from the city itself, in the new boroughs of Glendon and South Easton. Allentown also remained relatively untouched. Its iron mills and furnaces were remote from the town's commercial and residential center, and the largest plants lay up the Lehigh River, at Catasauqua, Coplay, and Hokendauqua. Scattered through the countryside, the iron mining and slate-quarrying centers of Hellertown, Orefield, and Slatington, as well as the early cement mills at Seigfried's Bridge and the Alburtis iron furnaces, lay beyond the view of the casual onlooker. Only students of such arcana as the federal *Census of Manufactures* and the county tax assessment lists could have recognized the extent to which the region had been industrialized by the middle of the 19th century. As for the newspapers, to which most people resorted for information about the world beyond their immediate experience, they were still primarily vehicles of public and commercial advertising. They had not yet developed a clear concept of news as a presentation of comprehensive viewpoints through a process of gathering and interpreting local and national events.

Thus, we can hardly fault the people of Lehigh and Northampton counties for their inability to foresee the social revolution that would result from the industrial one. Industry had, after all, been a familiar, if not dominant, feature of life in the Lehigh Valley since the completion of the Lehigh, Delaware, and Morris canals in the 1820s. While its effects on the landscape could not be ignored, these hardly seemed to extend to society. An early ballad about the men who built the Lehigh Canal clearly acknowledged their rowdiness:

When old Mauch Chunk was young,
Josiah used to say,
A man that labored hard should have
Six "Billy Cups" a day.
And so, with an unsparing hand,
The whiskey flood was flung,
And drunkards they were made by scores,
When old Mauch Chunk was young.

But the hard-drinking and hard-fisted canal builders and boatmen were, as the ballad suggests, regarded as amusing exceptions to the well-regulated lives of the people through whose towns and villages the waterway passed. The fact is that, to all appearances, economic development and population growth up to 1850 had not led to a social upheaval. Although Lehigh County's population had more than doubled between 1820

and 1850, the number of criminal cases brought before the Quarter Sessions Courts actually declined by more than half. From the standpoint of those living at mid-century, there seemed to be no reason to believe that industrial progress posed a threat to the social order.

But, with astonishing suddenness, public and private order began to collapse. No dramatic event caused the catastrophe. It was simply that older, more personal institutions of family and community government, while being able to contain and control a certain amount of increase in the quantity and diversity of the population, reached a critical point and faltered. Although Lehigh County's population between 1850 and 1860 increased only 30 percent, the number of criminal cases that came before the county court increased from 40 to 115, a jump of 288 percent. Between 1860 and the depression year of 1877, the number of criminal cases grew from 155 to 334 (190 percent), while the population increased just over 50 percent. Moreover, the kinds of crimes committed changed from relatively peaceful ones, violations of liquor laws and the fathering of illegitimate children, to violent and ugly crimes against persons and property—assaults, rapes, murders, frauds, and burglaries. Crimes against public morals, which had been virtually unknown in the first half of the century, became common, as prostitutes and bawdy houses became notorious features on certain streets in Allentown, Bethlehem, and Easton—as well as in the smaller industrial villages of the region. Such disorder could not be easily ignored, for it was all too visible. As the *Catasauqua Dispatch*

noted in April of 1880,

The pays of the several corporations last week made our streets very lively, and considerable money changed hands. To offset the pleasure of increasing wages, is that, in many cases, of increasing drunkenness, not alone confined to matured men, but participated in by minors and women. Our streets the past ten days have been perambulated by more inebriate persons than for some time in the past five years, and this has had the effect of arousing people to the necessity of praying relief of the court in refusing licenses to some of the hell holes parading under the titles of hotels, taverns, and restaurants.

On a more ominous note, the *Lehigh Valley Daily News* editorialized in November of 1868,

The practice of carrying "billies" and "pistols" by young men and rowdies, is extensively indulged in, and should be severely punished. A few examples would have a salutory effect in checking this dangerous evil.

The *Macungie Weekly Progress* of May 1888 addressed itself to another aspect of the problem of public order:

The Allentown Sunday Critic *devotes two columns in the last issue of describing the immorality of the Palace Skating Rink, at the foot of Hamilton Street Hill, now known to vulgar fame as Griffith's "merry-go-round," and faithfully portrays the habitues and their*

behavior in that place of sin, as the above paper calls it. Very young girls congregate there and meet young and old men, and their conduct is disgraceful in the extreme. If half is true as stated, it is surprising that such a crying evil has been allowed to exist in our county seat, and public indignation should be turned in the direction of closing up the vile place.

Although the majority of the population remained stolidly law abiding, the fact that so many appeared to be flouting law and convention was profoundly disturbing to those who were not.

If criminality and vice had been restricted to the industrial work force and to working-class neighborhoods, it might have been discounted as a regrettable but inevitable necessity of modern life. But this was not the case. The majority of defendants in criminal cases were not drunken representatives of one or another of the immigrant groups which had been moving into the Lehigh Valley since the 1830s. They were, overwhelmingly, people of Pennsylvania-German descent. Nor were they all of working-class origins for, as court records show, even respectable middle- and upper-class families were being shattered by alcoholism, venereal disease, suicide, and adultery. The sons and daughters of well-to-do merchants and professionals seemed no more controllable than the children of factory hands. Nor were problems of maintaining public and private order confined to the cities. Crime, vice, violence, madness, and suicide were even to be found in the rural townships. No level of society was unaffected.

The local press, taking its cue from big-city newspapers, tried valiantly to give the crisis a political and moral cast. For, if the problems were merely due to bad people—to immigrants or labor agitators, to tramps or the unchurched—it would seem more manageable. Accordingly, the editors raged about political corruption, about lawlessness in industrial wards, and the evils of saloons. They tried to ignore problems by making them humorous, depicting the Irish as comic drunkards, describing the antics of the "soiled doves" and vagrants brought before the Mayor's Court. But the news rather than the editorials and humorous fillers told the real story. No one, in towns where everyone knew everyone else, could ignore the poignancy of the death of a local watchmaker reported in the *Allentown Democrat* of October 1, 1884:

On Friday morning, J. Peter Roeder, a German watchmaker doing business in Romig's building, near the Court House, was found lying dead in a small private alley above Gordon Street, between Fifth and

ABOVE
Canal commerce opened the way to the industrialization of the Lehigh Valley. Barges carried coal throughout the valley's river and canal system and kept the iron mills' blast furnaces burning. Nonmotorized barges, pulled from the bank, were part of a technique called "towpath navigation." (Windsor)

FACING PAGE
One mile north of Coplay stands the village of Portland, so named because its only industrial establishment is Saylor's Portland cement works. This cement received its name from its first use in London. There the cement was used to create the Portland stone that can still be seen throughout the English capital. From *Autumn Leaves Upon the Lehigh* by Frank H. Taylor

TOP
This photo shows slate workers at an unidentified quarry in Lehigh Valley in the 1880s. Despite the physical dangers of quarrying, children worked 10-hour days just as adults did. (NCHGS)

ABOVE
The name of the town of Slatington suggests the town's major industry. The dozen firms quarrying here sent slate to destinations all over the U.S. and Europe. The oldest company operating here was the Lehigh Slate Company. From *Autumn Leaves Upon the Lehigh* by Frank H. Taylor

Sixth. He had been on a deep debauch for weeks, and on Tuesday evening visited a saloon in the neighborhood where he met his death. After leaving the saloon he was found lying on Gordon Street by several boys . . . who then dragged him into the alley, thinking he might there sleep off the effects of the intoxicants that had made him helpless. He was heard groaning by the near neighbors, but not looked after, since his condition was not regarded with any seriousness. Early in the morning, however, he was found dead on an ash pile, face downwards, and from appearances had been dead about five or six hours. The deceased was about forty-five years old and leaves a wife and six small children.

A death of this sort was not a private event, for his widow and children would continue to live in the community. At one time, church and family would have intervened to discourage the father's sprees and protect the widow and children. William Eckert, who later became a respectable Allentown merchant and a major real estate developer, described in a brief autobiography, how his family and how religion saved him from drink in the 1840s:

My father-in-law started my brother-in-law, Adam H. Eckert, and myself, in business. We worked faithfully for a while, but could not stand prosperity, and through gambling and drink we soon had no business, no stock, no shop. . . .

I then began to work for John F. Ruhe & Son, and was with them continuously for almost five years. After that I continued to work when it suited my fancy, and to waste my substance in riotous living, hoping, however, when I was in my sober thoughts that the day would come when I would be saved from the curse. . . . One day, with some of my companions in sin, I started to roam through the country, and a few days later I found myself in bed at Mechanicsville, sick from my debauchery and without a penny in my pocket. I started to walk to Catasauqua, with the intention of raising money there to buy more drink. . . .

Then the crisis came. While the glass was yet pressed to my lips, I besought the good lord to save me from my enemy, rum, and I went from that place with the determination that I would lead a different life. On my way from the tavern I stopped at a crossroad about a quarter of a mile away, and there I stood in the snow fully fifteen minutes, fighting the battle against drink, asking that God would give me strength to enable me to turn homeward and become a better man. The answer to my prayer came in a peculiar manner. While in the midst of a desperate struggle against my great enemy, a horse and sleigh came along in the direction of my home. I asked the man

The cornerstone on Ziegel's Church dates to May 16, 1796, making the building one of the oldest religious structures in Lehigh County. (LCHS)

ABOVE
Lutheran and Reformed congregations joined in 1741 to create the Union Church. The two congregations worshipped together in churches such as the one in Neff, shown here. (LCHS)

RIGHT
The Zion's Reformed Church stands in downtown Allentown. The Liberty Bell was hidden beneath the floor of this church from September 25, 1777 to June 1778. This church features a two-tower design with a limited transept and nave anteroom. (LCHS)

whether I could ride along, and he cheerfully granted my request. On the way I said to the driver, whose name was Fogelman, "Now I am saved, for today I have taken the last drop of liquor for my lifetime." He had confidence in what I said, and practically demonstrated it by inviting me to accompany him to his home for dinner, which I accepted. . . . From Mr. Fogelman's house I returned home, and my father gave me his usual and much-deserved lecture. I interrupted him and told him of my resolution never to drink again and from that day to this I have, with the help of God, kept my promise to my father.

Buoyed by the confidence of Mr. Fogelman and his family and forgiven by his father, Eckert's resolution to save himself from his "great enemy" was supported by his kin, who created new business opportunities for him, and by the church, which eventually made him a deacon of Zion Reformed Church. His rehabilitation was not easy:

After I had conquered rum I had considerable trouble to establish my good intentions and gain the confidence of my fellow men. For three years I struggled to make ends meet, during which time my good wife passed through a severe illness, and oftentimes I did not have ten cents to my name; but I prayed and hoped for the best, and at last everybody seemed to have confidence in me.

But however difficult, he was not alone in his struggle. Family, church, and a community of concern worked together to return him to sobriety and usefulness. J. Peter Roeder, 40 years later, could not expect that kind of aid. Nor could the unfortunate family he left behind.

If the newspapers were filled with tragic items that denoted a deep social crisis, the court records told the tale in even greater detail. One divorce case, involving a couple who had been married for 20 years and had two teenage children, suggested the dimensions of the crisis:

The evidence discloses the following facts: that one Mollie Young, a widow, kept a house of ill-repute at the corner of Hall and Turner Streets in the City of Allentown. That her reputation for chastity was not good. That men and women, singly and in couples were seen to enter her house both in the daytime and at night. That lewd women frequented the place. That upon one occasion, two boys and two girls, the girls in quite short dresses, came out of her house in the morning and while going up Hall St. were laughingly heard to say "that we had a good time last night, if our parents would only know where we had been." That in the summer time a beer wagon stops there every

day and unloads boxes containing bottles.

That the respondent . . . was a frequenter of the house of Mollie Young. That he was frequently seen to enter the house both in the daytime and at night. That on one occasion he was seen in the act of putting on his pants on the second floor in a rear room; on another occasion he was seen in the cellar at nine o'clock in the evening. He was frequently seen in the yard and the house. . . . That he shovelled the snow in front of Mollie Young's house while his wife was shovelling the snow in front of her house. . . .

Why should a man who had been a faithful husband and father for 20 years suddenly take up residence in a house of ill-repute? And who were the parents who did not know where their children had been the night before? The City Fathers shut down the bawdy houses and hired more police, but to no avail. For the real problem, as it became increasingly apparent, lay not with those who profited from immorality, but with the inability of apparently respectable citizens to resist immorality. Something had to be done to restore the religious and familial institutions which had once held the community together.

The older institutions of family and church could not deal with the problems of order as effectively as they had in the past, although they tried valiantly to do so. Between 1850 and 1875, dozens of new churches were established in the Lehigh Valley—14 in Allentown alone. While many of these churches were formed by the older Reformed, Lutheran, and Moravian denominations, many represented newer groups—the Roman Catholics and Jews—as well as a host of Protestant sects, including Episcopalians, Baptists, Methodists, and Evangelicals. The churches did not restrict themselves to liturgical exercises. They were active in the realm of education. All maintained Sunday schools for the young and Bible classes for adults. The Moravians established Moravian College in 1863, the Lutherans set up Muhlenberg College in 1867, and, in 1868, the Reformed Church created the Allentown College for Women (now Cedar Crest). The Roman Catholics by the 1870s were operating parochial schools in the valley. In addition, church members were active in charitable and relief organizations directed at aiding the unfortunate and reaching out to the unchurched.

Curiously, all this ecclesiastical activity, however vigorous, was limited in its impact. For underlying much of it was discontent and dissension within congregations. In the 1860s, the Lutherans, both locally and on a statewide level, split over questions of language and liturgy. Comparable quarrels affected both the Reformed and the Roman Catholic churches. In the 1890s,

ABOVE
This is the chapel at Muhlenberg College, built in brick neo-Gothic style. The college was named after a Pennsylvania German, Reverend Henry Melchoir Muhlenberg, who was influential in Penn's experiment with religious freedom in the New World. (LCHS)

RIGHT
Henry Melchoir Muhlenberg immigrated to America in 1742 and was assigned to the United Congregation of Lutherans in Philadelphia. He eventually became the patriarch of the Lutheran church. (NCHGS)

the Evangelical Church broke apart over the question of the authority of bishops. Many of these quarrels led to acrimonious court battles between congregational factions over control of church assets. Many, disgusted with the unchristian conduct of their fellow congregants, left older churches to join new ones. Thus, for example, William Eckert left his deaconate at Zion's Reformed in Allentown to join the United Brethren. His cousin Charles Eckert joined the Presbyterians. All this ferment tended to divide and weaken the role of churches as forces of community authority. As the number of religious options increased, religious allegiance became an individual matter and ministers became reluctant to act dictatorially or to take positions on controversial matters for fear of alienating their congregations. Thus, while organized religion flourished, its power over the population declined. As sociologist James Bossard concluded in his 1918 pamphlet, *The Churches of Allentown: A Statistical Study*:

The church comes into actual contact, and influences, but a minority of the people in this city. Even if its influence upon this minority is all that can be desired, there remains the majority to be considered. Whatever of religious, moral, and ethical influence that is brought to bear upon this majority under actually existing conditions, must come from some other source. Whatever standards of conduct are evolved, whatever sense of values is developed, whatever conceptions of right and wrong are formed, whatever notion of individual and social responsibility is held, all these are, among the majority of the citizenship of Allentown, the product of other forces than the direct touch of the religious agencies and organizations.

The churches, while they remained important, could not by themselves deal with the crisis of order.

The family was no more able than the church to deal with the crisis. For industrialism altered relations between family members in ways that weakened its overall authority. The family farm or workshop of the pre-industrial period depended on the labor and skills of all family members from the youngest to the oldest. The young were thus kept under surveillance at all times. But the family had no place in factories and offices. Mothers and fathers, who once shared the burdens of work and childrearing, had to act in widely separated spheres, the man in the impersonal world of work, the woman in the home. This division of labor set up a basis for differences of opinion which frequently set husbands and wives at odds—often sending husbands to the less pressured atmosphere of the saloon.

LEFT
Zion's Church in Upper Milford Township, was one of the parishes of the Reverend Eli Keller. The imposing structure shows two galleries of windows in the nave and a row of crypt windows. (LCHS)

ABOVE
Produce from neighboring farms fills baskets in front of an Allentown market on Hamilton Street. Notice the display of flour in the window. (LCHS)

ABOVE
Workers in a shoe factory are
surrounded by examples of their
craft in this photograph from
about 1888. (LCHS)

FACING PAGE, TOP
The early 20th century saw a
revival of the severe romanesque
style popular during the
previous century. This photo
shows an example of that style
in the nearly complete Blue
Church near Limeport (c.
1920). (LCHS)

FACING PAGE, BOTTOM
This is the Catholic Church of
the Immaculate Conception on
Ridge Avenue in Allentown.
The church was built by
members of the city's Irish
Catholic community following
an 1868 quarrel with the
German Catholics. Courtesy,
Charles D. Snelling Collection

Certainly the widespread employment of women and children in industry altered the character of family authority. As Bossard noted:

The writer recalls how, as a boy at the close of the last century, he wrestled with the invitation of the "Small Boys Wanted Here" sign which adorned the doorways and outside walls of the mills, weighing their call, with the promise of ready cash, against the parental mandate to continue a school career. Such signs, together with such as "Girls Wanted," "Women Wanted," and "Young Children Wanted," were for almost three decades familiar sights, staring passersby in the face day after day.

In some ways the employment of women and children had positive advantages. As Bossard pointed out:

While the head of the family worked in the various establishments in and about the city, the women and children of the household could contribute their share to the family income. Many an older family today owns its own home as a result of this earlier prosperity, when practically every member of the family was in receipt of a pay envelope.

But industry also had adverse effects on family life, especially on the authority of parents. When Bossard was conducting his study of Allentown churches, he surveyed the activities of those not attending services:

Most of the people encountered on the streets were young people—an almost endless procession of young men and women, for the most part in their teens or slightly over, walking back and forth, looking and waiting to be looked at, wooing and willing to be wooed. Undoubtedly, the parents of many of these young people believed that they were in church. This excuse is often necessary in order to obtain parental consent to leave home on a Sunday evening. But the writer is convinced that there is, in this city, a most marked laxity of parental control over the younger members of the family.

During the summer of 1917, as this thesis was being written, a United States Army Ambulance Camp was located within the boundaries of the city. As many as 8,000 young men were stationed in this camp—Camp Crane—during the summer and early fall. During this entire time, the writer, as a member of the staff of a morning newspaper, was obliged to be on the street at all hours of the night. The number of young girls, many with their hair in braids, who promenaded on the streets every evening of the week, is almost

unbelievable. Insistently the question presented itself to the writer: Where are the parents of these girls?

Of course, in the case of girls over sixteen years of age, certain local facts have their bearing. Very many of these girls work in the numerous silk mills of the city. They are self-supporting for the most part. They probably contribute to the family income. This gives them undue independence of parental supervision. When a seventeen year old girl helps to pay the landlord or the grocer, it is somewhat difficult for parents to interfere with the "pleasure" of their daughter.

It was bad enough for young women of 17 to behave this way. It was even worse, however, when children barely in their teens were kept out of school to support their families or to take care of their younger siblings while their parents worked. Again and again, factory inspector Annie Leisenring found cases in which parents had connived with factory owners to falsify working papers and thus permit their children to find places in the mills or in the streets. Ralph Holben, who wrote his 1923 doctoral dissertation, *Poverty in Relation to Education*, based on the case records of Allentown's Associated Charities, pointed out that sending children to work rather than to school produced unhappy social consequences:

The savage struggle for existence dictates no other choice than a grim determination to capitalize the human assets of the family, while it is still possible to do so. Poverty, in its most squalid phases, produces poverty of thought, with social and economic consequences which, it is not difficult to imagine, thus resembles an endless chain. Poverty of thought of parents, expressed in terms of perverted educational attitudes, eventuates in curtailed education of children. This spells curtailed opportunity which admits only to the ranks of delinquency, dependency, and their train of ills, and so in the succeeding generation we come back to where we started, only to find poverty and its concomitant, poverty of thought, continuing its deadly chain of cause and effect, interminably.

The unsupervised young were a haunting specter of American industrial centers in the last third of the 19th century: children whose parents were working 12 hours a day, 7 days a week, left to shift for themselves in the streets and alleys; children working in shops and factories, no longer as apprentices whose masters regarded them in a fatherly fashion, but as miserable manual laborers doing for a few cents a day jobs that no adult would do; and children running errands in the saloons and brothels, many becoming corrupted themselves before attaining adolescence. These young people made up the mobs which had, during the great railroad strike of 1877, looted and burned shops and stoned the militia in Reading, Pittsburgh, Baltimore, and Chicago. It was to them that John Eaton, first U.S. Commissioner of Education, referred when he wrote, in 1878, that the nation would have to "weigh the cost of the mob and the tramp against the cost of universal public education."

The newspapers could moralize about the misdeeds of responsible adults. The churches could reach out to reform them through their teachings. But only the most hardened social Darwinist would argue that the infant child of Ann McGinley, found dead of exposure in the streets of Allentown's Sixth Ward in September of 1879, deserved its fate, or that the 14-year-old boy whose arm was chewed up in the machinery of a shoe factory in the same year should, from any reasonable standpoint, have been forced into the "struggle for existence" from which the "fittest" were supposed to emerge. And even if only the poor were affected by the breakdown in family life—which was not the case—their misfortunes could not be isolated from the rest of society. Children of the poor, afflicted with lice, syphilis, tuberculosis, and other contagious diseases were a clear and present danger to the whole community, besides being pitiable. And the very presence of a submerged and oppressed mass in a supposedly Christian and democratic community brutalized and hardened its sensibilities. However anxious the well-to-do may have been to preserve property and order, the presence of the poor in large numbers posed difficult ethical and practical questions. It was hard for professed Christians to ignore the ever-growing impoverishment of the working classes, especially the suffering of children who were in no way responsible for their poverty; no less so for the professed democrats to support a system in which the majority would, if present trends continued, soon consist of the poor and the foreign-born.

Thus, the institutions of community, even as they began to respond to these challenges in the 1860s and 1870s, were limited in what they could do. Even government was not prepared to deal with the new responsibilities forced upon it by urban and industrial growth. To begin with, the Pennsylvania-Germans had always opposed big government. They preferred to leave major social tasks to families and voluntary associations—and with good reason—for they knew that big government created opportunities for political corruption. No sooner had Allentown, the valley's first incorporated municipality, taken on the enormous burdens of overseeing the paving of the city's streets, the laying of water and sewer lines, and the main-

LEFT
Annie Weiser Leisenring was one of the state's earliest factory inspectors. Performing her job uncompromisingly, she visited many Lehigh Valley factories during the late 1800s and reported all substandard conditions to the chief inspector in Harrisburg. As a female German professional, she had to withstand multiple prejudices. Courtesy, Pennsylvania Historical and Museum Commission

ABOVE
Water surrounds Allentown. The city, flanked by the Lehigh and the Little Lehigh rivers, is bounded in front by Jordan Brook, named after the river in the Bible. From *Autumn Leaves Upon the Lehigh* by Frank H. Taylor

Northampton Street in Easton looking west from Center Square typifies the commercial business district of a small American town of the 1880s. (NCHGS)

tenance of public health and safety, than it discovered how difficult it was to keep public servants and those with whom they contracted honest and frugal. As early as 1875, the Common Council was forced to investigate the conduct of the Water Department. In 1884, chicanery was discovered in the awarding of city paving contracts. The building of the Gordon Street storm sewer provided an endless topic of debate between those who claimed it essential to render the street safe during heavy rains and their opponents, who asserted that the project was merely a means for spreading the public largesse among a coterie of political favorites.

If the physical tasks of city administration were difficult to handle, the social burdens were nearly overwhelming. In 1875 alone, for example, over 4,000 homeless persons had to be lodged and fed in the city's jails. In 1881, smallpox broke out in a family of cigar makers on Gordon Street. It spread from them to their fellow employees at the Ruhe Brothers' cigar factory and into the general population. The city had to enact drastic quarantine measures and mount a massive inoculation program. By the end of the summer of 1881, over 10,000 persons had been inoculated—almost half of the city's population. Although city government had proved effective in this instance, there was no guarantee that it would be so fortunate in the future. As the city health officer pointed out in 1885, as he discussed the fall's rash of cases of typhoid:

. . . it is a well accepted fact that typhoid fever emanates pre-eminently from decomposition of animal and vegetable matter; and our records show that when such a condition of things is at its height we have the most cases. It becomes us right here to make an earnest appeal for a "Garbage System," whereby said garbage be removed regularly, and not allowed to remain on piles and heaps until the police are attracted by its offensive odors, or neighbors become quarrelsome by each one throwing it the farthest away from his house and invariably close to some other one's door. If anything is inconsistant with sanitation, hygiene, or good morals, this certainly is; and the history of the larger cities clearly demonstrates that the "Garbage System" is the only way of driving out this evil.

But implementing social and public health programs was expensive and many people doubted the competence of government to enact them.

Their doubts were not entirely misplaced. The corrupt condition of government on all levels was a major element in the post-Civil War crisis of order. The cities were particularly afflicted by "rings" of politicians who, on a reduced level, were as venal as New York's notorious Boss Tweed. The growth of political machines was a complicated phenomenon. Their growth can be linked to the failure of traditional community institutions as well as to the growing need for government services. Political bosses could do things for those who supported them which families and churches could not. When a boss saw to it that a major supporter was awarded a municipal contract for street-paving, pipe-laying, or constructing a public edifice, he was in a position to ask that the supporter hire a certain number of politically loyal laborers. Similarly, appointments to such city agencies as the police and fire departments were governed by political loyalty rather than fitness to do the job. Thus the boss could supply jobs to the unemployed and, by the judicious awarding of contracts, create jobs, in exchange for votes. The boss could, by using public funds and public power in certain ways, both enrich himself and his friends and, at the same time, give the poor assistance that no other agency could provide.

But however much the boss benefited his constituency, his impact on public order was negative. Scarce financial resources were wasted in unnecessary and extravagant public projects, such as the new (in 1861) Northampton County Courthouse in Easton. Its location, a goodly distance from the center of town, had been dictated, reformers claimed, by the real estate interests of certain prominent Democratic politicians, whose holdings adjacent to the new structure would gain enormously in value. One disgruntled citizen, attorney Alexander E. Brown, addressed the following poetic attack on the project to County Commissioner Jacob Houck:

These are the wise men who showed their skill
By planting this nuisance on top of the hill,
Regardless of safety, regardless of time,
Or the necks of the people compelled to climb;
For when the court was called it was all the same—
The young or old, the halt or the lame—
They must mount with the lawyers who climb up the hills,
To visit the clerks with the awful long bills,
Who wrote in the house that Houck built.

Political corruption had its amusing sides. But it also had its less comic elements, especially in its impact on the electoral process. With substantial financial interests, as well as scores of patronage jobs, riding on the outcome of elections, political contests became violent. Vote-buying, with money, with liquor, and

The Church of the Sacred Heart of Jesus was built by the German members of Allentown's Catholic community in the early 1870s. This was the first Catholic Church in downtown Allentown. Courtesy, Charles D. Snelling Collection

with promises of government favors, became common. Intimidation of voters and outright ballot fraud marred the democratic process. In North Whitehall Township, for example, when a citizen challenged the vote of a man he knew to have voted earlier in the city of Allentown, he was set upon and beaten by a gang of eight men. The gang had apparently been sent out from the city to cast multiple ballots (anticipating James M. Curley's dictum, "vote early, vote often") and to harass the opposition. Through the 1870s and 1880s, German and Irish mobs, inflamed by rum and oratory, battled in the streets at election time.

This last aspect of bossism, its playing on the rivalries between ethnic, religious, and economic groups, had a particularly destructive impact on the integrity of the Lehigh Valley's communities. As long as any numerically significant group felt that its interests were distinct from those of others, cooperation and consensus in rebuilding the social order could not be achieved. The region was fortunate in that its immigrants never translated ethnic rivalries into class conflict, as the Irish miners at Mauch Chunk did in organizing the terrorist group, the Molly McGuires. Nevertheless, conflicts between groups in the area were frequent and violent. One case in the Lehigh County court records, the murder of Lawrence Hickey, an Englishman, by Robert Thomas, a Welshman, at Catasauqua in 1868, indicates not only the pervasiveness of such conflicts, but also the way in which they were viewed. Both men were drinking in the crowded bar of the United States Hotel. Hickey, though only 22, had a reputation as a belligerent drunk. He began quarrelling with the bartender. Within minutes, he was standing in the middle of the tap room declaring that he could "whip the best Irishman, Dutchman, or Welshman in the house." Robert Thomas rose from the card table where he had been sitting. Raising his fist, he knocked Hickey down. He then vindicated his national pride by stomping the prone man, breaking his jaw and causing internal injuries. The insensible victim was then thrown out into the street, where his body lay until some acquaintances found him and carried him home, where he died two days later, without regaining consciousness. All the witnesses' accounts of the crime are remarkable in their lack of passion. They described the event as though it was the sort of thing that happened all the time—as it very likely did.

This conflict was different only in degree from the quarrel between German and Irish communicants which, on St. Patrick's day of 1866, shattered the unity of Allentown's Roman Catholic community. The two groups had coexisted uneasily for many years, struggling over the nationality of their priests and the language in which church business was to be conducted. Although no records survive to tell exactly what took place between the Irish and German Catholics in March of 1866, it must have been rather dramatic. By the first week of April, both the Irish priest, Father McEnroe, and the German curate, Father Kaelin, had left the parish for other assignments, and the German and Irish parishioners were refusing to meet together for worship. A prolonged battle between the factions ensued over control of the old church on Ridge Avenue. It was eventually sold at public auction in 1869. The Irish, who were the high bidders, took control of the structure. The Germans, who had managed to retain the parish records and other movable property, established their own congregation, *Herz Jesu Kirche* (Sacred Heart Church) on North 4th Street.

Ironically, the major actors in the rebuilding of public and private order in the Lehigh Valley's towns and cities proved to be the area's businessmen. Their peculiar importance was due to several things. First, they were relatively united as a group. Whatever ethnic, religious, and political differences separated them, they had in common a more compelling interest: the desire to make money. Crime, violence, and public disorder was not conducive to profit-making. Thus, in confronting the crisis, businessmen began to come together to present a united front in favor of stability and order. Secondly, the crisis of public order coincided with a major economic problem, the Panic of 1873, and the collapse of the anthracite iron industry due to improved Bessemer technology, which used the bituminous coal of western Pennsylvania. The entrepreneurs of the Lehigh Valley not only faced the short-term economic dislocation resulting from the panic and the national depression that followed it, but also a long-term problem, resulting from the obsolescence of the region's major industry.

The cities and towns of the Lehigh Valley responded in different ways to this challenge. Easton did the least. Its businessmen had, on the whole, been less than wholehearted in their support of industry. And, in any case, the major foundries and mills lay outside the city, across the Delaware at Phillipsburg, at Glendon, and South Easton. They appear to have been content to let industry decline and let its troublesome work force move elsewhere. The business leaders of Allentown and Bethlehem were far less passive. Allentonians, recognizing that the enormous growth of their town had been sustained by the iron industry, quickly acted to attract new manufacturing enterprises. They formed the Allentown Board

Education prospered along with industry in the Lehigh Valley. This is Pardee Hall at Lafayette College in Easton in about 1873. Also shown here is the college's library and reading room, built in the classic English manner. From *Autumn Leaves Upon the Lehigh* by Frank H. Taylor

TOP
The Adelaide Silk Mill of the Phoenix Silk company was a major Allentown industry. Mills such as this one made the Lehigh Valley one of the nation's textile centers. Courtesy, Charles D. Snelling

ABOVE
On July 9, 1888, an explosion occurred in the Adelaide Mill of the Phoenix Silk Company in Allentown on the southwest corner of Race and Linden streets. Compare the size of the men to the great driving wheel inside the mill. (LCHS)

ABOVE RIGHT
These are the works of the Bethlehem Iron Company as they appeared in 1865. Construction began in 1860 with the erection of an iron rail mill, a puddle mill, and a blast furnace. From *Autumn Leaves Upon the Lehigh* by Frank H. Taylor

of Trade which, by 1881, had succeeded in attracting investors from Paterson, New Jersey, to establish the Phoenix Silk Manufacturing Company. Businessmen, working together, offered a factory site in the center of town, as well as a subscription to a substantial portion of the company's stock. The opening of the mill in the fall of 1881 was a public celebration attended by several thousand spectators, as well as prominent persons from New York and New Jersey. The Phoenix company was the first of many which would come to the area in succeeding decades, making the valley one of the textile manufacturing centers of the nation. Another coup for the Board of Trade was the decision of the Iowa Barb Wire Company to locate its plant in Allentown. The company had originally been situated in Johnstown. It moved to South Easton in the early 1880s, but finding its prospects limited there, finally settled in Allentown, where it grew to enormous size.

The result of these actions was a diversification of the city's economy. No longer dependent on a single industry, it would

be relatively immune to the technological changes and swings in the business cycle. And diversity, rather than concentration on a single industry like iron, promoted a continuation of cooperative civic-mindedness in the business community, permitting it both to continue to encourage the relocation of businesses from other places (Mack Truck, for example, would come to Allentown from New York in 1905), and to begin to deal, beyond the economic realm, with the problems of government and society.

Bethlehem was also active in its response to the collapse of order, though it followed a course of action different from both Allentown's and Easton's. The major factor in determining its response was the fact that its iron industry was peculiarly innovative. Thus, when the iron masters of Lehigh County persisted in their attachment to anthracite and cast iron, the Bethlehem Iron Company, under the guidance of John Fritz, was quick to adopt the new Bessemer technique, which produced a stronger and longer-lasting product. Always one step

ahead of the competition, Fritz and Bethlehem Iron prospered in times when other men failed. In spite of the Panic of 1873, Bethlehem Iron, as one of the few companies in the United States capable of making steel rails, was ready to fill orders from railroad companies, which had, until then, been forced to import their rails from England. Similarly, when the federal government began to rebuild the U.S. Navy in the mid-1880s, the company was one of the few able to offer iron plate equal in quality to that produced in Germany. Soon it expanded its operations into the production of heavy forgings for naval canons. The steel industry prospered through this difficult period, and prospering along with it, Bethlehem grew far beyond its bucolic beginnings as a religious commune.

But Bethlehem's growth followed a very different pattern from Allentown's. The town had not, since the advent of industry and the influx of non-Moravians, really possessed a unified sense of community. The Moravians kept to their side of the river and the Yankee industrialists and their polyglot

ABOVE
This excavation at the Chapman Slate Quarry measured 240 feet in depth by 300 feet in width by 820 feet in length. Slate was used for roofing, stairs, blackboards, billiard tables, and many other purposes. The darkness of the sky shown in the painting was caused by smoke from the massive amount of coal used to process slate. From *Autumn Leaves Upon the Lehigh* by Frank H. Taylor

FACING PAGE, TOP
The Easton National Bank building represented the sense of economic stability necessary to attract new businesses to the town. Easton's development came first in the Lehigh Valley before 1850, but Allentown and Bethlehem began with a better industrial environment. (NCHGS)

FACING PAGE, BOTTOM
This is a painting of the first locomotive built in the South Easton shops. The wooden cab has brass ornamentation. The name on the cab, Anthracite, refers to the type of hard coal that was the primary source of the Valley's—and the railroad's—prosperity. (NCHGS)

work force filled the fields and farms of west and south Bethlehem with factories and houses of varying degrees of grandeur. Unlike Allentown, Bethlehem early developed exclusive neighborhoods that separated the rich from the poor and capitalist from laborer. With the enormous concentration of wealth and power in the hands of the small group that controlled the Lehigh Valley Railroad and the Bethlehem Iron Company, Asa Packer and his descendants—the Sayres, the Lindermans, the Wilburs, and others—there was little need to achieve social order through consensus and cooperation. This group simply imposed its solutions on the people, not only by providing work for them, but also by financing charitable enterprises, schools, churches, and St. Luke's Hospital, which served their obvious needs. Fragmented as it was, Bethlehem and its people were neither acutely aware of one another's problems, nor did they feel compelled to restore a sense of community which had never existed in the first place. Nevertheless, all groups were active, each in its own way, in dealing with the social crisis. The Moravians, with their long history of missionary work, were quick to turn their attention to the problems of Bethlehem's poor. And the Episcopalian-Yankee entrepreneurs were no less active, for the Episcopal Church had originated the "Social Gospel" to deal with England's problems of industrial poverty.

The region's response to the challenge of industrialism and to the search for industrial order in the last quarter of the 19th century was diverse. Bethlehem remained a center of heavy industry, prosperous, but lacking in unity. Allentown developed a diversified and largely commercial economy, its industrial sector characterized by many smaller plants rather than being dominated by a single huge enterprise such as Bethlehem Iron. This diversity was the product of the cooperative actions of the city's businessmen. Easton, though sustained by the busy arteries of transportation that flowed through it, was content to deal with industrial problems by discouraging industry—a pattern that would eventually change (in 1901, 30 years after Allentown, its businessmen would organize a Board of Trade). Economic stability was the first and certainly the most important step towards the restoration of order in government, in society, and in the private lives of the citizenry. Fortunately, the business leaders of the Lehigh Valley, especially those of Allentown and Bethlehem, were farsighted enough to know that their economic achievements were only the beginning of their larger task. Having laid a firm economic foundation, they were ready to proceed with the construction of a new order.

These row houses on Seventh Street in Allentown typify the urban growth that accompanied the rise of industry in the Lehigh Valley. Inexpensive and attractive housing was an important factor in bringing new industry to Allentown after the depression of the 1870s.

TOWARD COMMUNITY: 1880-1960

In the fall of 1914, the Coopersburg Neighborhood Association and the Moravian Country Church Commission published a remarkable pamphlet entitled *The Coopersburg Survey, Being a Study of the Community around Coopersburg, Lehigh County, Pennsylvania.* This "social inventory," as it called itself, in many ways summarized the transformation of society and social outlook in the Lehigh Valley in the 40 years since the catastrophic depression of the 1870s. Citizens, businessmen, and public officials had confronted the hard fact that the future of the region could not be guided either by moralizing or turning away from the realities of industrial life. The problems resulting from industrial and urban growth could only be engaged and dealt with by the whole populace organizing itself to determine community needs, to ascertain community resources, and to direct the community's energies to common purposes. Little Coopersburg with its "750 souls" was doing what the larger settlements in the valley had been striving to do for four decades.

The effort that led to the publication of *Coopersburg Survey* had begun a year earlier. The local Moravian congregation called a public meeting to discuss community problems. The townspeople met on a January evening. Before they adjourned, they had created a comprehensive agency, the Coopersburg Neighborhood Association, which, in turn, delegated its tasks to five committees: industrial, recreation, civic improvement, health and hygiene, home and school, and publicity. The asso-

ciation was willing to confront the whole range of community issues. Rather than imposing a scheme of order based on government dollars and policies, the association, made up of the existing organizations of the community—schools, fraternal orders, and businesses—proposed to use its own resources to solve its own problems.

The association proceeded with a will. Its Industrial Committee acted as a board of trade, seeking to attract new commercial and manufacturing enterprises. To do so, it purchased a large tract of land and advertised free factory sites for industries willing to locate in Coopersburg. This industrial park scheme had a dual motive. On the one hand, it served to attract new enterprises. On the other, it ensured that the companies that came were ones willing to serve the community's best interests. As the committee's report noted, the industrial park scheme would give it "absolute control" over what sorts of firms came into the community. (They probably wanted to discourage companies like the Gabriel Hosiery Mills, the town's largest employer, which had moved to Coopersburg from Allentown in 1903. The Gabriels were notorious for their use of child labor at a time when most other employers in the Lehigh Valley had abandoned the practice.) Acknowledging that a shortage of adequate housing discouraged industrial growth, the committee organized a savings and loan association. This too had a dual purpose, not only enlarging the amount of capital available for home building, but also encouraging economic virtues among the young, who would otherwise squander their earnings in saloons or other unsavory places. As the *Survey* noted, "a special effort was made to enlist young men in the ranks of the stockholders and in this way many have become regular savers."

The Civic Improvement Committee took as its main task the gathering of data for a social census to assess the problems and resources of the community. It also devoted its energies to developing town spirit, sponsoring, among other things, the creation of a Coopersburg slogan, motto, hymn, and flag. When the railroad station burned, the committee arranged substitute accommodations for travelers and secured commitments from the railroad company to construct a new facility. The Recreation Committee sponsored the organization of an assortment of groups and facilities to ensure the socially productive use of leisure time, especially among the young. By the end of 1914, a Coopersburg orchestra, band, and glee club were put together, as well as a boy scout troup. Talent shows, plays, and concerts were produced, and a town baseball team was recruited and provided with a playing field. Plans were drawn up for the construction of a community park, which was to include picnic grounds, a swimming "pond," and tennis courts. The Home and School Committee functioned as a parent-teachers association, coordinating the socializing role of schools and families. Working with the Recreation Committee, it sponsored social events that brought townspeople of all ages together. These included pageants illustrating the history of the town, which reminded the citizens of their common heritage. Finally, the Health and Hygiene Committee and the Religion and Morals Committees sought to identify and correct sources of physical and spiritual malaise.

Coopersburg's activities were a microcosm of the reordering of political, social, and economic life that had been taking place in the Lehigh Valley's larger urban centers, especially Bethlehem and Allentown, since the 1880s. And it was a portent of the direction these communities would take in the course of the 20th century. The essence of this reorganization was determined cooperative action among all groups to promote economic progress and, at the same time, to meet the human needs that could no longer be answered by the family and the locality alone. Because the basis of this reorganization was in the private sector, particularly commerce and manufacturing, and because the economic characteristics of the Lehigh Valley's communities differed (Allentown's being diversified and controlled by many companies; Bethlehem's being heavily industrial and dominated by a single great manufacturing firm, Bethlehem Iron; and Easton's being primarily commercial), the actual forms that community reorganization took varied, tending to emphasize the differences rather than the similarities between communities. As each worked cooperatively to come to grips with its own problems, each, although informed by a common cooperative sensibility, began to develop along diverging paths.

Bethlehem: Corporation and Community

The cooperative community-oriented sensibility that informed the transformation of the towns and cities of the Lehigh Valley had complex roots—origins that differed from place to place. Bethlehem's transformation is instructive in this regard. Historically, the town had always possessed a communitarian orientation. The Moravian Church, which had founded the town, had been a communal organization, subsuming individual interests, including economic ones, to the general welfare. But the failure of the Moravian's exclusive settlement and the fact that their scheme of community organization was exclusively focused on church members tended to inhibit rather than encourage a community approach to social problems later in the century, when Bethlehem had become religiously and ethnically diverse.

Nevertheless, there were other strands of the Moravian tradition that would lend themselves to such an approach. The first was the Moravian's early interest in interchurch cooperation, which led the sect to complement rather than compete with other denominations. The second was the Moravian tradition of missionary work, which in the 18th and early 19th centuries had been primarily directed to Indians. The social challenges of the post-Civil War period revived the importance of these themes, turning the church, as the Coopersburg example suggests, away from exclusivity toward inclusive communitarianism in cooperation with business and other religious denominations.

But just as the Moravians were only one element in Bethlehem, so their renewed social commitment was only one component in the broad task of community reconstruction. A second element involved the group of Yankee industrialists who had settled and developed South Bethlehem. Led by Asa Packer and his associates, the Wilburs, Sayres, and Lindermans, this group was characterized by that notable New England trait, the propensity to do things through institutions. Just as they had busily transformed the economy of the region through aggressive corporate activity in railroading, banking, and manufacturing, so they, with equal ardor, founded charitable, religious, and educational enterprises, most notably, Lehigh University (1865), St. Luke's Hospital (1871), and the Episcopal churches. Religion was a powerful motivating force for this group. They were enthusiastic Episcopalians, the denomination that pioneered the "social gospel," the particular mission of the church among the poor, and which was also aggressive in converting newly rich commercial and industrial classes which, in turn, were motivated to reach out to redeem the unchurched poor.

Another important aspect of this group was its Yankee practicality, which led its members to do business with whomever would serve its interests, regardless of creed or national origin. Such openness was essential to cooperative efforts. Thus, although the Packer group and the Moravians each pursued their own paths at the outset, the foundation was in place for a cooperative and community-oriented approach to the problems of urban industrialism.

The third and perhaps most important component of communitarianism was economic, emanating from the peculiar character of Bethlehem's largest industries, the Bethlehem Iron Company and the Lehigh Valley Railroad. Industry is generally thought of as a source of social problems rather than a solution to them. In fact, both characteristics are present. As a source of

TOP
The dedication of Comenius
Hall in 1892 marked the
opening of Moravian College
and Theological Seminary. The
school occupies the same
location today. (NCHGS)

ABOVE
Packer Hall of Lehigh University
was named after Asa Packer, the
university's founder, and
dedicated on June 20, 1869.
Until 1958, when it became the
University Center, the hall held
lecture rooms, the president's
office, a chapel, the university's
archives, and the library.
Courtesy, Linderman Library-
Lehigh University, Bethlehem

problems, industry is, first and foremost, self-interested: its primary object is to make profits for its stockholders. To do so in the highly competitive context of the late 19th century's "age of enterprise" required many actions which were not, in the short term, in the community interest. Production costs had to be rigorously controlled in order to undersell competitors. And the most flexible dimension of production cost was labor. Wages could be cut, hours lengthened, and the speed of production increased or decreased with market demand. And if workers didn't like it, there was little to be done, for the labor market was flooded with immigrants, any of whom would happily fill positions vacated by the discontented.

Technical innovation was another method of increasing competitiveness, an area in which the Bethlehem Iron Company was particularly notable. This company pioneered the introduction of Bessemer converters for steelmaking (giving the company a head start in domestic production of steel rails) and achieved a near monopoly in the production of armor plate for naval vessels. After the turn of the century, Bethlehem pioneered the development of structural steel, the material that made possible America's soaring bridges and towering skyscrapers. Innovation helped the company to compete with its rivals. It also created hundreds of jobs. And, as mechanization simplified work tasks, eliminating the need for large numbers of highly skilled craftsmen, these jobs were filled by immigrants, who were mercilessly exploited as the steelmakers struggled for survival.

The railroads were just as pressed by competition. The Lehigh Valley Railroad and the coal mines upriver, which supplied the bulk of its business, had no monopoly. The mines and foundries of the mighty Philadelphia-controlled Philadelphia & Reading Railroad and its assorted canal, mining, and manufacturing affiliates, also dealt in anthracite, iron, transportation, and land. To the north, the New York-controlled Delaware & Hudson and Delaware, Lackawanna & Western Railroads controlled the coal fields in the Scranton and Carbondale area and, like their southern neighbors, also manufactured iron and steel and moved them by their own transportation network of railways and canals to the rich urban markets. The Lehigh Valley Railroad did not even dominate the region's access to New York City, competing with the Central Railroad of New Jersey and several other lines for this profitable route. Not surprisingly, railroad workers were subjected to the same pressures on wages, hours, and working conditions that affected laborers in the steel industry: wages were low, hours were long, working conditions

Taken in the 1930s this photograph by Walker Evans vividly depicts the living conditions of workers in Bethlehem. Hemmed in by electric poles and jammed against the mill wall, the houses perch unsurely on the slide toward urban neglect. Courtesy, Library of Congress Collection

Walker Evans' series of famous cityscapes in the 1930s included this view of the Bethlehem train station. Courtesy, Library of Congress Collection

were dangerous, and job security was nonexistent.

The deplorable situation of the growing population of industrial workers necessarily affected the character of the communities in which the workers lived. When railroad and steel workers were unable to earn enough to support their families, their wives and children were forced to leave their homes and schools to seek employment themselves. As family life disintegrated, illiteracy and delinquency spread among the young, who could no longer be properly supervised. Many fathers found solace with their meager wages in saloons and brothels. Living conditions, even where the company supplied housing, were poor. Older structures built to house single families housed many. Unmarried workers crowded in barracks, sometimes sleeping in shifts. Without garbage collection, running water, or indoor plumbing, public health deteriorated as this industrial population, its resistance sapped by brutal working and living conditions, fell prey to epidemics of typhoid, cholera, and pneumonia. Not surprisingly, by the 1870s some of the workers began to be receptive to the appeals of trade unionists and other more radical voices.

Because it was a buyer's market for labor, unionization and radicalism had limited success in the Lehigh Valley. The unions were effective only among skilled workers who, because it took so long to train them, were not easily replaceable—and who, because most of them were native-born, had a greater sense of solidarity than the immigrants, who did not even share a common language. Thus ironworkers, whose tasks were specialized and required substantial training, managed to organize trade unions under the banner of the Knights of Labor by the late 1870s. But the steelworkers, whose jobs were largely unskilled, did not. Had the two groups worked together, they would have undoubtedly been able to better their situations. But the craft unions, made up of natives and northern European immigrants, would have nothing to do with the unskilled Italians and Slavs.

A similar situation prevailed on the railroads. The skilled men in charge of operating the trains—the engineers, firemen, brakemen, and mechanics—organized themselves by the 1870s. But they stood aloof from the unskilled, replaceable immigrants who built and maintained the tracks and who loaded and unloaded freight. Although these unions achieved limited improvements in the wages and working conditions of their members, they did not serve as sources of broader reforms in the communities of the Lehigh Valley. The broader reform initiative came, ironically, from the corporations themselves.

The first reform impulse originated on the railroads. As the size and speed of trains increased and the companies struggled to undercut their competitors, the probability and potential cost of major accidents increased dramatically. After a rash of disastrous accidents in various parts of the United States, the public, shippers, and the insurance underwriters began to demand improvements in safety standards from the railroad companies. Some of these could be implemented by technological improvements, such as air brakes, automatic couplers, stronger car construction, and interlocking signal systems. But for improved machinery to be effective, it had to be operated by men who were alert and committed to the safety of the public and to the protection of the company's property. By the mid-1890s, railroad executives and other industrialists began to come to grips with their social responsibilities by encouraging the establishment of branches of the YMCA to serve their employees. These organizations provided more than just food and shelter, as Stuart Brandes notes in *American Welfare Capitalism:*

> They also typically housed baths, libraries, athletic facilities, classes on railroad work, and, significantly, Bible classes and religious meetings. The underlying theory was that well-housed, well-fed, clean, properly-educated Christians do not strike, or at least were less likely to do so than those with different life styles.

We cannot determine what part altruism played in such corporate good works. It is clear, however, that the employers regarded such reforms as cost-effective measures that increased the safety and efficiency of their operations.

A similar thing happened in the iron and steel industry. In the mid-1870s, entrepreneurs, led by Andrew Carnegie, began to introduce cost-accounting methods first developed by the railroads and by the nation's first industrial trust, the Standard Oil Company. This innovation enabled the steel men for the first time to accurately calculate the cost of production and, more importantly, to identify those aspects of the productive process which could, by the invention of labor-saving devices, by integration of the manufacturing process, and by more effective deployment of the work force, be made more efficient. The impact of cost accounting was dramatic. Those who used it were able, within an astonishingly short time, to gobble up smaller and less efficient competitors. By 1901, with the creation of United States Steel, nearly all the steel companies in the United States had been consolidated into a single gigantic firm. Even smaller companies, like the Bethlehem Iron Company, followed Carnegie's lead, introducing new, more cost-effective equipment and integrating their manufacturing activities with control of transportation facilities, raw materials, and marketing.

Cost accounting had a dual impact on labor. Its short-term effect was a lowering of the level of skills needed to produce steel, thus permitting the hiring of cheaper non-union labor, and a deterioration of working conditions as the manufacturers raced to produce more cheaply and quickly than their rivals. But the logic of cost accounting as it affected labor ultimately had to come to terms with the fact that workers were not themselves machines. The complex issues of human motivation had to be subject to the same rigorous analysis as the productive process itself. This interest in human engineering took two forms. The first, involving time-motion studies and the effort to rationalize and simplify the work-task itself, had its beginnings at Bethlehem Iron. In 1898, Joseph Wharton, the company's most powerful stockholder, persuaded the directors to hire a young man named Frederick W. Taylor who had written a provocative paper on methods of maximizing worker output.

Taylor's scientific approach to analyzing and improving the output of workers was astonishingly simple. He noticed, for example, that Bethlehem Iron employed from 400 to 600 men as laborers. Their job primarily involved shoveling: they moved coal, limestone, and iron ore from railroad cars to trackside piles, and from those piles to the company's three blast and seven open-hearth furnaces. He observed that the optimum weight per load for a shoveler was 21 pounds—but, because the men preferred to own their own shovels, which they used for all the various shoveling jobs, they did not work efficiently. A worker might go from shoveling iron ore, at 30 pounds per load, to rice coal, at 4 pounds per load. Obviously, what was needed to maximize productivity was the right tool for the right job. Taylor suggested that the company supply the shovels, large ones for light loads, small ones for the heavy, each capable of holding a load of 21 pounds.

Taylor did not confine his attention to tools. He also introduced a bonus system, which rewarded workers for high productivity. Taylor was not a popular man at Bethlehem Iron. Management resented him because he was forcing changes in factory organization which, even if profitable, ruffled their conservative sensibilities. Bethlehem was a more paternally run operation than the Carnegie Works. Each shop operated on its own, under the authority of its foreman. Bethlehem's president, Robert Linderman, who was more of a banker than a manufacturer, did not want to have to make decisions that he had been accustomed to leaving to others. Middle management disliked

Taylor because his reforms undercut their authority. And the workers resented a system that placed them in competition with one another. Taylor was fired in April of 1901. He went on to write several books about his Bethlehem experiments and is today acclaimed as the "Father of Scientific Management."

The second variant of cost-accounting, which focused on the worker rather than the work-task, was first developed by Andrew Carnegie in the 1880s. It was based on the simple observation that men who work 12 hours per day, 7 days per week do not work very efficiently and tend to be indifferent to their employers' interests. Carnegie instituted three eight-hour shifts in his steel-rail mills. While this forced a 17 percent increase in wage costs, the increase in productivity was so dramatic that it more than paid for itself. A colleague of Carnegie's, the president of the Allegheny Railroad Company, followed his example, reducing the work week from seven to five and a half days. The result was the virtual elimination of absenteeism. Before long, Carnegie recognized that if workingmen could be brought to be devoted to their employers with the same loyalty that they brought to their union leaders, companies would benefit enormously. He began to experiment with stock-option and profit-sharing plans, as well as keeping lines of communication open between management and the workers. His interest in reform spread beyond his factories to the communities in which they operated, to schools, hospitals, and libraries, as well as to the creation of pension plans to support injured and retired workers. His eventual involvement in the establishment of America's first philanthropic foundations was a continuation of the reforms that he had first developed as a steelmaker.

Carnegie's work came to Bethlehem with Charles M. Schwab who, having worked with Carnegie and J.P. Morgan to create United States Steel, stepped down from its presidency to buy out and run its tiny rival, the Bethlehem Iron Company. Schwab had worked at Carnegie's side since 1879 and was thoroughly familiar with his methods, especially in the management of the work force. He had been brought in from Carnegie's Braddock plant to settle the bloody Homestead strike of 1892. And he did so in his own inimitable style—a style which might have been taken word-for-word from Carnegie's 1886 essay, "An Employer's View of Labor" in which he stated:

It is notable that bitter strikes seldom occur in small establishments where the owner comes into direct contact with his men, and knows their qualities, their struggles, and their aspirations.

LEFT
This Walker Evans photograph shows a gospel mission in Bethlehem. Courtesy, Library of Congress Collection

ABOVE
The labor of immigrants such as these men in Bethlehem permitted an expansion of the steel-producing capabilities of Lehigh Valley industries. Even in the work place, however, immigrant groups maintained their ethnic divisions. Courtesy, Bethlehem Steel Corporation

This photo provides an interesting view of working men at play in 1911. In their outlandish uniforms they look like refugees from about six circuses. Courtesy, Bethlehem Steel Corporation

Strong personalities dominated the early days of the iron industry. As chairman of the board of Bethlehem Steel, Charles M. Schwab (right) transformed the company from a small specialized iron manufacturer into one of the nation's great industrial concerns. John Fritz (far right) constructed and operated the Bethlehem Steel rolling mills. He was a leading innovator in iron production. Courtesy, W. Bruce Drinkhouse, NCHGS

Accordingly, Schwab personally and individually greeted the men as they returned to the Homestead Works, promising them that all would be permitted to retain their jobs, that their grievances would be given a full hearing, and that they would retain the financial benefits they had possessed before the strike. He was astonishingly successful in revitalizing the plant. Labor and management alike regarded him as a wonder-worker. Within three years he had become president of all of Carnegie's steelmaking operations.

When Charles M. Schwab took over the management of Bethlehem Steel in 1904, he had an immense task before him. Although the innovations brought to the company by John Fritz under the Packer-Linderman regime were still in place, the technology of steelmaking and the development of new markets in shipbuilding, armaments, structural steel, and the then-infant automobile industry, meant that the company would have to be run energetically. Not only was it in competition with the immense United States Steel, but it had been indifferently managed and was deeply in debt. While making sweeping changes in the organization and scope of company operations, he did not lose sight of the importance of the human element. As he stated in a speech to the American Society of Mechanical Engineers in 1927:

Our job is primarily to make steel, but it is being made under a system which must be justified. If this system does not enable men to live on an increasingly higher plane, if it does not allow them to fulfill their desires and satisfy their reasonable wants, then it is natural that the system itself should fail.

Unless the workers should benefit from company profits, identifying themselves with their employer's interests, Schwab argued, not only would the company itself fail, but the capitalist system as well. His argument, like Carnegie's, some 40 years earlier, combined ideals and self-interest. For Schwab recognized that well-paid, contented workers not only labored more efficiently, but also, in spending their wages, stimulated the entire economy, creating more jobs, more factories, and higher wages and profits.

Under Schwab, the company took on a very different character. Rather than just being a place where people worked, it reached out to reorganize their lives. Ambitious workmen could look forward to being promoted into management, much as Carnegie and Schwab had been. The company harnessed the leisure time of its workmen and executives to promote team spirit. The workers were encouraged to organize competitive athletic teams and musical and social clubs, for which the company underwrote the cost and supplied prizes. The executives were encouraged to organize the Saucon Valley Country Club, where golf and tennis served the same purpose as baseball and soccer for the workers. The company constructed hundreds of houses for its workers, purchasing vast tracts of land in proximity to its works.

Schwab was also a leader in the effort to unify Bethlehem as a community. What is now a single city was, until 1918, a collection of distended and uncoordinated boroughs, the major components being the old Moravian borough, Bethlehem, and the bustling industrial center, South Bethlehem. While progressive business elements had been agitating for unification since the early 1890s, they encountered powerful opposition, particularly from South Bethlehem politicians whose working-class-based power would necessarily be diluted by an inclusive city government that included non-industrial areas. The unification movement could not be easily stopped, especially as it could be demonstrated that disunity was economically damaging to the prospects of the area: new companies were reluctant to locate in a place with inadequate transit, water, and sanitation systems. Financial distress persuaded some to change their minds. In 1904, following a recession, Bethlehem annexed West Bethlehem, leaving only Northampton Heights and South Bethlehem in opposition. In that year Schwab entered the picture, as he assumed active management at Bethlehem Steel.

The Steel's expansion beyond the bounds of South Bethlehem began to pull things together, as did Schwab's involvement with the area's transit system and public utilities. More important, however, was his willingness to work closely with unification leaders from the three boroughs. He became actively involved with the Joint Bridge Commission, which proposed to connect the two Bethlehems with a bridge across the Lehigh, the "Hill to Hill Bridge." He also involved the company in financing various cooperative activities like the Bethlehem Steel Band, the Lehigh Valley Symphony Orchestra, and the Bach Choir, which brought citizens of all the boroughs together as participants and spectators. In 1915, the company created eight acres of playing fields for athletic events in North Bethlehem—thereby constructing the first public park in the city.

Finally, the coming of the First World War and the rising tide of prosperity and patriotism, in which Schwab was a partic-

ABOVE
Massive cranes such as this one kept pace with the steel industry's growing production. This rail loading dock was photographed at Bethlehem Steel's Stanton division in about 1918. Courtesy, Bethlehem Public Library

RIGHT
This is one of Walker Evans' photographs depicting worker housing in Bethlehem in the 1930s. Courtesy, Library of Congress Collection

ularly visible leader, helped to overcome remaining resistance to unification. After an intense promotional campaign led by Bethlehem's merchants and manufacturers,the citizens voted by an overwhelming majority to unite the boroughs of Bethlehem and South Bethlehem. The importance of Bethlehem Steel as a central part of the unification movement was attested to by the fact that Archibald Johnston, a vice-president of the company, was elected by acclamation as first mayor of the united city.

While Bethlehem Steel was unquestionably the most important single element in the creation of Bethlehem as a progressive modern city and in efforts to reintegrate the community, the dominance of this giant corporation in municipal affairs and its penetration of virtually every aspect of the lives of the citizens gave the city a peculiar character. However open the Steel's corporate structure may have been to workers with luck and pluck, it was, like all successful modern corporations, distinctively hierarchical in character—divided into levels of influence, affluence, and authority. And however much Charles M. Schwab and "his boys" rhapsodized about the importance of teamwork and the commonality of the interests of workers and management, the community inevitably reflected the differences in power, wealth, and national origin. The corporate and commercial rich lived in imposing mansions along Delaware Avenue and, by the 1920s, were laying out sizable estates in the countryside outside the city. They lived a life unto themselves, sending their children to private schools and colleges, socializing with one another in private clubs. Their tastes, interests, and aspirations were governed by national fashions. Even Schwab himself, although he built a house in Bethlehem, spent most of his time in New York, leaving the daily tasks of administering Bethlehem Steel's far-flung industrial empire (which included shipyards in Virginia, Texas, California, and Massachusetts; iron mines in Latin America; and bridge-building projects all over the world) to trusted lieutenants like Eugene Grace.

The industrial work force, on the other hand, while certainly better off after 1920, was still concentrated in South Side neighborhoods close to the plant. While joined together by political interests and such institutions as the public schools, the workers were fragmented by their diverse national and religious backgrounds. They too were a world unto themselves. Bethlehem, in other words, never fully achieved a unified sense of community, mirroring as it did the status order of the corporation and the intergroup rivalries of the immigrants. Workers who believed in the communitarian rhetoric of management and its middle-class allies, were reminded soon enough of who held the real power in the town.

In 1910, when poorly organized workers walked out in a protest against low wages and poor working conditions, the company called in strikebreakers and the state constabulary. Many businessmen initially sympathized with the strike and freely extended credit to the protesters. But when President Schwab threatened to close down the works unless the merchants rallied to his support, they were quick to denounce what the Bethlehem Globe-Times called the "misled men on strike" and the influence of "unscrupulous non-resident agitators." Their willingness to parrot the company line must have seemed curious to the workers, whose plight was termed by Outlook, a progressive magazine that boasted former president Theodore Roosevelt as an editor, as "a reproach and a shame, not only to this company, but to the Nation and the State that allow them." The Federal Council of Churches, after conducting an investigation of conditions at Bethlehem, described the situation as "a disgrace to civilization." Labor historian David Brody states that the Terre Haute (Indiana) Post sent a reporter to South Bethlehem before the Christmas season of 1912. The reporter

described the life of an immigrant whose family lived in three meanly furnished, unheated rooms. The worn-looking mother had recently given birth without a doctor, and the baby had the only blanket in the house. The father, a seven day a week man, had not been home at the birth, nor would he be on Christmas day. The article ended: "The Christmas spirit? Oh, I didn't see much of it around the mills of Bethlehem in Pennsylvania."

The company successfully broke the 1910 strike, but the adverse publicity it received from the national press and from several government investigations made it a pyrrhic victory.

Bethlehem Steel learned something from the strike of 1910: it had to face the fact that it was accountable for the discrepancies between rhetoric and reality. And conditions did improve with wartime prosperity and, after a brief slump, again during the boom years of the twenties. The company and the business community, working through the churches, the public schools, and such groups as the Boy Scouts and the YMCA, energetically promoted Americanization, teaching the English language and American history, along with middle-class life-styles and aspirations. The children of immigrant workers took advantage of opportunities for schooling, which enabled them to acquire more highly paid, skilled manual and white-collar jobs, both in

Bridges such as this one required massive amounts of steel from companies like Bethlehem Steel. This open lattice-work design used thousands of girders and hundreds of thousands of rivets. Courtesy, Bethlehem Steel Corporation

and out of the company.

Many immigrants and their sons became businessmen and professionals: John Gosztonyi not only founded the first Slavic-language newspaper in the United States, he also operated a successful bank and transportation agency, and served as the Northampton County Court interpreter; John F. Stefko, a Hungarian, having completed his education at the South Bethlehem Business College, went into banking and operated a travel agency; Antonio Castellucci, after several years at the Steel, resumed his trade as shoemaker, which he had learned in his native Italy. Carefully saving and reinvesting, he soon became a large-scale labor contractor and real estate developer, as well as a banker and travel agent.

The city directories give the clearest indications of immigrant success in the new world. In 1920, the Bethlehem city directory listed no attorneys or physicians who can be identified as members of the new immigrant groups. Nor did it list any immigrant social organizations. By 1929, 2 of the 25 lawyers and 6 of the 66 physicians were Italian, Hungarian, or Slavic in origin. Over the nine-year period, the ethnics had succeeded in establishing two incorporated banks, two weekly newspapers, and a large number of social organizations, many of them mutual assistance societies. More dramatic, however, was the rising importance of ethnic small businessmen—grocers, confectioners, druggists, and craftsmen—who, though they had started at Bethlehem Steel, had managed to achieve middle-class status.

For all this success, however, the immigrants remained a divided and politically ineffective group. In order to maintain control of the work force and to discourage unionization efforts, Bethlehem Steel and other employers fostered rivalries between national groups. As Mike Stofko, a union organizer, reminisced:

On bull gangs they'd mix the nationalities to keep you in line. You got there in the morning before work and the Italians would be off in one corner talking among themselves. The Slavs would be all together talking among themselves in their language. The Dutch in another.

The Dutch always got to be leaders, because they were around longer, I guess. They hated us. We hated them. They'd split us up and drive us, drive us hard all day. Called us "hunks" and stuff like that.

Not until the mid-1930s, when the Steel had been forced to lay off two-thirds of its 15,000-man work force, did Bethlehem's laboring men manage to overcome their differences and move toward effective unionization. The Steelworker's Organizing Committee, supported by the C.I.O.—and with its right to organize recognized by the New Deal's labor legislation—by 1938 succeeded in giving labor a united voice in Bethlehem. Although this movement was opposed by the company, the excesses of anti-unionism, which brought bloodshed and violence to other communities, were largely avoided here. The Bethlehem Steel Company's management, led by Schwab's protégé, Eugene Grace, was more progressive than most. Its ideals of "good industrial housekeeping" and its recognition of impending world war and the lucrative contracts that mobilization would bring, undoubtedly shaped its relatively clement attitude toward the unions. While consolidating the ethnics as an economic and political interest group, unionization led Bethlehem away from, rather than toward, the old goal of community integration. Even as a united group, ethnic penetration of the city's political structure was minimal: no southern or eastern European held a major elective or appointive office in city government until the 1960s.

If Bethlehem failed to reintegrate itself as a single community except in a geographical sense, it did succeed in becoming a city of communities, each with its own distinctive character. Whether one looked at the manicured estates of the Steel executives in the Saucon Valley, the modestly elegant townhouses in the Moravian section, or the small residences of the South Side with their tiny but spectacular gardens, each displayed a fully developed sense of itself—pride and integrity. As the center of heavy industry in the Lehigh Valley, employing not only Bethlehemites, but also thousands of breadwinners from Easton and Allentown, Bethlehem necessarily had to pay the price of being a "gritty city," both in the physical sense of being dominated by industrial structures and in the social sense of mirroring the vast range of skills and backgrounds needed by a huge firm like Bethlehem Steel. As a city whose fortunes were dependent on a single industry, Bethlehem's prosperity has necessarily been an uncertain thing, varying with the demand for the company's products. The Great Depression of the 1930s was a catastrophe for the town. But Bethlehem bounced back during the Second World War. Even with the phasing out of many of the Steel's heavier manufacturing operations in Bethlehem, the city remains the company's research and administrative center, and continues to provide thousands of skilled and unskilled jobs. Bethlehem Steel, unlike many other old industrial firms in the Northeast, maintained its commitment to the place which gave it birth. And Bethlehem, whether one views it as a gritty city or as a historical monument, remains as lively and diverse as its many communities.

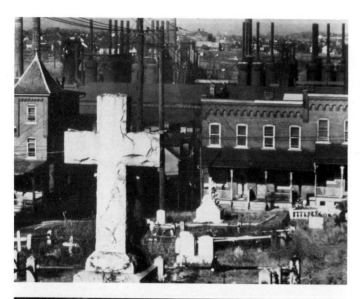

TOP
This Walker Evans photo shows
that urban crowding had pushed
house porches right onto the
cemetery by the 1930s. Behind,
the mill's chimneys loom like
another set of gravestones.
Courtesy, Library of Congress
Collection

ABOVE
Pennsylvania Germans
predominate among ethnic
groups in Allentown. This man,
Clayden Handwerk (born
October 14, 1890), is descended
from German immigrants of
1769. Mr. Handwerk grows
potatoes in Handwerkstadt,
Heidelberg Township. Photo by
Adrienne Snelling

Allentown: Cooperation Conquers

As in Bethlehem, progressive businessmen led the effort to
deal with Allentown's social and economic problems. But,
although their goals were similar, the Allentonians used quite
different methods from those employed in Bethlehem. There
were two basic reasons for this difference. The first involved the
fact that Allentown's industrial and commercial experience was
more extensive than Bethlehem's. Where the iron industry did
not become a central factor in Bethlehem's economic life until
the 1870s, it had been the central factor in Allentown's growth
since the mid-1840s. As L.C. Gobron noted in his florid but
accurate historical pamphlet, *Souvenir of Allentown* (1916):

*Our merchants profited so long as the iron industry was
prosperous. They gave no thought to the future. They lived only in the
present, never dreaming that the tide of prosperity might cease flowing
their way. One day they awakened to the folly of putting all their
industrial eggs in one basket, for when the panic of 1873 came the
basket toppled over and the eggs were broken. In other words, when
the panic came Allentown was "flat on its back," to use a slang
phrase. The iron industries shut down and no city in the United States
suffered more from that panic than unhappy—we might say
unwise—Allentown. Hundreds if not thousands of people were out of
work. Merchants failed by the score.*

*These were dark days for Allentown. Nor were the clouds soon
dispelled. They hung over the city for about nine years. . . .*

In the wake of the disasters of the 1870s, according to Gobron,
the business community determined that "never again should
Allentown be dependent on only one branch of industry." A
board of trade was organized, which not only advertised the
attractiveness of Allentown as a place for new businesses to
locate, but also provided very substantial financial incentives to
encourage them to do so. The effort was astonishingly successful. As Gobron noted:

*Here and there new industries on a small scale were established,
but the great move made toward a greater industrial Allentown was
in 1881, when Allentown capitalists furnished the money for the erection of the Adelaide Silk Mill. This was the first great step forward,
and Allentown since that time has not ceased taking big steps. Since
that time, the Adelaide Mill has become one of the greatest silk mills
in the country. Five years later came the Pioneer Mill and the same
year the Iowa Barb Wire Company. . . . Furniture factories went up.
Old shoe factories were enlarged and new ones erected. The manufac-*

Allentown's diversification
included recognition of the
city's earlier agrarian roots. This
photograph from the 1900s
shows that hay wagons were still
seen on city streets. (LCHS)

Downtown Allentown had a
light frosting of snow for
Christmas 1897. Electric utility
poles had grown as tall as four-
story buildings. (LCHS)

ture of cigars became an important part of the industrial life of the city. *The Allentown Spinning Mill was erected. All these industries were encouraged by local capitalists, with the result that industrially Allentown has been growing at such a rate that sister cities have been outstripped in the race. What has been the result of having these diversified industries? The result is that since 1873 panics have come and panics have gone; but in none of them did Allentown suffer to any great extent.*

The second reason for Allentown's distinctive response to the crisis of the late 19th century lay in the nature of the business community itself. Unlike Bethlehem, which was sharply divided between Moravians and Yankees, Allentown's capitalists were overwhelmingly Pennsylvania-Germans. For them, there was more at stake in responding to the crisis of the 1870s than mere economic recovery. They were equally concerned with the survival of Pennsylvania-German culture. Accordingly, their response was strikingly cooperative. As Gobron stated:

If we were asked the question, "Who has rendered Allentown the greater amount of service?" we should unhesitatingly give the credit to those loyal and progressive citizens of Allentown who, after viewing the financial ruin left by the panic which had its inception in 1873, opened their purses when capitalists in other cities closed theirs and held on to what money they had, and said, "From these ruins a greater and more prosperous Allentown shall arise." There were among the number men who had ample means and who could have locked their strong boxes and told the town "go hang." There were among the number men of scanty means, but they came forward with their mites ... . All of them were strong men when strong men were needed. Most of them lived to see their hopes realized.

Unlike Bethlehem, which chose to rebuild itself on the basis of a single large industrial corporation, Allentown determined to create an economic foundation which would serve the interests of the already existing community of Pennsylvania-Germans. They could do so because they possessed, from the beginning, a clear sense of who they were and what they wanted to achieve. Thus, rather than competing against one another and taking advantage of one another's misfortunes, they worked together to create an economic environment which would, in turn, favor the growth of a particular way of life, a way of life in which people were valued not for what they did or how much they had, but for who they were. It was

this ideal of community that led Allentown's entrepreneurs to act as openhandedly as they did in the 1870s and in subsequent economic crises.

Diversification was only one goal of the city's economic strategy. The other, which was no less important, was to gain control of the direction of Allentown's economic development. For, the economy, up through the 1870s, had not only been narrowly based on one industry—iron—it had also depended largely on the capital and expertise of non-Allentonians, who controlled the iron industry, the canal, the railroads, and much of the city's capital. Gaining economic autonomy required, more than anything else, a willingness to be innovative—a sensitivity to the currents of science and invention and to the national economic needs that Allentown could supply. For without friendliness to innovation, the predominance of more open-minded outsiders would be guaranteed, as had happened in the earlier development of the iron industry. Allentonians were, therefore, quick to move into the exploitation of the only remaining large-scale extractive industry: cement.

Although cement had been produced in the Lehigh Valley since the 1830s, it only began to become a major industry in the 1890s, with the rebuilding of American cities. Accompanying the birth of the skyscraper was the construction of sewers, water systems, streets, and bridges, all of which required newer and cheaper methods of construction—for which precast and reinforced concrete were ideal materials. And as railroads accommodated themselves to heavier and faster-rolling stock, it became necessary to replace trestles and causeways with more durable materials. Within a few years, the automobile would increase demand for paving materials still further. Allentown-based entrepreneurs, seeing their opportunity, moved ahead quickly. Not only were they technical innovators, pioneering in the large-scale manufacture of portland cement, they also worked hard to discover new uses for cement and concrete. Not content to confine their efforts to the Lehigh Valley, they explored and developed cement properties all over the United States. Thus, while the Lehigh Valley's share of national portland cement production dropped from 75 percent in 1897 to 30 percent in 1913, much of the production beyond the Lehigh Valley was in the hands of the businessmen of Allentown.

But the real thrust of activity guaranteeing Allentown's economic independence involved more local concerns, specifically control of credit, public utilities, and real estate. Without pooling and effectively mobilizing its own capital, outsiders could

The typesetting room of the *Call* and *Chronicle* newspapers was the place where Allentown's progress was put into print.

Newspapers both supported and criticized economic policies. (LCHS)

dictate the city's development, for industries were unlikely to locate in an area which could not provide them with this basic nutrient of expansion. Without community control of public utilities, outsiders could discourage industrial and residential growth by declining to provide needed services. And without control of its own real estate, the physical expansion of the city could be curtailed or led in directions incompatible with the interests of the community. In taking the credit situation in hand, the Allentown entrepreneurs pursued a three-pronged strategy. First, they endeavored to mobilize the savings of the "little" people—the shopkeepers, craftsmen, and industrial workers—by encouraging the formation of savings and loan societies. These societies served a dual purpose, social and economic. As the Allentown *Chronicle and News* noted in March of 1875,

nowhere are building associations so numerous in proportion to population as in Allentown and we believe it is universally acknowledged that they have very materially assisted in producing a practice of saving and economy among our mechanics and laboring men, and others of small means, and have assisted many a man to a comfortable home who otherwise would never have achieved the means of providing himself with that great blessing.

The blessing was that those of small means, rather than being alienated from society, came to see themselves as having a stake in it. And having such a stake, they were more likely to be hardworking, industrious, and reliable. Further, because these associations acted essentially as mutual benefit societies, their capital not only being derived from the savings of members, but their major investment vehicle being the financing of mortgages for members, they fostered precisely the kinds of communitarian attitudes of self-help and common concern that the business leadership wanted to foster on a larger scale. Further, by encouraging those of small means to help themselves by cooperating to pool and reinvest their own earnings for their own benefit, larger-scale capital was freed up for more major industrial and commercial undertakings. Finally, large-scale building activity by small-holders stimulated the building trades, supporting not only craftsmen and developers, but also brickyards, lumberyards, planing mills, cornice works, and the furniture industry. And, the more attractive residential housing the city had, the more eligible it was as a location for new commercial and manufacturing enterprises.

The second thrust of the entrepreneurs' effort to control

ABOVE
Originally established as a picnic grove and trout hatchery by Solomon Dorney in the 1860s, Dorney Park took on its present form as an amusement park after 1900. Purchased at that time by the Allentown & Reading Traction Company, the park became a major traffic generator for the rural trolley line. Today, Dorney Park is considered by many to be one of the best old-fashioned amusement parks still operating. Courtesy, Call Chronicle Newspapers, Inc.

RIGHT
Trolleys represented the most widely used form of early mass transportation. This trolley was used on the line that connected Allentown and Dorney Park. (LCHS)

their access to capital involved the formation of local commercial banks, institutions whose primary function was to serve the business community by pooling the capital of stockholders and depositors and investing it, through loans, notes, mortgages, and stock purchases, back into the local economy. While Allentown had only two commercial banks as of 1870—the Allentown National Bank (founded in 1855) and the Second National Bank of Allentown (founded in 1863)—between 1870 and 1910, four more were established, all of them controlled entirely by Allentonians and, by 1914, representing an aggregate capital of almost $15 million. Prudently managed and paying high dividends, these banks provided the means for attracting new industries and underwriting the expansion of older ones.

Although nominally in competition with one another, all worked together cooperatively to promote local interests. Coordination was sustained by the tightly-knit nature of the business community. The bank directors were connected to one another through blood and marriage. Many were in other businesses together. Business and family connections were reinforced in other ways. Many members of Allentown's business and professional elite had gone to the Allentown High School together and had gone on to graduate from Muhlenberg College. Many belonged to the Livingston Club, where the city's business and professional men met both for business and pleasure. Also important in tying the community leaders together were memberships in such fraternal organizations as the Masons and Elks, work in service organizations like the Board of Trade and its successor, the Chamber of Commerce, and service on the governing boards of such philanthropic institutions as the Y.M.C.A., the Allentown Hospital and the Associated Charities of Allentown.

Businessmen were also active politically. Many businessmen served as mayor, as aldermen, city councilmen, and as members of the school board. Their involvement with one another and with the life and problems of the community led, by the turn of the century, to a common viewpoint about the needs of the city and its citizens. This led, in turn, to a diminution of partisan conflict. Both Democrats and Republicans—at least as far as local issues were concerned—supported and sustained one another's efforts to build a better Allentown. Thus changes in city administration, rather than being disruptive, were characterized by continuity, each mayor building on the achievements of his predecessor. Coming away from the disasters of the 1870s, the bankers were among the first to learn that they could do well by doing good.

Theodore Roosevelt came to the Lehigh Valley during the campaign of 1914. Here he exercises his famous speech-making style from the balcony of the Hotel Allen in Allentown. (LCHS)

The Clover Club Picnic on August 9, 1892 was typical of the social activities of fraternal business clubs. Even at this summer outing, complete with band, many of the men are still wearing coats and ties. (LCHS)

Early Lehigh Valley agribusinessman General Harry Clay Trexler rides the range in style as he tours his orchards in Orefield in 1915. Farming was only one of Trexler's many interests. He also founded the Pennsylvania Power and Light Company and was a co-founder of the Lehigh Portland Cement Company and the Lehigh Transit Company. With him are his farm manager, John Linde, and his superintendent, Percy Fenstermacher. Courtesy, Harry C. Trexler Estate

Colonel Edward M. Young, one of the founders of Lehigh Portland Cement Company in 1897, served as its secretary and president until his death in 1932. Here Colonel Young appears in front of the Portland Cement Company's Perfect Safety Record Monument in 1930. Courtesy, Barbara Y. Benner Collection

But as prosperous as Allentown's commercial banks might have been, the city and its enterprises still required infusions of outside capital, especially for major undertakings like the creation of a nationwide cement industry, the reorganization of the Lehigh Valley Transit Company, and the establishment, in the 1920s, of the Pennsylvania Power and Light Company. Obviously, where this capital came from made a difference in terms of the elements of control outside investors might exercise. To turn to Philadelphia, which had a vested interest in dominating development in the Lehigh Valley, would be to invite disaster. But New York was another matter; all New York investors wanted was a good return on their investments. Accordingly, when Allentonians sought major underwriting for new ventures, they turned to New York rather than Philadelphia, thereby retaining control of the city's economic fortunes.

With capital in hand, control of public utilities and real estate was fairly easy to achieve. The city's rapid transit system and electric power supply, although begun by Allentonians, were taken over and consolidated by outsiders in the 1890s. Like many such efforts, the promoters overextended themselves and, by 1903, the Lehigh Valley Traction Company, which had a virtual monopoly of electric railway operations in the region, went into receivership. The Allentonians' chance had come. In 1905, a group led by cement and lumber magnate Harry Clay Trexler and his associate Edward M. Young—and including Bethlehemites Charles M. Schwab and Warren Wilbur—bought up the system. They proceeded to aggressively upgrade the system—not only purchasing new rolling stock, rationalizing routes and schedules, and rebuilding shops and rights-of-way (most notably in the construction of the 8th Street Bridge connecting South Allentown with the rest of the city)—but also creating an express service from Allentown to Philadelphia to rival the Lehigh Valley Railroad's own passenger trains. More importantly, the new city routes opened up Allentown's West End as a residential area, bringing what had once been bucolic groves and remote farms within minutes of Center Square.

Control of the Lehigh Valley Traction Company brought with it control of Allentown's electrical generating plant, which the company had been operating as a subsidiary. Trexler separated the two and, working with New York investment bankers, began to develop the small subsidiary into a regional giant, the Pennsylvania Power and Light Company. This company enabled Allentown and other cities in the valley to develop free from the designs of the Philadelphia-controlled

Metropolitan Edison Company. This freedom was of more than symbolic importance, for in an area attempting to attract new industries, control of electric rates and availability of electric service were an important matter. The P.P.&L. building, designed by architect Wallace K. Harrison, who later went on to take a leading role in the design of New York's Rockefeller Center, stands as an important symbol of the Lehigh Valley's achievement of economic self-determination.

A similar strategy was followed in the telephone field. In 1900, Allentown was served by two telephone companies, the Philadelphia-controlled Bell Telephone Company of Pennsylvania and the locally controlled Lehigh Telephone Company. The two companies struggled for regional dominance, buying up smaller systems and duplicating service. (It is said that the Lehigh was able to hold its own against the more powerful Bell company because the Lehigh was a pioneer in the use of dial telephones, whereas the Bell relied on operators to connect parties. Apparently the Pennsylvania-Germans, uncomfortable with the thought that operators might eavesdrop on their conversations, preferred dial phones.) In 1910, however, the Lehigh Telephone Company went into receivership, was taken over by another Bell rival, the American Union Telephone Company, which, in turn, filed for bankruptcy in 1913. Once again, Harry Clay Trexler and Edward M. Young stepped in, and, using New York capital, bought up American Union's Pennsylvania properties, and reorganized them as the Consolidated Telephone Company. In 1930, the Consolidated merged with the Bell Company—but the price of the merger was a seat on Bell's board of directors for Harry Clay Trexler, thus giving the valley a continued voice in company policy. Allentonians also managed to become directors of the Lehigh Valley Railroad and, more importantly, the Allentown Terminal Railroad, which gave them power to determine the placement of freight and passenger facilities in the city.

With public utilities under control and a ready supply of capital, the stage was set for the orderly expansion of the city. Between 1901 and 1908, the city annexed over 600 acres west of 17th Street. Much of this property was already owned by large-scale developers like Harry Clay Trexler, who also owned lumber yards, planing mills, and brick factories in the area. Because Trexler and his associates had definite ideas about what constituted a livable city, they wanted to ensure that the new areas were consonant with their concepts. In addition to creating model developments, such as the area around West Park, the city's first public park, Trexler and his associates promoted

the organization of a city planning commission. Its far-sighted plans anticipated and provided for patterns of residence and transportation, particularly the automobile, decades in advance of actual need. The motive in making Allentown an orderly and beautiful city was not merely aesthetic. As Trexler remarked in connection with his acquisition of the lands which are now Hickory Run State Park,

we are fast approaching a time when the work week will be shortened to 35 or 40 hours and we will have to provide recreational areas for our people to enjoy during their idle time, if we are to avoid anarchism and communism.

It was the same concern with social order that led him to remark that while he himself had little interest in belonging to a church, he would not want to live in a community without churches. This concern led him to personally finance the first boy scout troops in Lehigh County and to underwrite organized activities in the city's playgrounds.

It was one thing to create the elements of economic and physical order in Allentown. It was another, however, to regenerate a social order, especially one capable of including the immigrants who, especially after 1880, were flocking to Allentown to work in its new mills, factories, and stores. Fortunately, Allentonians were especially well prepared to do this, for their experience with the immigrants of the period 1830-1880 had altered their outlook toward *auslanders*. To begin with, the Pennsylvania-Germans themselves were, though long in America, still a threatened and, in many cases, a despised minority—which gave them a sympathy for groups suffering comparable discrimination. Further, German culture had been somewhat inclusive from the outset, when the early Lutherans and Reformed German immigrants had had to accommodate to one anothers' ways.

When, in the 1830s, Jewish and Roman Catholic immigrants from Germany began to gravitate to Allentown in considerable numbers, the townspeople had little trouble accepting them. Intermarriages and business partnerships quickly obscured religious differences and emphasized their common Germanic heritage. Even the new immigrant's social organizations, like the Lehigh Saengerbund (a music society founded in 1858) included, along with the newcomers, many old Lehigh Valley names like Trexler and Kern.

The newcomers were valued for their industriousness and skills. Because many of them were educated professionals,

After taking control of the electric railway operations in Allentown, Harry Clay Trexler and Edward Young expanded the service. The 8th Street Bridge (shown under construction) was the largest reinforced concrete structure in the world—and a showcase for the products of Lehigh Portland Cement Company. Courtesy, Mrs. Paul Willistein

trained in the great universities of Europe, they were a source of pride to the Pennsylvania-Germans who had for so long labored under the stigma of being thought ignorant and backward by their Anglo-Saxon neighbors. And the newcomers were undoubtedly delighted to find the strangeness of the new world mitigated by communities of people who spoke their language and shared their values.

The new German immigrants became wealthy and prominent. They included men like G.A. Aschbach, a civil engineer and Allentown's first trained architect who was hired by local entrepreneurs to survey rights-of-way for their railroads. The city employed him to design its schoolhouses and to lay out the first accurate topographical maps of Allentown. The Lehigh County Prison, which still stands today, was an Aschbach product. He also taught many of the architects and engineers who would shape the city's future appearance. William Danowsky, a German of Polish extraction, was an inventor in addition to being a successful physician and druggist. In 1850, he constructed a small gas generator to supply fuel for cooking and illuminating in his own household. His neighbors, seeing the cleanliness and convenience of gas, prevailed upon him to supply their needs as well—which he did for those willing to provide themselves with inflatable rubber or leather bags in which to transport and store it. Within a decade, his hobby had become the basis of a gas generating and distribution system which served the entire city. He finally gave up his medical practice to devote himself to constructing gas works in other parts of Pennsylvania, including Williamsport, Danville, and Tamaqua.

The Schnurmans, a German-Jewish family who came to Allentown in the 1840s and 1850s, were another success story. Two brothers, Meyer and Henry Schnurman, and their nephew, Joseph Schnurman, arrived in Allentown by circuitous routes. Meyer emigrated from Germany in 1854. Arriving in New York, he began peddling merchandise from a wagon through the surrounding countryside. Once he had accumulated enough capital, he established a horse-dealing business which operated throughout the United States and Europe. He made a fortune selling horses to the government during the Civil War. He eventually settled in Allentown and devoted himself to banking and real estate development. His brother, Henry Schnurman, came to Philadelphia in 1830. There he established a general store and married a Quaker girl of ancient Pennsylvania lineage, Clementine Penrose. After two of his children died in a scarlet fever epidemic, he moved to Allen-

LEFT TOP
Louise Leisenring was the first female county probation officer. Here she appears at the time of her graduation from Allentown College for Women (now called Cedar Crest College). After becoming a widow, she raised her family alone. Courtesy, Eleanor Leisenring

LEFT MIDDLE
Of old Pennsylvania-German stock, James L. Schaadt was an outstanding lawyer. He served as deputy warden of the Lehigh County Prison, district attorney, and mayor of Allentown from 1899 to 1902. He was an advocate of an enlightened approach to the problems of young people. During his tenure as mayor, the city started garbage collection services and asphalted streets. (LCHS)

LEFT
The John F. Drayton family is one of Allentown's oldest and most respected black families. The family migrated to Allentown in 1924 from Charleston, South Carolina. Mr. John Drayton died in 1973 after retiring from Bethlehem Steel in 1953. (LCHM)

ABOVE
The Victory Drummers formed in 1914 to see soldiers off to service in World War I. The average age of this particular group of Eastonians was 62 years when they were organized. (NCHGS)

town. Although his business was destroyed in the fire of 1848, he became a leader in the city's commercial renaissance. He also established the famous Blue Jacket Flour Mills and was a major producer of commercial fertilizers.

Joseph Schnurman, Meyer and Henry's nephew, joined his uncle Henry in Allentown in 1849. After spending some time in New York in his uncle Meyer's horse business, he returned to the Lehigh Valley. There Joseph played a role in the aftermath of the Panic of 1873 comparable to that played by Henry after the fire of 1848. He was a leader in the revival of the construction industry. Lacking ready capital, he persuaded craftsmen to accept payment in merchandise, which put men to work who would otherwise have been idle. This trading system soon became the basis for much of Allentown's small-scale residential development. Joseph's son, Harry J. Schnurman, is credited with being the inventor of the trading stamp. The Schnurmans prospered in Allentown and were fully accepted as members of the community. While never abandoning their own faith, they supported organizations of other denominations: Henry Schnurman was a pew-holder in the Presbyterian Church and his children attended its Sunday school. The Schnurman children intermarried with old valley families, as well as with other Jewish families. Such stories of acceptance and success were not exceptional in Allentown—they were the rule.

It was one thing for Allentonians to welcome German immigrants. But the Irish and other non-Germans who came after them—Italians, Poles, eastern European Jews, Belgians, Frenchmen, Hungarians, Slavs, and Syrians—posed a problem. For their habits, values, and languages were different. But they were neither unskilled nor lacking in ambition. Since Allentown was not a port-of-entry like New York, its many diversified industries tended to attract newcomers whose abilities were marketable and who had been in America long enough to have learned how to market themselves. Of the immigrants applying for citizenship in Lehigh County in 1907, for example, the average age was 27 and the average period of residence in the United States, eight years. While many listed themselves as laborers, the majority possessed an impressive range of skills: brewers, bricklayers, carpenters, silk weavers, tailors, merchants, shoemakers, and machinists.

The business community decided to extend to them the same opportunities that had been offered to others. For, however exotic some of them might seem, they all had the makings of good citizens, good workers, and good customers.

Rather than being exploited, fathers received decent wages to support their families, which in turn allowed mothers to stay at home to supervise their children and to send them to school instead of work. The use of child labor was emphatically discouraged. Mortgage money was made available to encourage home ownership. And they were supported in their efforts to create a rich associational life which not only bound them together for mutual assistance, but also wove them into the fabric of the community. Harry Clay Trexler lent the Russian Jews money to construct their first synagogue; his wife was a major financial benefactor of the religious organizations of Allentown's small black community. Both were major contributors to Catholic charities, particularly Sacred Heart Hospital. Catholic and Protestant business and professional leaders worked closely together to ensure the welfare of the whole community, natives and immigrants alike.

It did not take long for the promise of American life to eliminate whatever tendencies may have existed among the new immigrants to hold themselves aloof from full participation in the community. Allentown offered excellent free education in the public schools and parochial education at low cost; and education was the key, both to economic success and assimilation. Economic opportunities were freely offered. Hugh Crilly, perhaps the most successful member of Allentown's post-Civil War Irish community, made his fortune in fulfilling contracts offered by the traction companies and local government. Similarly, the McDermott family grew wealthy as engineers and pioneers in the use of structural steel. No less successful were Italian families like the Billeras, the Pasquariellos, and the Moggios, who distinguished themselves as manufacturers of silk and other textiles. Certainly the town's greatest success story involved the Iacocca family, members of which prospered as real estate developers, artists, and restaurateurs. Lido (Lee) Iacocca, a graduate of Allentown High School and Lehigh University, served as president of the Ford Motor Company and later as president of the Chrysler Corporation.

In the Jewish community, no one did more to bring about Allentown's commercial success than Max Hess, while the Senderowitz clan, which came to town in the 1890s, made the city one of the national centers of the garment industry. The Syrians, who began to arrive in Allentown at the turn of the century, showed remarkable talents for business and politics and, although surely the most exotic of the city's ethnic groups, were quick to achieve success and acceptance in the community. Opportunities, acceptance, and associational life made

FAR LEFT
Charles Hess founded the Hess Brothers department store in Allentown together with his brother, Max. Their store became one of Allentown's largest retail outlets. Courtesy, Betty D. Hess Collection

LEFT
Morris Senderowitz was one of Allentown's many success stories. Arriving in the Lehigh Valley from Russia at the turn of the century, he became involved in the manufacture of men's underwear. The company he founded, the Royal Manufacturing Company, is one of the nation's leading producers of this essential commodity. Courtesy, Call Chronicle Newspapers, Inc.

ABOVE
Certainly the most visible and exciting feature of the Lehigh Valley's participation in the First World War was Camp Crane. At this training center for the United States Army Ambulance Corps, over 7,000 young men learned their duties in the makeshift camp erected on the Allentown Fairgrounds. Courtesy, Call-Chronicle Newspapers, Inc.

divisive ethnic and class consciousness an impossibility in Allentown.

While political radicalism gained footholds in other industrial centers, it garnered little support in Allentown. Labor unions were accepted as a necessary part of industrial life, so the "Age of Industrial Violence," 1910-1920, passed Allentown by. Populists and Socialists received only a handful of votes in the elections of the 1890s and the years leading up to the First World War.

The Pennsylvania-Germans had managed to make the melting pot work. Surprisingly, they had done so without forcing the immigrants to forsake their origins. Where most American communities brought about assimilation by compelling immigrants to accept middle-class standards as defined by the Protestant Anglo-Saxon majority, the Pennsylvania-Germans of Allentown, having struggled long and hard both to maintain their ethnic identity and to make it consonant with mainstream economic success, recognized the value and importance of ethnic heritage as a source of pride and strength. Thus, while they encouraged the immigrants to help themselves by fostering the intactness of families and of religious and social life within the subcultures, they also created a host of organizations, ranging in interest from the parks and playgrounds through parades and public schools, which brought the whole community together and permitted it to see the necessity for cooperation and consensus.

Allentown's task of social and economic reconstruction was largely complete by the 1920s. Although a city of nearly 100,000 people, it maintained the sensibility of a small town in the best sense of the term. Through the schools, churches, neighborhoods, and the fine mesh of social organizations, everyone knew everyone else and felt a distinct obligation toward their city and their fellow citizens. The stable neighborhoods, inhabited by families which had lived in the same places for generation after generation, were models of cleanliness and safety. This remarkable degree of social integration contributed to Allentown's economic stability. The city seemed immune to the swings of the business cycle. This proved to be true in the Great Depression of the 1930s, as men like Harry Clay Trexler made huge interest-free loans to local government in order to permit it to meet its payroll and the bankers and businessmen pooled their resources to prevent failures and foreclosures. Allentown ended the 1930s with more plants in operation than it had had in the boom year of 1929. While Bethlehem and Easton either lost population or grew hardly at all, Allentown

FACING PAGE TOP
Allentown celebrated the end of the First World War with a parade down Hamilton Street. Despite the gloomy weather, a mood of jubilation prevailed. Courtesy, Barbara Y. Benner Collection.

FACING PAGE BOTTOM
Mack Trucks, Inc. employed many Allentown residents. The company manufactured this fire truck in the 1920s. Notice the use of solid rubber tires and a chain-driven rear axle. (LCHS)

ABOVE
Residential districts such as this one attracted new investors and entrepreneurs to Allentown in the 1890s. Sidewalks and trees marked middle class neighborhoods.

Allentown's leading hotel, the Americus, dominated the downtown sector. The hotel's ballroom featured many of the famous big bands between 1920 and 1940. Courtesy, Pennsylvania Historical and Museum Commission

continued its steady growth.

Allentown achieved a distinctive character, which made it different from the run of large provincial cities. While a notable manufacturing center, it was particularly famed as a rich and diverse commercial mecca. Its department stores were legendary, particularly Hess Brothers. Although a relative latecomer (it was founded in the 1890s by Max and Charles Hess), the concern attained a national reputation in the 1930s through the fertile imagination and merchandising genius of Max Hess, Jr. He is justly considered to be one of the founding fathers of the modern American department store. He made Hess Brothers the equal of the best establishments in New York.

No less well-known were the city's fine hotels, the Traylor and the Americus, whose ballrooms were graced by the most famous bands of the period (1920-1940). (Mealy's Auditorium was also a well-attended jazz showplace.) Most notable of all were the city's spectacular parks and playgrounds. They were brought into being by a coalition of community-minded progressives led by newspaper publisher David A. Miller; editor Percy Ruhe and his wife, Amy; politicians like James L. Schaadt and Malcolm Gross; and business leaders like Harry Clay Trexler. At his death in 1934, Trexler would leave his multimillion-dollar estate to a publicly appointed board of trustees to administer for the benefit of the community and, in particular, its system of parks and playgrounds.

While other cities in the Northeast withered, Allentown flourished. When old industries, like slate and ironmaking, died off, they were replaced by new ones, like Western Electric, Alpo Pet Foods, and Air Products and Chemicals, the nation's leading producer of industrial gases. As L.C. Gobron noted at the turn of the century, those who redeemed Allentown from the ruin of the 1870s "builded wisely for future generations." And even in the second half of the 20th century, thanks to their foresighted efforts, Allentown remained a place to stay, not a place to leave.

Places of Unrealized Promise

While Allentown and Bethlehem experienced enormous growth after 1880, their populations increasing by over 500 percent, Easton languished. It possessed only 30 percent more inhabitants in 1930 than it had contained in 1880. And after 1930 its population actually declined. By 1960, only half of Easton's housing, most of it built before 1939, was owner-occupied. A third of the city's housing was rated as unsound.

LEFT
As editor of the *Allentown Morning Call* for nearly 50 years, Percy Ruhe brought non-partisan community-oriented journalism to newspaper readers in the Lehigh Valley. With his wife, Amy, he was an advocate of the city's fine system of parks and playgrounds, and it was through their eloquence that the system became a reality. Courtesy, Call Chronicle Newspapers, Inc.

ABOVE
Arthur Haas, a lifelong resident of Seipstown, is pictured loading 10-gallon milk cans onto a new Mack milk truck. The milk was pasteurized and bottled at the Allentown Dairy Company. (LCHS)

Easton's average household size was only 2.94, indicating that the city's inhabitants were predominantly older people whose children had grown up and moved away. Of the 15 most populous communities in Lehigh and Northampton counties, the median number of school years completed by the inhabitants of Easton rated eleventh, with a median of 9.5 years of schooling. Easton's problems were more severe than those of its neighbors in the Lehigh Valley.

But it would be highly misleading to write off Easton as a failure. It would be more accurate to say that Easton, much as it had since its foundation as the first major settlement in the Lehigh Valley, had anticipated the trends that would eventually affect all the towns and cities in the region. These trends were, for the most part, beyond Easton's control. They involved two basic factors: first, the overall decline in the industrial economy of the Northeast; second, the regionalization of the economy of the Lehigh Valley.

Easton's economy had been based on coal and transportation—the network of railroads and canals which, in passing through the city, had carried anthracite to the homes and factories of the Northeast. After 1920, coal, railroads, and canals began to decline in economic importance. A series of disastrous coal strikes in the mid-1920s permitted oil to displace coal as a major fuel for manufacturing and heating purposes. With the rise of the automobile and the motor truck as major forms of transportation, the importance of coal and the older forms of transportation connected with it declined precipitously. Anthracite coal production reached its peak in 1917, when Pennsylvania produced almost 100 million tons of black diamonds. By 1955, only 26 million tons were produced, the smallest amount since 1878. Although the national economy grew enormously during that period the amount of freight carried by American railroads increased only slightly and the number of passengers declined by more than half. More important, however, was the fact that Easton's industrial base, in terms of plant and equipment, was obsolescent—a situation that it shared with many other older Northeastern industrial centers. And labor costs were higher than in newer communities to the west and south. The town's geography also limited plant expansion. It was more advantageous for Easton industrialists to shut down their plants and locate elsewhere than to rebuild.

Perhaps Easton could have bucked the tide, as Allentown and Bethlehem did, by reordering their economic and social foundations. Certain elements in the city in the 1880s did attempt to follow Allentown's example by organizing a board of

Allentown rose above many of the problems caused by the Great Depression because of loans from civic-minded industrialists. The economic strain was supported by the whole population. Courtesy, Pennsylvania Historical and Museum Commission

By the late 1930s, Allentown showed all the blessings and curses of a thriving city. This view, looking north on Seventh Street, reveals that traffic jams accompanied prosperity. The objects over the street support the wires for the electric traction system. Courtesy, Pennsylvania Historical and Museum Commission

ABOVE
By 1906 Easton had been
dwarfed by the industrial and
commercial growth of her
neighbors, Allentown and
Bethlehem. This view of Easton
shows a jewelry store, a bank,
and a dry goods store. (NCHGS)

RIGHT
The floodwaters of the Delaware
River had not reached their high
point when this photo was taken
near Easton on October 10,
1903. The standard crowd of
near-suicidal gawkers belies the
force of the water hurling under
the bridge. (NCHGS)

trade to attract new industries. But Easton was unable to back its rhetoric with sufficiently substantial financial incentives. As a result, major industries like the Iowa Barb Wire Company, which later became a subsidiary of U.S. Steel, did not stay in Easton, but relocated in Allentown.

In the first decade of the 20th century, Eastonians tried again through their chamber of commerce. This time they achieved some success. Ingersoll-Rand, a giant producer of industrial machinery, built its plant across the Delaware in Phillipsburg, giving employment to thousands. The J.T. Baker and C.K. Williams chemical companies, the crayon manufacturer, Binney and Smith, Dixie Cup, and a number of textile concerns came to Easton in the 1920s. Hugh Moore, the head of Dixie Cup, took an active role in promoting Easton—to the extent of attempting, in the 1940s, to have it selected as the site for the United Nations. But even with these efforts, the city could only hold its own. It did not experience substantial growth.

The second feature of Easton's problem was more local, involving the economic regionalization of the Lehigh Valley. It is probably true that, up to the beginning of the First World War, much depended on the initiative and resources of particular communities. But after 1920, once the national economy and the place of its components had become largely fixed in character, opportunities of the sort that permitted Bethlehem Steel and the Lehigh Valley's cement industry to flourish largely ceased to exist. Because Easton started late in its task of reconstruction, its prospects were limited by the fact that Bethlehem had become the valley's industrial center and Allentown its commercial hub. New department stores were no more likely to be able to compete successfully with Hess's, Leh's, and Zollinger-Harned of Allentown than a revitalized Glendon Ironworks could have competed with Bethlehem Steel.

Further, suburbanization, the tendency of workers to live at considerable distances from their places of work, was already well underway in the Easton area by the 1920s. While Allentown dealt with this tendency by annexing large areas to the south and west of the city, Easton did not. And thus, while the number of inhabitants and housing units in townships adjacent to Easton increased substantially, this growth was not counted by the census-takers as being Easton's.

Eventually the same trends affected all the towns as had affected the cities of the Lehigh Valley. The towns of the slate belt went into eclipse as slate was replaced by cheaper, if less beautiful and durable, building materials. The cement industry, scattered through the rural townships of Lehigh and North-

ampton counties, also declined, as companies found it uneconomical to replace antiquated equipment and meet high labor costs, and the centers of the nation's construction activity shifted westward. The iron industry, which was still flourishing in places like Catasauqua as late as the 1920s, was overtaken by competitors. Even Bethlehem Steel reduced the level of its local manufacturing operations.

The Second World War, which gave valley residents both new prosperity and more cosmopolitan tastes, encouraged the movement away from the center cities toward the suburbs. While Allentown's population increased 11.7 percent between 1940 and 1960, the populations of adjacent communities, South Whitehall and Salisbury Townships—most of whose wage-earners worked in Allentown—increased 102.3 percent and 87.8 percent, respectively. And, much as Easton's industries had gravitated to the countryside in the 1920s, both new and old plants began to be located in once rural areas. Allentown's brewing industry, for example, which, until the 1950s had operated three plants in the center of the city, was replaced in the 1970s by a huge brewing and bottling plant at Fogelsville. While Mack Truck prospered from the switchover from railroads to highways, many of its new operating units were located in rural communities like Alburtis and Macungie rather than in Allentown itself. Similarly, when Air Products and Chemicals, one of the nation's largest manufacturers of industrial gases, decided to locate in the Lehigh Valley, it came to rural Trexlertown rather than to an older urban center.

It was no longer possible, in other words, to assess the economic fortunes of the Lehigh Valley in terms of its cities. For the cities had become interdependent. And they, in turn, had become inseparable from the surrounding countryside. In fact, taken as a region, the Lehigh Valley is more prosperous than Pennsylvania as a whole. It has met the challenges of the post-World War II period. But, the problems of the 1950s and 1960s have required concerted cooperative action. The promise of the Lehigh Valley could only be realized through an enlightened partnership between government, business, and the citizenry. Fortunately, the valley's past had prepared it unusually well to deal with the uncertainties of the future.

The trolley connection between Allentown and Bethlehem made its final run on June 8, 1955. The last trolley was photographed that day in Allentown on Hamilton Street. (LCHS)

PROSPECT AND RETROSPECT: 1960 TO THE PRESENT

Great changes often occur unnoticed. Through the Great Depression and the Second World War, the Lehigh Valley did not appear to be either better or worse off than any other section of the county. To be sure, these great events changed people's lives. The young people who came to maturity during the 1930s had to postpone some of their dreams, waiting to marry, waiting to have babies, delaying buying cars and homes until times were better—then waiting still longer while husbands and boyfriends went off to war. If the Depression made people postpone realizing their dreams, wartime prosperity brought dreams within reach. But, by the late 1940s and 1950s, the dreams were different from those of earlier generations. And the achievement of those dreams affected the valley more profoundly than anything since the coming of the first European settlers.

The young people who came to maturity in the 1930s and 1940s were different from their parents and grandparents. Even if of immigrant background, almost all were born in America—for changes in the immigration laws in the early 1920s had cut off the inpouring of the foreign-born. More than any other generation, this one had been subjected to the homogenizing influence of public schooling. The large high schools that had been built between 1910 and 1930 in the valley's major cities served not only those with academic interests, but those bound for manual and clerical vocations as well. The curricula of these institutions were profoundly influenced by the increasingly pro-

fessionalized training of teachers to impart national rather than regional or local standards of taste and ambition. But the schools were not the only instruments of nationalization. The new generation had grown up on movies made in Hollywood and radio broadcasts relayed from New York. They danced to records and to touring big bands which played a music common to the young throughout the country. Thousands of men and women had, as young adults, served in the military at bases throughout the United States and the world, seeing and experiencing things that their parents would not have even comprehended.

If the prewar years had, through education and experience, given the young new goals, the postwar years provided new opportunities for realizing them. The G.I. Bill brought higher education within the reach of virtually any veteran who wanted it and could qualify for it. Federally subsidized mortgages brought the suburban dream house with a lawn, a garage, and an automobile easily within reach. Highways like the rebuilt U.S. 22 tied the cities of the valley together and made it reasonable to consider commuting by automobile. With a revived national economy, the young could live and work almost anywhere—and many chose to leave the valley for places with greater opportunities. Subtly, gradually, things began to change. New houses began encroaching on the farmlands as the young moved away from the neighborhoods where they had grown up. And this movement was swelled by new families who came to the valley to work in its new industries. The rowhouses in the central cities began to be divided into apartments. Many stood empty. And the stores and shops began to suffer competition from the new shopping centers that were springing up to serve the suburbanites.

The changes of the postwar period were not merely physical ones. There was a basic change in sensibility that could be felt everywhere, in the city and in the countryside. The age of the great entrepreneurs, the Schwabs and Graces, the Trexlers and Youngs, who had run their businesses as personal possessions, had passed. Career managers, no less talented and competent, but infinitely less freewheeling in style, took their places. And with the great men, the vital connection of city and countryside passed as well. Once men like Harry Trexler brought prize alfalfa plants into his office in town to show off to his business associates. Henry Leh, the department store executive, was said to work with his hat on because he could not wait to get back out to his farm. The new men, accountable to stockholders, could not use their time in these ways, even if they had wanted to.

The Allentown Fair was a bellwether of changing sensibilities. Until the 1950s, it was still primarily an agricultural event. The trotting races were replaced by stock-car competitions and rock concerts. The exhibition buildings were displaced to make room for a larger midway and more parking

On his 85th birthday, David A. Miller (center), founder of the Call-Chronicle Newspapers, looks over local history with his two sons. On the left is Donald P. Miller, *Call-Chronicle* publisher at the time of this 1924 photo, and on the right is Samuel W. Miller. Courtesy, Call-Chronicle Newspapers, Inc.

space. Pennsylvania-German was no longer heard in the beer garden—which increasingly became a place for high school classmates to meet one another and less of a place for family reunions. Indeed, agriculture itself had changed. It became a business rather than a way of life. Small farmers sold out to larger ones. And the large farmers pooled their production and marketing resources in cooperatives and marketed their products nationally. Some, seeing that the future lay in the value of their land rather than in what it could produce, became large-scale real estate developers, creating housing tracts where fields of corn and orchards once thrived. The price of fulfilling the American dream was the loss of the valley's distinctive identity.

The cities were hard hit by the new postwar life-styles, though some were better equipped to deal with them than others. Allentown's farsighted city plan had anticipated the new developments and had not only provided for the shift to the automobile long in advance of its happening, but had also, in annexing so much land at the turn of the century, ensured that suburbanization would take place within city limits. Immediately after the war, the city's businessmen, led by men like Donald Miller, Harvey Farr, and C.E. Folwell, worked to adapt the downtown shopping district to new needs. They created the Park and Shop system, which kept the city's shops accessible to suburban patrons who came into town in their automobiles.

Convenient access was also ensured by the creation of one-way streets which eased the flow of traffic in and out of the commercial center.

The threat that new life-styles posed to old commercial centers like Allentown's "Miracle Mile" of shops and department stores was apparently easier to deal with than the more profound and less manageable threat to the area's industrial base. The industries that had been the Lehigh Valley's greatest sources of strength in the first half of the 20th century were, by the postwar period, on the wane. Silk manufacturing, which had made the valley the second largest silk center in the nation, was largely a thing of the past, as synthetic materials manufactured elsewhere gained in popularity. The cement industry was phasing out many of its local operations. The immense American Steel and Wire Company of Allentown had closed its doors during the 1930s. And many worried that Mack Truck was planning to move its plants out of the area. Finally Bethlehem Steel, the region's largest employer, was, as wartime production ceased, laying off many of its employees.

Some communities were able to act decisively on a local level to counter this trend. Little Emmaus, for example, was able to attract Air Products and Chemicals (which later relocated in Trexlertown), the Rodale Manufacturing Company, and the Rodale Press to replace its silk mills and iron foundries.

FAR LEFT TOP
Sisters House (right) was built in 1744. Bell House was erected in 1745. Bell House became the home of the first town clock in 1746. Courtesy, Adrienne Snelling

FAR LEFT CENTER
This softwood chest, built in 1788, was used to store clothes and linens and probably held a bridal trousseau. Chests such as this one took the place of built-in closets. (LCHS)

FAR LEFT BOTTOM
Birth certificates were known as "frakturs" among the Pennsylvania Germans. This hand-lettered and colored fraktur marked the birth of Salome to Lorentz and Maria Magdalena Schneider Neuhardt in 1789. (LCHS)

ABOVE
Jacob Geiger made this tall clock in about 1790 in Northampton, which is now Allentown. It is decorated with roses, strawberries, and cherries. (LCHS)

In March 1745 the Evangelical Reformed Church and the Evangelical Lutheran Church joined together to build the Heidelberg Union Church. This cemetery, located on a hillside adjacent to the church, is one of the oldest in Lehigh County, with headstones dated as early as 1760. Courtesy, Adrienne Snelling

BOTTOM LEFT
Marquis de LaFayette, wounded at the Battle of Brandywine, came to the Lehigh Valley to recuperate. He stayed at the home of George Frederick Beckel. Painting by Eleanor Barber. Courtesy, Moravian Museum of Bethlehem

BOTTOM RIGHT
George Taylor, a signer of the Declaration of Independence, lived in this house in Easton during the Revolutionary War. Preserved by the addition of modern features, the house no longer presents a colonial facade. Courtesy, Easton House and Tavern Preservation Association; photographer Adrienne Snelling

In the early morning of September 25, 1777, the Liberty Bell was placed in the basement of the German Reformed Church in Allentown for safekeeping. In June 1778 it was returned to Independence Hall in Philadelphia. Painting by Wil Behler. Courtesy, Liberty Bell Shrine

ABOVE
The Lehigh and Delaware rivers join with the Morris Canal at Easton. This painting by Mary Maxwell McCartney shows the junction of the crucial waterways as they appeared in 1840. (NCHGS)

FACING PAGE LEFT
George Wolfe was the founder of the Public School System in Pennsylvania. A native of Allen Township in Northampton County, he was a schoolteacher and principal of a private school near Bath, that later became known as the Wolf Academy. As governor of Pennsylvania from 1829-1835, he signed the Free School Act establishing the public school system. (NCHGS)

FACING PAGE CENTER
Mrs. Henry Schnurman was born Clementine Penrose in Bucks County, in 1810. She was a Quaker, as were her parents. She bore seven children and died in 1890. (LCHM)

FACING PAGE RIGHT
Henry Schnurman was born in 1809 in Germany. He came to the United States in 1830. He settled in Allentown in the 1840s and was successful in retail trade, real estate, and flour milling. A director of the Allentown National Bank, Schnurman died on March 8, 1875. (LCHM)

TOP
The decoration of cloth with stitching (samplers) began during the Renaissance. By the 19th century fabrics and patterns had changed, but the sampler remained a demonstration of a young girl's aptitude. This sampler was worked by Sarah Wagner, age 12. (NCHGS)

ABOVE
This chain suspension bridge was erected at Hamilton Street between 1812-1814 by the Lehigh Bridge Company. It was the first bridge to span the Lehigh River and travelers had to pay a toll to cross. (LCHS)

ABOVE
From a hilltop in western Lehigh County, we can see north to Kittatinny Ridge (Blue Mountain). The village of Kempton is below in the valley. Courtesy, Adrienne Snelling

FAR LEFT, LEFT
These two paintings by Gladys Lutz in 1971 depict Easter activities of the Pennsylvania Germans. On Shrove Tuesday they fasted while on Easter Monday the Germans visited relatives and friends. Courtesy, Gladys Lutz

144

TOP
These coverlets are a good example of Pennsylvania-German folk arts. The coverlets were made by weavers with hand-operated Jacquard looms between 1830 and 1870. Courtesy, LCHS; photographer, Adrienne Snelling

BOTTOM
Agriculture has always been the basis of Lehigh Valley's rural economy. This dairy farm operates in western Lehigh County. Courtesy, Adrienne Snelling

ABOVE
The Coplay Cement Manufacturing Company operated the Schoefer Kilns in Coplay Pennsylvania from 1892 to 1893. Coplay Cement was the pioneer producer of American Portland cement, an important product of Lehigh Valley industry in the 19th century. The kilns became a museum in 1976, dedicated to the Portland cement industry and operated by the County of Lehigh. (LCHS)

FACING PAGE BOTTOM
G. Lehman painted this view overlooking Easton and the Delaware River. In the foreground is a coal-laden barge, and across the river is Easton, expanding to cover the hills around it. (NCHGS)

LEFT
The Lock Ridge Furnace Museum in Alburtis was opened by Lehigh County in 1975 and dedicated to the anthracite iron industry that flourished in the Lehigh Valley during the 19th century. These furnaces were built by the Thomas Iron Company in 1868-1869. Courtesy, LCHS: photographer, Adrienne Snelling

TOP
German artist Frederick Wulff painted this view of the Volker residence as it appeared in 1855. The house, surrounded by a grape arbor, garden, barn, and orchids, shows the agrarian orientation of Allentown at the time. (LCHS)

BOTTOM
The rivers and canals of the Lehigh Valley played a crucial role in the economic development of the area. This hand-tinted photograph from 1910 shows an Easton boat approaching Lehigh Canal Lock 19. Courtesy, Pennsylvania Canal Society Collection, Canal Museum, Easton

LEFT
This painting by Clayton P. Yoder shows the junction of the Lehigh and Delaware rivers and the Morris canal in 1850. The ferry crossed by moving back and forth on a spanning line. Courtesy, Pennsylvania Canal Society, Canal Museum, Easton

ABOVE
Cities in the Lehigh Valley grew to industrial modernity from rural beginnings. This painting, circa 1850, shows an early, but substantial, Bethlehem and the surrounding fields and pastures. (NCHGS)

ABOVE
This hand-tinted 1910
photograph shows the meeting
of the Lehigh and Delaware
rivers at Easton. The great
railway bridge can be seen in the
background. Courtesy,
Pennsylvania Canal Society
Collection, Canal Museum,
Easton

RIGHT
This 1900 painting by Howard
Briesch of Bethlehem shows the
arrival of the beer boat, *Maid of
the Mist,* at Walnutport. The
boat belonged to Seitz's Brewery
in Easton. Courtesy,
Pennsylvania Canal Society,
Canal Museum, Easton

LEFT TOP
Canal traffic moved all day and night, so the lock operators lived in houses built right next to the lock. This hand-tinted photograph shows Lehigh Canal lock 143 and the locktender's house near Bethlehem. Courtesy, Pennsylvania Canal Society Collection, Canal Museum, Easton

LEFT BOTTOM
The Pennsylvania Power and Light Company building has been a longstanding landmark on the Allentown skyline. Courtesy, Karyl Lee Kibler Hall; photographer, Arthur D. Williams

ABOVE
The Lyric Theatre in Allentown appears in this hand-tinted postcard from 1907. After serving as a showcase for legitimate theatre and the greats of vaudeville, the Lyric became a burlesque house. It has recently been redeemed as Allentown's Symphony Hall. (LCHS)

Urban decay begins at the core of a city and grows out. Super Sunday represents a response to that problem by revitalizing Allentown's downtown sector.

Sidewalk sales, and ethnic food and music are featured on the mall. Courtesy, City of Allentown

Allentown persuaded such national firms as Western Electric, General Electric, and Bell Labs to locate in the city. But local initiative was not enough, for large-scale industrial redevelopment required not only space on which to construct new factories, but also a wide variety of services—police, fire, education, water and sewerage systems, and housing—that could only be made available cooperatively by the counties and municipalities working together.

In spite of the Lehigh Valley's historic tradition of community-mindedness, cooperation on a regional scale was not easy to achieve. The towns around Easton, for example, while they wanted the advantages of the city's municipal water and sewerage systems, were unwilling to consolidate politically because they did not want to take responsibility for the problems of reconstructing the inner city. Suburban villages around Allentown like Alburtis resisted the extension of city services because they felt that their cost was unreasonably burdensome. Many local political leaders in the countryside feared that they would lose influence in a shift toward regional government. But progressive leaders in commerce and industry, with the enthusiastic support of the local press, were gradually able to generate public support for their plans, especially as the recession of 1960-1961 underlined the unstable condition of the area's economy.

The first step to a regional approach to economic redevelopment was the creation of political institutions capable of acting on the common problems of all the communities in Lehigh and Northampton counties. Accordingly the Lehigh-Northampton County Joint Planning Commission was formed in 1961. Its major task was to study the valley's problems from a regional perspective in order to suggest regional rather than local solutions. Gathering and interpreting information from this standpoint was essential if the region were to benefit from state and federal industrial and community redevelopment funds which were beginning to be made available to the troubled older industrial cities. Such information was also essential to the planning process through which the region's human and material resources could be most effectively used. The commission produced a basic framework within which both city and country could benefit mutually from new economic undertakings.

The second step to the region's economic revival involved the reform of municipal and county government itself. Up through the late 1950s, government had basically been an affair of amateurs, public-spirited professionals and businessmen able to divide their time between politics and their private interests.

Part of the Allentown program of urban revitalization included the construction of a downtown mall. The mall, completed in 1973, appears here during construction. (LCHS)

ABOVE
Allentown Public Library, paid
for by contributions, opened in
June 1978. The library serves
the city with a collection of
210,000 volumes. Over half a
million people pass through its
doors annually. Courtesy,
Allentown Public Library

FACING PAGE TOP
Cedarbrook, the county home
for the aged, first opened in
about 1849. The home has 624
beds and is surrounded by 200
acres of open parkland owned by
Lehigh County. The building
was enlarged in 1973. Courtesy,
Richard Lane

FACING PAGE MIDDLE
Allentown Sacred Heart
Hospital Center, opened in
September 1974, is located on a
103-acre campus in suburban
Allentown. The main hospital

building is dedicated to Leonard
Parker Pool, a founder and the
first president of the hospital
center. Courtesy, Allentown
Sacred Heart Hospital

FACING PAGE BOTTOM
Allentown Hospital first opened
its doors in 1899. Since then,
the growing population has
necessitated expansion. This
artist's conception shows the
hospital as it will appear in 1984
at the completion of current
modernization. Courtesy,
Allentown Hospital.

This kind of government had its benefits: because mayors and councilmen were active in their communities in their private capacities, they kept government responsive to community needs. And, with a healthy private sector, the cities could pretty well run themselves. But the new problems of industrial and commercial decline required determined government action and high levels of professional expertise that exceeded the capabilities of the amateurs and of the older administrative forms. Led by Bethlehem in 1961, many of the valley's cities adopted "strong mayor" city charters which turned the administration of city agencies over to management professionals, and which brought the government directly into new areas of endeavor, including housing, community relations, and economic development. The county governments followed suit, creating administrative frameworks capable of perceiving regional problems and acting decisively to solve them.

Government could not, of course, solve the region's problems alone. Political reform was merely the basis for the all-important partnership between government, private enterprise, and the general public. By the late 1960s, the fruits of this partnership were becoming apparent. All three cities were engaged in massive urban renewal programs. Allentown, Bethlehem, and Easton were transforming all or part of their commercial and governmental centers into plazas and malls of great beauty. Deteriorated industrial and residential structures were cleared to make room for new buildings, playgrounds, and parking areas. Public transportation was improved by the expansion of the A.B.E. Airport and, in the early 1970s, by the creation of a public entity, the Lehigh and Northampton Transportation Authority (LANTA) to operate the region's bus routes.

Attracted by the availability of capital, tax-incentives, and first-rate public services, new industries came to the valley. These included a giant new brewery and a host of companies, some old and some new, which located themselves in the Allentown-Bethlehem Lehigh Industrial Park and in the Forks Township Industrial Park outside of Easton.

The nonprofit sector also grew dramatically. In 1956, all the communities of the region, under the leadership of the Lutheran Church, pooled their resources to create the Muhlenberg Medical Center, a 300-bed facility for the chronically ill. In the mid-1960s, efforts began to approach the valley's health care problems regionally. This resulted in the construction of the Allentown-Sacred Heart Medical Center in Salisbury Township, an ultramodern facility which made the most advanced medical technology available to all the citizens of the

Parks and playgrounds ensure a healthy city. This photo shows children and adults enjoying maypoles on Romper Day in 1961. (LCHS)

area. Both Lehigh and Northampton counties rebuilt their old almshouses into splendid new facilities for the aged and dependent. These endeavors complemented the already excellent health care available through Easton, Allentown, Sacred Heart, Osteopathic, and Saint Luke's hospitals, the Allentown State Hospital, the Good Shepherd Rehabilitation Center, the Phoebe-Deaconness Home, and the Holy Family Manor.

The region's colleges—Lehigh, Lafayette, Muhlenberg, Moravian, and Cedar Crest—all expanded their enrollments and facilities. New institutions were brought into being, including community colleges in Lehigh and Northampton counties, United Wesleyan College, Pinebrook Junior College, and the College of St. Francis de Sales. New parks, libraries, and museums were brought into being under both public and private auspices. The Trexler Game Preserve, through the creative joint use of public and private funds, established a children's zoo. The Lehigh County Historical Society joined forces with the Lehigh County government to maintain a group of historic sites and homes. One of the most spectacular of these joint ventures, the Lock Ridge Furnace park and museum at Alburtis, was carried out with major assistance from Bethlehem Steel. Allentown's old Presbyterian Church became the Allentown Art Museum. The core of its collection was an invaluable gift of objets d'art, spanning the Gothic to the Baroque periods, from the estate of Samuel H. Kress, a Cherryville native who founded the Kress chain of discount stores. The historic center of Bethlehem complemented its holdings of Moravian archives and memorabilia with museums devoted to fire fighting, Victoriana, and the town's industrial past.

Easton turned its abandoned canals into an asset through an operating museum devoted to the canals' great days. This group has not confined its interests to Easton alone. It has actively promoted the rehabilitation of canal "rights-of-way" as parks and historic monuments. And it has played an important role in underlining the value of the region's industrial achievements of past and present. More generally, Northampton County was benefited by public and private efforts to create distinctive recreation areas. These include Lake Minsi, the Jacobsburg State Park (which contains one of the few surviving stands of virgin forest in the Northeast) and Louise Moore Park, the gift of the widow of philanthropist and industrialist Hugh Moore.

Religious organizations have played an important part in maintaining the high level of nonprofit activity in the Lehigh Valley. Beyond their charitable and educational contributions, many new churches have been built to accommodate the population shift toward the suburbs. The old churches have become the homes of new and growing Hispanic and Afro-American denominations. Perhaps the most important religious contribution of the postwar period involved the naming, in 1961, of Allentown's St. Catherine of Siena Church as a cathedral and center of a new Catholic diocese encompassing Lehigh, Northampton, Berks, Carbon, and Schuylkill counties. Long the dream of Allentown's Catholic leadership, this achievement was an important morale booster to all the citizens of the Lehigh Valley region. These non-profit enterprises have not been unprofitable. Beyond enriching life for the residents of the Lehigh Valley, they have brought in thousands of new people—as tourists, students, and employees of business and industry.

The determination of government and business to maintain the economic stability and quality of life in the Lehigh Valley has been matched by enthusiastic action by private citizens. If the young people of the 1930s and 1940s fled the cities after the war, the generations coming to maturity in the 1960s and 1970s showed a new appreciation for what had been left behind. Urban homesteading by individuals and preservation efforts by such groups as the Old Allentown Preservation Association redeemed whole neighborhoods from deterioration. The old houses were admired not only for their solid construction and splendid craftsmanship, but also for their energy efficiency and convenience to shopping, work, and leisure activities. Young and old worked together in Bethlehem to save the historic Sun Inn and other important structures. In Easton, Historic Easton, Inc. succeeded in saving many notable structures from the wrecking ball. But energies were not merely devoted to buildings. For the younger generation, the fully Americanized grandchildren of immigrants, came to reappreciate their origins and to prize their unique customs and traditions. Many worked hard to retrieve the memories and artifacts of the past and make them a part of the working present.

As the people of the Lehigh Valley celebrate Pennsylvania's tercentennial, they continue, as they always have, to struggle with adversity. Historically energetic, ingenious, and willing to cooperate, they are holding their own. Having valued and appreciated the past, they have learned from it. And they are using it to build, as their forebears did, a new community— inclusive, tolerant, and progressive—which will surely weather the storms of the 21st century as well as its predecessors weathered those of the 18th, 19th, and 20th.

The Glendon Iron Works were founded in 1843 by Charles Jackson, Jr., of Boston. By the mid 1850s the anthracite-burning Glendon works produced 22,000 tons of pig iron annually. Jackson was the nephew of Patrick Tracy Jackson, the father of the American factory system. Courtesy, Pennsylvania Canal Society Collection, Canal Museum, Easton

CHAPTER EIGHT

PARTNERS
IN PROGRESS

The strength of the Lehigh Valley is the diversity of its industry and business, as well as the broad and varied skills of its citizens.

This diversity stems from the pioneers, the farmers who came here from the palatinate and carved their homes out of the wilderness. They dug the ore they found in the scanty local deposits, smelted it in charcoal furnaces, then fashioned the tools they needed, to clear and cultivate their fields and build their shelters, on their simple forges. They made rifles to protect themselves and their families and to kill game for their food. When the women weren't helping in the fields and forests, they spun flax and carded wool to make the clothing their families required.

As the population grew, expanded by more arrivals from European countries, people began working together outside their homes—merging their skills in mills, factories, and industrial enclaves.

The crude-iron foundries of the pioneers eventually became the steel mills that manufacture the structural pieces and the plate other area plants fabricate to build the tallest skyscrapers and the strongest bridges, the armor plate for military ships and tanks, many of the components for millions of automobiles, and the assorted heavy machinery other American workmen produce each year.

From home-loom weaving, the people of the Lehigh Valley moved into the massive mills—which at one time made Allentown the second largest silk-weaving center in the United States—and later into sewing trades to produce clothing sold under some of this country's best-known labels. They made shoes and ladies' handbags, tools and typewriters, pipes and wire, mining and milling machinery, horseshoes and musical instruments, military aircraft, and a thousand and one components that lost their identity as some of the nation's largest manufacturing plants used them on their own production lines.

They still manufacture many of these products, but they also produce transistors and the other miniature components that have revolutionized communications, electrical appliances and devices, hydraulic equipment, massive industrial pumps, and equipment that manufactured the fuel used to fire the rockets that sent men to the moon. They also operate knitting mills and printing plants, publish newspapers and magazines, and experiment with new ways to keep feeding the world's mushrooming population and to conserve energy.

That agriculture still is a leading industry, though no longer a major employer, is evident in the productive farms scattered across the magnificent countryside—in the broad fields of potatoes, corn, wheat, and alfalfa, as well as orchards producing thousands of bushels of luscious apples and peaches.

From the beginning the residents of the Lehigh Valley had churches and schools. As the area developed they built colleges and hospitals, libraries and museums, and preserved the historical landmarks. They established facilities to serve the business community, as well as others that provide for day-to-day living and to enhance life.

The stories of some who have been partners in this progress are told on the following pages of this history. They and the people they employ are important factors in the economic strength that has made the Lehigh Valley Pennsylvania's third largest market area, and in every season one of the most pleasant and prosperous.

ALLENTOWN BUSINESS SCHOOL

The typewriter had just been invented and hadn't made its appearance in the Lehigh Valley when W.L. Blackman organized the Allentown Business College in 1869. That also was the year Allentown's public schools held their first high school commencement, graduating three students with appropriate exercises in the First Presbyterian Church, then at Fifth and Court streets.

For more than a century, the college and its successors have been preparing both men and women for the increasingly demanding roles in business, industrial, and professional offices in this and other communities. Because many records were lost in a fire, the exact number who attended is uncertain. Several thousand who studied in the school, however, have left their mark in the Lehigh Valley and elsewhere. Many have become influential community leaders.

Today the school is accredited by the Accrediting Commission of the Association of Independent Colleges and Schools, approved for an 1,800-hour program leading to Associate in

Allentown Business School is located in the Center Square Building at 11 North Seventh Street.

Specialized Business Degrees in Business Administration, Fashion Merchandising, and Secretarial Science. These courses can be completed in about 18 months. Choices also include Advanced Diplomas in General Business, Junior Fashion Merchandising, Medical Transcription, Receptionist, and Stenography. Specialized business degrees include options in Data Processing, management-marketing, and travel. Secretarial science options include Executive, Legal, and Medical Office Assistant/Secretarial courses. The academic schedule is on the quarter system with terms beginning in September, January, March, and July. Students may begin their studies in any of these terms. There also are night classes.

Although it meets a definite need in the community and for many young people, the school always has been a private institution, providing its own facilities and operating without tax support.

C.W. Blackman, who served as the first president, incorporated his school as a college in 1897. His successors were N.S. Biery and John W. Oberly. In those years the school operated on the second floor of a building near Ninth and Hamilton streets, on what now is the site of the Allentown Hilton.

In 1958, after Oberly retired and closed the college, Richard T. Hope opened the Allentown Business School at 801 Hamilton Street. The International Correspondence Schools of Scranton became owners in 1968 and expanded the curriculum to include broader areas of business administration, general business, and training for executive secretaries, medical secretaries, and receptionists. The school now is a wholly owned entity of the National Education Corporation. Barbara N. Thomas, the director, heads a faculty of 17 and a staff of nine.

Throughout its history, the school has been in the heart of the main Allentown business area. It now occupies the Center Square Building at 11 North Seventh Street. There its facilities include spacious classrooms, computers, and other equipment used in modern business and social areas.

The student body is a diverse group of high school graduates from the cities, suburbs, and rural areas of the community and includes various ethnic backgrounds, age levels, experience, interests, and needs. The school is dedicated to providing all of them with a variety of quality educational programs that are sound in concept, implemented by a competent and dedicated faculty, and geared to serve those seeking a solid foundation of business knowledge and skills required to obtain employment in their chosen field. It has been unusually successful in placing those it trains.

ALLENTOWN PNEUMATIC GUN COMPANY

The Allentown Pneumatic Gun Company, leading producer of equipment used to build and strengthen with cement in projects where retaining forms would be costly and difficult to erect, is one of the industries that delivers a Lehigh Valley product around the world.

With the pneumatic gun, powered by compressed air, cementitious materials can be blown against any clean surface with a force that promotes quick and lasting bonding. The method is equally effective in new construction and for repairs of older structures. It has been used, for example, to build architectural showpieces like the TWA Terminal at John F. Kennedy International Airport in New York; to rebuild the deteriorating arches and roadway of old concrete bridges, like the Alburtis L. Meyers (Eighth Street) Bridge in Allentown; and to preserve the old wooden pilings of the pier at Newport Beach, California, which were encased in a three-inch coating of Gunite. It also is used to install and repair refractory linings in furnaces and high-temperature processing equipment.

The gun is the development of Carlton Akeley, curator of the Field Museum of Natural History in Chicago, who developed it to recreate the structure of mammals for permanent display. Samuel W. Traylor, Sr., Allentown industrialist, bought the rights to the gun, patented in 1911, and with W.J. Roberts, Sr., and B.C. Collier, his associates in the Traylor Engineering and Manufacturing Co., produced and marketed it. They also introduced the patented Gunite process. William C. Roberts, the grandson of both Roberts and Collier, became president of the firm in 1969.

The company, now independent, operates from its headquarters at 614 North 18th Street, Allentown, and has a plant at 480 Mickley Road, Whitehall Township. It produces several models of the simple, effective machine, some mounted on trailer chassis with the essential mixing equipment, and a wide range of accessories. Basically, however, the gun is the same product that was first manufactured in Allentown in 1911, a machine that for some 70 years has proved effective for a wide range of construction in almost every country in the world.

An early local project was the Lehigh Country Club swimming pool built in 1935 and still in use. Mines and tunnels throughout the world use the Allentown pneumatic gun for support and sealing. Hundreds of dams have been repaired and over 1,000 miles of irrigation channels constructed with the gun. One of the largest projects ever completed was Disneyworld, virtually all built of Gunite.

All the major steel, aluminum, oil, and chemical companies use the Gunite process daily to make repairs to the linings inside their furnaces and vessels, shooting on refractory and insulating materials.

Patents long since have expired but the uses for the tool in construction and industry continue to expand.

LEFT
The pneumatic gun is a relatively simple tool in which compressed air is used to shoot cementitious products used in new construction and in repairs without building forms.

BELOW
Cement guns are used to place concrete pneumatically as this workman is doing in the walls of a tunnel.

AMERICUS HOTEL

The Americus Hotel, on the Sixth and Hamilton street corner where Abraham Gangewere built a two-story frame hotel in 1810, is the oldest and largest hotel in Allentown.

Although the Americus has passed through a succession of ownerships since it was formally opened in September 1927, it maintains much of the elegance and most of the conveniences long associated with the grand hotels of the period when the 14-story building took its place on the city's skyline.

The Americus, built by a group headed by A.D. Gomery, an Allentown produce wholesaler, carries the name of the explorer for whom America was named. The Spanish decor in the lobby and other public rooms recognizes the country under whose flag he sailed to the New World.

Andrew Sordoni, Wilkes-Barre hotelman and contractor and a former state senator, bought the hotel from a bond holders' organization in 1944 and, after substantial refurbishing, it became a part of his Sterling chain which operated hotels in Wilkes-Barre, Scranton, Montrose, Shenandoah, and Binghamton. In November 1965 Sordoni's American Hotel Realty Corporation sold the hotel to Albert Moffa, a young Allentown entrepreneur who enthusiastically undertook the job of redeveloping it, for $500,000. It had cost $2.5 million to build.

Moffa reduced the number of guest rooms from the original 326 to 247 in order to enlarge some of the smaller ones and developed the top floor into the Skyline banquet room, which seats 300 and offers a magnificent view of the city and its environs.

Elsewhere in the hotel, most of the original facilities and decor were retained. The two-story ballroom, with its floor-to-ceiling windows, a balcony, and adjoining dining room, provides comfortable seating for up to 500 and may be approached either from the main lobby or a pleasant mezzanine. A cocktail area is located just two steps above the lobby and has direct access to the dining room and ballroom.

What once was a grotto dining room on the lower level has been converted into a motion picture theater with full stereo equipment and seating for 200. It is used regularly by church groups and is available to other organizations. The Forum, a street-entrance restaurant, has been created out of the ground floor space once occupied by five separate stores that were centered on the corner. There also are several private dining rooms for small meetings and parties.

ABOVE
Strangers have found lodging in an inn at Sixth and Hamilton streets, now the site of the Americus Hotel, since Abraham Gangawere built the two-story frame American Hotel in 1810. This three-and-one-half story building was erected about 1860. The stage brought passengers from the railroad a few blocks away.

LEFT
The Americus Hotel at Sixth and Hamilton streets is Allentown's oldest and largest hotel.

All guest rooms have been refurnished and are equipped with television. Approximately 100 rooms are rented to permanent guests, leaving about 140 for transients. It can guarantee up to 100 rooms for conventions and offers the use of the ballroom for sessions.

What Moffa lacked in experience as a hotelman he has made up by his enthusiasm and the back-breaking work he put into rejuvenating the deteriorating property he took over. Born in Allentown, the son of a shoemaker, he owned and operated several small motion picture theaters in and around the city and had a theater sound service before buying the Americus.

As was the case with all his other undertakings, the Americus has been a challenging enterprise for Al Moffa, to which he is dedicated to fulfilling the dreams of many and again making it Allentown's grand hotel.

APPEL-JEWELER, INC.

For well over a century Appel-Jeweler, Inc., of Allentown has been widely recognized as one of the nation's top jewelry stores. For many of these years it also has been a museum in which people may browse either to admire or to acquire what they enjoy seeing: precious gems exquisitely set, and treasures designed and created by artists and artisans in all parts of the world.

Founded by Jacob Massey in 1860 at 738 Hamilton Street, it is one of the oldest jewelry stores in the country. In 1893 the store was moved to 619 Hamilton Street and a few years later to the site it now occupies.

Wilson H. Appel purchased the business in 1897 and it has been in the family ever since. His son, Carl W. Appel, joined him in 1923 a few months after graduating from Lehigh University with a degree in electrical engineering. Since his father's death in 1934 he has owned and operated the business. The store was expanded in 1961-62, when an adjoining property was added to accommodate increasing lines of fine china, crystal, silver, porcelain, and art objects. The basement is featured as the Continental Gift Shop.

Trained by the American Gem Society to evaluate the cutting, color, clarity, and carat weight of diamonds and to interpret their significance to customers, Appel has been a member of that prestigious organization for almost 50 years. An associate in the store also is trained and affiliated. Regardless of

their size, Appel diamonds appear to have a distinctive brilliance. All have been selected in accordance with Gem Society standards. Equal care is given to the selection of all gemstones. Among these is the superb 259.25-carat Appel amethyst, once in the Hapsburg Collection.

If a store can be judged by the company it keeps in the choice of its wares, then Appel's in Allentown is in the most select group. Its silver includes Reed & Barton, Gorham, Towle, Lunt, Wallace, Kirk, Stieff, International, Tuttle, Newbury Crafters, Frank Smith, Buccellati, and Christofle. In its wide range of fine china and porcelain patterns are many by Wedgwood, Lenox, Cybis, Gorham, Royal Doulton, Royal Worcester, Royal Crown Derby, Spode, Minton, Rosenthal, Herend, Aynsley, Ceralene, Haviland, Oxford, Bernardaud, Royal Copenhagen, Bing and Grondahl, Fitz & Floyd, Villeroy & Boch, and Hutschenreuther. Crystal includes Waterford, Baccarat, Lalique, Val St. Lambert, Swarovski, Lenox, Gorham, Seneca, Stuart, and Ceská. Gorham, Reed & Barton, Kirk, Stieff, Hampshire Lance, Towle, Royal Holland, Lunt, and Boardman are included in its pewter collection. Fine linens are of matching quality. The store's watches include Rolex, Baum and Mercier, Movado, Concord, Piaget, and Longines-Wittnauer.

Appel's was among the first retail stores to handle Boehm porcelains and has a magnificent collection of its birds, flowers, and animals. Many other collector lines are represented among its porcelain figurines and selected art objects. Good taste, not price, controls its choices.

The bronze-trimmed marble and glass facade is an appropriate introduction to the elegance that is the hallmark of Appel-Jeweler, Inc. The Boehm porcelains in the foreground of the china-crystal-silver department are just a few examples of the treasures behind the doors with the Lalique crystal doorpulls.

THOMAS A. ARMBRUSTER, INC.

Thomas A. Armbruster, who began his career as a builder when he was a high school student helping his father erect and renovate homes in the Jim Thorpe area of Carbon County, now heads and directs one of the largest and most successful building contracting firms in the Lehigh Valley.

In recent years, the construction work done by Thomas A. Armbruster, Inc., has run between $10 million and $15 million a year with major contracts ranging from about $500,000 to more than $6 million. The company has built churches and hospital units, industrial plants and warehouses, office buildings and apartments for the elderly, retail stores, banks, public facilities such as wastewater treatment plants, park and recreational developments, and has completed many extensive renovation projects.

Armbruster came to Allentown in 1953 and worked for other contractors a short time before establishing his own business in 1954. Operating as a single proprietorship, he built

Episcopal House, a high-rise apartment for the elderly, was built by Thomas A. Armbruster, Inc.

St. Thomas More Roman Catholic Church in South Whitehall Township, Lehigh County, is one of the architectural gems of the area erected by Thomas A. Armbruster, Inc.

homes in the Parkway Manor section on Allentown's western periphery, in the Lehigh Parkway area, in Whitehall Township, Hellertown, Coopersburg, and other suburban communities.

The business was incorporated in 1958; in that year it bid successfully to erect one of the fraternity houses Muhlenberg College was building for on-campus residence groups. The next year it built St. Timothy's Lutheran Church, a pentagon-shaped structure at Walnut and Ott streets. Among the other churches in the area the firm erected are Faith Presbyterian Church in Emmaus and St. Thomas More Roman Catholic Church, the circular structure whose walls are brilliantly studded with thousands of small pieces of stained glass that bring rich colors into the building during the day and present a glorious view from the outside when the sanctuary is lighted at night. Armbruster also constructed the school and the convent on the St. Thomas More campus on Flexer Avenue, just outside Allentown's western city limits.

Schools Armbruster built include the Northern Lehigh High School and Sports Center, a $6.8-million project in Slatington; the William A. Shoemaker School in Macungie; the $2.4-million elementary school in Jim Thorpe; and a $2.2-million elementary school for the Whitehall-Coplay School District. It also built the oncology addition to the Wilkes-Barre Hospital, the unit that houses two linear accelerators.

Among the industrial projects it completed are the $4.5-million manufacturing plant additions to the Binney & Smith Crayola crayon operation on the sylvan campus in Forks Township, near Easton; the $6.2-million frozen food facilities for

ABOVE
The William Shoemaker School in Macungie is one of several public school buildings constructed by Thomas A. Armbruster, Inc.

TOP
Another project by Thomas A. Armbruster, Inc., is Prosser Hall, a women's dormitory at Muhlenberg College, Allentown.

Beatrice Foods, the $4-million Olin Corporation chemical plant, the $4-million Cotter Company warehouse and paint plant, and the National Can Company plant, all at Fogelsville; the $3.8-million Olean Tile Company plant in Quakertown; and the specialty gas plant at Haucks Station for Air Products and Chemicals, a $2.75-million project.

It erected Episcopal House, a high-rise apartment for the elderly, in Reading; the main office of the Lafayette Trust Company in Easton; additions to the Merchants National Bank in Allentown; the Strawbridge and Clothier Clover Department Store in Whitehall Township; the Lehigh Valley Motor Club building in Allentown; and the $2.7-million Rodale Press operating center in Emmaus.

The company also has undertaken the reinforced concrete work for new office and laboratory units at the Air Products

and Chemical plant in Trexlertown, for the new $38-million Coplay Cement plant near Nazareth, for the Bethlehem wastewater treatment plant, the brewhouse addition to the F and M Schaefer operation in Fogelsville, and for Allentown's Hilton Hotel and Conference Center. Armbruster did the construction on two Susquehanna Riverland projects for the Pennsylvania Power & Light Company near its Berwick nuclear power plant, and developed the 100-acre French Creek State Park in Berks County and the 110-acre Promised Land State Park in Pike County.

Among the projects under way in 1982 were complete alterations to transform the former J.B. VanSciver furniture building at 10th and Hamilton streets, Allentown, into additional office space for the Pennsylvania Power and Light Company, and the firm's Carbondale Service Center. Together, these projects will cost approximately $6 million. Also under way are a process water facility at Western Electric's Allentown operation and additions to the Caloric Company's plant and warehouse in Topton. In the first five months of 1982 the corporation was involved in projects with a total price tag of about $100 million.

Armbruster operates from its own building in a pleasant rural setting along Twin Ponds Road in Trexlertown. It customarily has a staff of between 150 and 175, including a registered architect who has designed some of the structures the company erects.

Most of the work the firm has done was awarded after competitive bidding. However, it also works on a fixed-price basis and serves as a construction manager for the owner when a project has been designed and bid.

Thomas A. Armbruster, founder of the organization, is its president and chief operating officer. Other officers are Bruno N. Bianchini, a registered architect in Pennsylvania and New Jersey, vice-president/marketing and design services coordination; Carl H. Wieder, vice-president/estimating; Betty Lou Klinedinst, vice-president/contract management; Fred T. Armbruster, vice-president/project supervision; Kenneth G. Knapp, Jr., secretary; and Dominic B. Sorrentino, treasurer. Armbruster also has a staff of 11 project superintendents, some of whom have been with the firm for more than 20 years.

Thomas A. Armbruster, Inc., is a long-standing member of the Lehigh Valley Contractors' Association, which Mr. Armbruster has served as an officer and director. He also is chairman of the Building Advisory Council for Architectural Engineering at Pennsylvania State University.

B & M PROVISION COMPANY

The Lehigh Valley has always been noted as a region where people cared about fine food. Until the 20th century, hotels, restaurants, stores, clubs, and schools obtained what they needed to keep those they served fed and happy by dealing directly with farmers and with a variety of specialty suppliers—fruit and vegetable dealers, butchers, confectioners, dairies, and grocers. But with the enormous growth in the number and size of service institutions and in their volume of business, the trade of provisioning became a necessary development that could supply the full range of wholesale food needs through a single outlet. Among the pioneers in this field was the B & M Provision Company.

In May 1940, as the Lehigh Valley was returning to prosperity after the Great Depression, two enterprising men, Karl Everett and Charles W. Moser, founded the E & M Provision Company. When Everett went off to war in 1941, he sold his share of the new business to Russell T. Bloss, long associated with the wholesale meat business as a salesman and manager for Swift & Company. Experience and hard work paid off and the enterprise, which was renamed the B & M Provision Company, grew steadily. Charles W. Moser died in 1958 and the remaining partner, Russell T. Bloss, brought his brother, Elwood Bloss, into the firm.

In 1969 Matthew Bloss and Richard S. Oravec, both with long experience in the meat and frozen food business, joined B & M. Oravec was named vice-president, taking charge of the firm's hotel, restaurant, and institutional concerns. Within the year he became a partner, buying out Russell Bloss' interest on his retirement. When Matthew and Elwood Bloss retired, he purchased their shares and became president and chief operating officer of the company. He brought his son, Richard Oravec, Jr., into the firm as general manager and his daughter, Joan Marie Oravec, as secretary.

The B & M Provision Company has grown enormously over the past 42 years. Beginning on South Seventh Street in center city Allentown with a small 200-square-foot cooler and a single open truck, it supplied local customers. The growth of its business forced it to relocate, first to a large building at 101 Ridge Avenue and, finally, to North Graham Street in East Allentown. From its new plant, with a 60,000-square-foot cooler and a fleet of refrigerated trucks, the firm serves a large area, covering not only the Lehigh Valley, but parts of New Jersey as well.

Much has changed in the Lehigh Valley over the past century, but not its appetite for fine food. And B & M works hard to satisfy that appetite. It supplies beef, pork, lamb, and veal in any size portion, from individual servings to whole carcasses, as well as bacon and cold cuts. It also carries a full line of dairy products, seafood, and produce. Although its primary concern is servicing stores, restaurants, hospitals, and schools, B & M also operates a retail outlet at its plant on Graham Street, offering individuals the same fine-quality products that have made the company a Lehigh Valley institution.

From its plant at North Graham Street in East Allentown, with a 60,000-square-foot cooler and a fleet of refrigerated trucks, B & M Provision Company serves a large area, covering not only the Lehigh Valley, but parts of New Jersey as well.

BALLIETSVILLE INN

For more than 230 years, under a succession of owners and with changing cuisines, the Ballietsville Inn has provided comfortable surroundings to enjoy a pleasant evening and a well-prepared, superbly served dinner with friends.

Opened in 1750 by Paulus Balliet, who on June 22, 1746, was licensed to "operate an inn on a frequently travelled road" in Whitehall Township, northwest of Allentown, it has remained in continuous operation since. Richard Wotring Gemmel, who with Joseph J. Hartmann has operated the inn since 1971, is a direct descendant of Abraham Wotring, father of Paulus Balliet's wife, Maria Magdalena.

Originally called the Whitehall Inn, the establishment was a sturdy log cabin in the middle of a virgin forest. For more than 100 years it was a station for the stagecoaches traveling between Philadelphia, Easton, and Mauch Chunk, and a haven for settlers during the French and Indian War. It also housed a post office and in its early years was an Indian trading post. Much of the early social and business life of the community was centered at the inn. The present brick building was erected in 1840 to replace the original log structure. It was built over the walls of Fort Balliet, to which early settlers fled when they feared attacks by Indians.

Gemmel, who had a lifetime dream of operating the old inn with which his forebears had been identified, and Hartmann, a Swiss-trained hotelman with whom he was associated in the Chalet Suisse in Philadelphia, visited the area in April 1971 and saw a "for sale" sign in the window of the establishment. Two days later they purchased it.

Gemmel and Hartmann, who learned the business from his father (owner of a famed ski resort near St. Moritz), then served apprenticeships in Lucerne and Lausanne before studying in a hotel school in Lucerne, share the management of the inn. Gemmel learned the art of the business from Hartmann during their association in Philadelphia.

In refurbishing the two-centuries-old building, the owners maintained its colonial charm. The first dining room, now the Emperor Room, accommodated 32 guests. Within six months it was inadequate and a second room, now known as the Chalet Suisse, was opened to expand the seating capacity to 100 guests. The old barroom was transformed into a tastefully styled cocktail lounge.

Under its present ownership the Ballietsville Inn has established a reputation for the finest Swiss and French cuisine and

Originally opened as the Whitehall Inn, later functioning as an Indian trading post and a station for the stagecoaches traveling between Philadelphia, Easton, and Mauch Chunk, the present-day Ballietsville Inn is owned by Joseph J. Hartmann (left) and Richard Wotring Gemmel (right).

service. The establishment, which also caters for dinners held elsewhere in the Lehigh Valley, has received several prestigious awards for its service and cordiality and the high quality of its menus and food. Its greatest compliment is the roster of returning guests, many of them from other parts of the country, who make it a point to visit Ballietsville and its famous inn.

THE BESECKE GROUP

The Besecke Group, with headquarters at One Bethlehem Plaza, is a combination of widely diversified companies with the skills, expertise, and affiliations for assisting both corporate and individual clients in finding solutions to financial and estate-planning problems.

Organized in 1975 by Juergen A. Besecke, an executive trained in insurance planning and counseling, the firm's emphasis is on serving those able to benefit from the creative personal attention of a specialist who has either the tools that will help them or knows how to find them quickly. In a relatively few years the organization has developed a clientele of some 3,000. Among them are small business concerns, their owners, managers, and shareholders, and many individual professionals. It has set up more than 150 pension plans covering many hundreds of persons.

Advanced financial planning for both business organizations and individuals has been made increasingly imperative because of inflation, four major tax bills in five years, and increasing federal and state regulations.

The Besecke Group's resources enable it to assist those faced with problems of reducing business taxes, protecting estates for heirs, continuing a business after the death of a partner, or preparing for the sale, merger, or purchase of an operation or one of its divisions. The company helps business managers attract and retain key executives, remain competitive in employee-benefit programs, and reduce health-care costs and insurance

Juergen A. Besecke, agent of Penn Mutual Life Insurance Company.

payments. It serves professionals in matters of practice management and of assuring the continuation of income during disability or upon retirement. Assistance also is available for young professionals confronted with the costs of establishing their own offices and financial-record systems.

As professional insurance counselors, The Besecke Group works with employee benefits—including pensions, group life and health insurance programs, voluntary benefits, and employee-benefit analyses. This area also includes matters such as executive and professional compensation services, deferred compensation, estate analyses and planning, tax shelters, and business strategy planning. Among the latter it counsels on key-employee insurance, business continuation insurance, and protection for professional corporations.

To offer the broadest range of services, The Besecke Group has these key affiliate relationships: The Stewart-Biborosch Agency, a life-insurance resource offering advanced estate-planning concepts and full capability for expert backup in business and professional insurance needs; Juergen A. Besecke Associates, an agency specializing in financial planning, estate planning, disability, and group and commercial lines of insurance; M.L. Stewart Associates and its subsidiary, Independence Square Pension Planners Inc., which provides services in corporate, Keogh, SEP, and IRA pension and profit-sharing plans; Financial Brokers Inc., a company specializing in business and professional financing; Personal Economics Group, a New York corporation which offers access to limited partnerships in real estate and in oil and gas production, a device primarily for use as tax shelters; and the Mutual Association for Professional Services, which provides established professionals or those in residency programs, internships, or graduate schools with assistance in loans and mortgages, practice management, insurance coverage, and other basic financial needs for the business side of the practice. The Besecke Group's primary carrier is the Penn Mutual Life Insurance Company.

Juergen A. Besecke, a graduate of Abington High School (near Philadelphia), received his formal business education at Bloomsburg State College following three years of military service. He entered the insurance field with M.L. Stewart Company in Philadelphia in 1973, and in 1974 came to Bethlehem as the district manager of the Penn Mutual Insurance Company. He resigned the management responsibilities in 1978 to devote full time to the broader financial business he had established three years previously and has become one of the top producers of Penn Mutual Life Insurance Company.

To best serve the individual needs of his own firm's clients, Juergen A. Besecke now has affiliations with 25 of the nation's leading life insurance companies. His key associates are his wife, Colleen R. Besecke, a licensed agent; Sandra Gorkos, executive secretary, who coordinates all client programs, provides information for clients, and handles the administrative aspects of the business; Lois Howell, who provides the technical research for customer planning and client service; Karen Klinger, responsible for detailing group coverage and pension programs; and Paul Blow, who works to maintain close relationships with clients to make certain their policies are adequate for changing situations.

Another very busy associate in The Besecke Group is the Star computer, with direct access to the Penn Mutual Computer Center in Philadelphia. In moments it provides the Bethlehem-based organization with the facts, the numbers, and the available plans and alternatives for an individual client's program. Juergen A. Besecke is planning some further additions to The Besecke Group to provide even more clients with expanding services they will need and desire as they plan for their financial futures.

Juergen A. Besecke and his staff (left to right): Sandra A. Gorkos, Paul D. Blow, Karen Klinger, and Lois Howell. Seated is Besecke.

169

BEYER-BARBER, INC.

Beyer-Barber, Inc., is an organization of 40 professionals with the corporate tools needed to provide employee benefit and actuarial consulting services to a wide range of employers throughout the Lehigh Valley.

Organized in 1943 by Harold W. (Jake) Beyer and Aman M. Barber, Sr., the firm has installed pension plans for more than 1,600 employers. The largest plan has some 53,000 participants; in the smallest there is only one.

Clients include agricultural enterprises, all hospitals in the area, nursing homes, newspapers, banks and savings and loan associations, a wide spectrum of manufacturing concerns and industrial operations, building contractors, credit bureaus, department stores and smaller retail operations, the city of Allentown and many other municipalities, labor unions, the Allentown-Bethlehem-Easton Airport, wholesale and retail food-service establishments, bottling companies, breweries, and others.

The corporation, with headquarters at 515 Linden Street, Allentown, operates through three wholly owned subsidiaries:

Leaders of the Beyer-Barber team are (left to right) Bernard J. Gordich, president; Donald S. Guman, executive vice-president; Aman M. Barber, Jr., chairman of the board and chief executive officer (seated); and Julian Rappaport, treasurer.

Barber and Company, Inc., general agent for Travelers Insurance, Dominion Life of Canada, Hartford Life Insurance Company, and access to between 50 and 75 other firms dealing in life and health insurance and financial services relating to insurance; Hard Assets Inc., a subsidiary dealing in mergers, acquisitions, and divestitures, and matters such as tax-leverage leasing, real estate syndication, and lease-back arrangements; and Collateral Capital Inc., engaged in financing, including second-mortgage programs and commercial lending.

Initially, Beyer and Barber—with the help of a part-time secretary—designed and installed a pension plan for their first client. Today the professional staff provides the technical competence and expertise necessary to design, install, and service all types of employee-benefit plans. The firm also assists management in evaluating the merits of self-insurance and serves as a contract administrator for all types of benefit plans, including pension, health, disability, and dental plans.

Beyer-Barber specialists keep the company's clients abreast of the constantly changing government rules and regulations for retirement plans, stock options, employee stock ownership plans, estate planning, executive compensation, group insurance, and many other areas.

The founders of the organization operated it until their death. There now are two stockholders: Aman M. Barber, Jr., chairman of the board and chief executive officer; and Donald S. Guman, executive vice-president. Barber, a chartered life underwriter, serves as president of the Allentown Economic Development Corporation and is a member of the Lehigh County Chamber of Commerce. Guman, also a chartered life underwriter, is a member of the Allentown Lions. Bernard J. Gordich, a lawyer admitted to practice in Pennsylvania and New York, formerly a director and president of the Statewide Insurance Company and Banner Casualty Company of New York and currently a member of Allentown Rotary, is president. Julian Rappaport, a chartered life underwriter and certified public accountant, is treasurer. He also serves on the board of governors of the Jewish Community Center; is chairman of the Endowment Fund of the Lehigh County Blind Association, president of the Livingston Club, chairman of the board of Israel Bonds, and treasurer of Endowment Fund, Temple Beth El.

The firm and its individual members maintain affiliations with more than a score of professional organizations, and both the firm and its officers are heavily engaged in civic duties and responsibilities.

BINNEY & SMITH INC.

Binney & Smith, with headquarters and a major plant on a sylvan campus near Easton, is the Lehigh Valley's most colorful industry.

The company, producer of world-famous Crayola crayons, was established in Peekskill, New York, in 1864 by Joseph W. Binney, who came to America and began the manufacture of hardwood charcoal and lampblack. In 1867 his son, Edwin, and a nephew, C. Harold Smith, joined him in a partnership that became a distributor in New York City for charcoal, lampblack, and imported colors—including red oxide used to manufacture the then-popular red paint for barns.

At the beginning of the 20th century, Binney bought an old water-powered mill along the Bushkill Creek, near Easton, to grind soapstone used in many industries as foundry filler. The mill was also used to grind scrap slate from nearby quarries to make slate pencils then sold to schools. A line of a relatively dust-free blackboard chalk quickly followed.

In their visits to schools, the company's salesmen discovered that the colored-wax crayons then in use were too expensive for children. Experiments that began with the production of black-wax crayons to mark barrels led to the introduction of Crayola crayons in 1903. The name was coined by Binney's wife, a schoolteacher, from the French word for crayon and the "ola" ending then in use in other oil-derived products. From 8 colors in a box that sold for a nickel, the line was expanded to its present rainbow range of 72 colors and shades, including fluorescents.

Products marketed under the Crayola name and produced by Binney & Smith now include children's paints, markers and chalks—as well as numerous activity items designed for creative expression.

At its plant in Winfield, Kansas, the firm also manufactures a line of fine-arts materials marketed under the name of Liquitex. Brushes are manufactured at its plant in the Dominican Republic. Binney & Smith also has operations in Canada and England, a partnership in Mexico, a distributorship in Australia, and sales in more than 60 countries.

Of the organization's 1,600 employees, approximately 900 work at the Easton operation where the impressive headquarters building erected in 1976 is located on a 73.4-acre site in Forks Township. One major production plant on the site covers 11 acres under roof.

The 1903 Crayola crayon box.

World headquarters of Binney & Smith, producers of Crayola crayons, are in this spacious building on a sylvan campus in Forks Township near Easton, Pennsylvania.

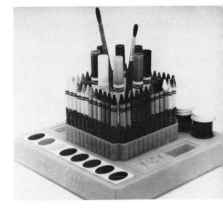

ABOVE
Crayola crayons once were made by hand-pouring batches of hot colored wax into these molds and ejecting the long colored tubes by hand after they hardened. The crayons were then labeled and packaged by hand by area families.

RIGHT
The revolving Crayola Caddy, introduced several years ago, is based on a "play center" concept.

Under the leadership of Jack F. Kofoed, chairman of the board, president, chief executive officer, and chief operating officer, company earnings were up 50 percent to a record $8.8 million on sales that increased from $94 million in 1980 to $120 million in 1981. In 1982 Binney & Smith began a $15-million expansion program.

BIXLER'S, AMERICA'S OLDEST JEWELERS

Bixler's, whose Easton jewelry store is the oldest in America continuously owned and operated by the same family, has been in business since 1785—when Christian Bixler III came from Reading to establish himself as a clock maker and silversmith in a village with a population of under 700.

Serving his apprenticeship under John Keim, a master clock maker in Reading, Bixler (a former soldier in the American Revolution) worked in his father's clock store before coming to Easton in Northampton County. He bought his first property at the corner of Bank and Northampton streets from John Penn, son of William Penn, and began business in the home and shop he built on the site.

Although Bixler's, now at 24 Centre Square, has been at five locations, all of them have been within a block of the original site. In 1976, rather than expand into a shopping center, the firm opened a second store on Bethlehem's historic Main Street.

According to the original ledger, still in the family's possession, the founder made 465 clocks between 1784 and 1812. Most were tall grandfather clocks, highly prized then, as now. Several are still in the family and are museum pieces in Bixler stores. A perfectionist in clock making, Bixler was able to attain a degree of accuracy that rivaled jeweled movements by carefully drilling and polishing pivot holes.

Bixler also was well known for the fine silverware he crafted,

Bixler's, in Easton, is America's oldest jewelry store continuously owned by one family.

LEFT
Christian Bixler III, founder of the jewelry store that has been in the same family almost 200 years. (Photo courtesy of the Winterthur Museum Libraries.)

ABOVE
In 1976 Bixler's opened this second store, with a Victorian-style front, on Bethlehem's historic Main Street.

including spoons, a few ladles, and sugar tongs. All were in the traditional colonial-fiddle pattern and were made from the prospective purchaser's silver coins or sheet silver.

In about 1825 his two sons, William and Daniel L., acquired the enterprise and continued under the name of W. and D.L. Bixler. Although William later left the operation, Daniel maintained it and passed it on to his sons, Rush and C. Willis Bixler.

Arthur B. Bixler, son of C. Willis, became the fourth generation to own and operate the firm. When he died in 1945 it came under the management of his daughter, Kathryn, and her husband, Kenneth H. Mitman, a registered jeweler and former vice-president of the American Gem Society. Their son, Philip Bixler Mitman, now is president and treasurer and their daughter, Joyce Mitman Welken, is vice-president and secretary. Ken continues as chairman of the board.

The unique front of the Easton store has leaded glass windows and a foundation of stones from a wall of the city's first church. The Bethlehem store on historic Main Street has a Victorian design.

Part of the community for almost two centuries, Bixler's has old traditions—but its merchandise is thoroughly contemporary. The stores sell only selected high-quality diamonds and gems with a wide choice of distinctive and fashionable settings. The many gift items they offer include fine porcelain, silver, china, crystal, and contemporary gift merchandise.

The Bixler's staff includes eight registered jewelers of the American Gem Society, a Certified Gemologist, and three registered bridal consultants.

BROWN, FULFORD AND MUNSIE, INC.

Brown, Fulford and Munsie, Inc., a general insurance firm with offices in the Farr Building at 739 Hamilton Street, Allentown, has been serving the Lehigh Valley community for more than 85 years.

Established by the late Ray S. Brown on August 1, 1897, when another insurance office that employed him refused to raise his eight-dollar-a-week salary, the organization had a succession of partnerships before it was incorporated in 1978. Through the years, all members of the firm have been leaders in the insurance business and in the development of the Lehigh Valley.

Brown wrote his first policy for the trust department of the Allentown National Bank, now the First National Bank, and for many years handled all insurance on the properties of the late General Harry C. Trexler, whose estate has become the multimillion-dollar trust that helps meet many community needs. After Trexler's death, Brown was named appraiser for the estate's widespread agricultural properties.

Russell Fulford came into the firm as Brown's partner in 1939. A graduate of Lafayette College, he spent four years as a fire protection engineer with the Underwriters Bureau of the Middle and Southern States and 10 years as a special agent for Fireman's Fund Insurance Company. His position in the community is indicated by some of the posts he held: director of the First National Bank of Allentown and a member of its executive committee, trustee of Muhlenberg College, vice-president of the Good Shepherd Home, and a former president of the Lehigh Community Chest, now the United Fund.

After Brown's death in 1956, he operated the agency as an individual until Donald G. Munsie, also formerly with Firemen's Fund, joined him in 1957 to form the partnership of Brown, Fulford and Munsie.

The business was incorporated in 1978 when the two partners sold the firm to George Coffin III, president of Coffin Associates, an Easton insurance firm, and James T. Brennan, president and secretary of the Herbert R. Frye General Insurance Company of Bethlehem. Fulford continues as chairman of the board, with Coffin as president and Brennan as secretary-treasurer.

Brown, Fulford and Munsie, Inc., represents six of the nation's leading property and casualty insurance companies, including Firemen's Fund since 1911, Royal since 1915, and the St. Paul Companies since 1942. A broker's license gives it access to others to meet every insurance need, except life insurance, for a wide range of clients. These include Allentown's two colleges, many large and small manufacturing concerns and mercantile establishments, financial institutions, the properties of the Lehigh County Historical Society, and hundreds of homeowners scattered throughout the area.

Ray S. Brown, founder of the firm later to be incorporated as Brown, Fulford and Munsie.

Russell Fulford, chairman of the board of Brown, Fulford and Munsie, Inc.

BLUE CROSS OF LEHIGH VALLEY

Blue Cross of Lehigh Valley is the mechanism for which 425,000 subscribers in Lehigh and Northampton counties are served by the effective and economical provision of hospital benefits and related health care programs that positively impact upon the health care delivery system.

It is one of 70 individual Blue Cross hospital insurance plans in the United States and Puerto Rico and five in Canada and Jamaica. All are independent and operate without profit. They have an umbrella, however, under which a patient with Blue Cross insurance receives the benefits to which his policy entitles him anywhere in any one of 6,500 hospitals. In recent years coverage has been expanded to offer group plans to pay for extended periods of hospital care and for prescription drugs.

Blue Cross came to the Lehigh Valley in the early 1930s when David B. Skillman, president of the Easton Hospital board of trustees, proposed a prepayment plan for hospital bills similar to the one established a few years before at Baylor Hospital, Dallas, Texas, for schoolteachers. Organized as the Easton Hospital Association, the plan offered 21 days of hospital care without charge and a 25-percent discount on all bills for seven weeks thereafter to individuals who paid $10 a year. This was the first prepayment hospital plan in Pennsylvania. In little more than two years it had a membership of 10,250.

To limit the liabilities of Easton Hospital, the plan was incorporated in 1938 as the Hospital Service Plan of Easton. Growing demands for the insured service prompted St. Luke's Hospital of Bethlehem, the Allentown General Hospital, and the Sacred Heart Hospital of Allentown to join Easton Hospital in 1938 in organizing the Hospital Service Plan of Lehigh Valley.

A short time later the organization entered into an agreement under which the newly formed Hospital Service Plan of Philadelphia and the Lehigh Valley Plan shared the services of E.A. Van Steenwyck, a former schoolteacher who was the founder and first executive of the Hospital Association of Minnesota, as their director. It was Van Steenwyck who began using a blue cross on his literature and stationery. In 1939 the blue cross was officially adopted by the American Hospital Association. In 1972 ownership of the symbol passed to the Blue Cross Association. A year later, a new symbol was introduced: a blue Greek cross with a stylized human figure in its center.

Van Steenwyck served until 1962 when he was succeeded by Earl G. Wray, Jr., who had been associated with the Lehigh Valley organization since 1950. Wray, who became president when titles were changed, retired in 1978. He was succeeded by Harold M. Petersen, formerly vice-president of financial services of Blue Cross-Blue Shield of North Carolina.

Offices were moved to the Hunsicker Building at 19 North Seventh Street, Allentown, in 1938 and to a new building at 1221 Hamilton Street in 1970. There it also serves as an agent for Pennsylvania Blue Shield. It now has approximately 275 employees.

Member hospitals are the Allentown Hospital, Allentown and Sacred Heart Hospital Center, Allentown Osteopathic Hospital, Easton Hospital, Good Shepherd Home and Rehabilitation Hospital in Allentown, Muhlenberg Medical Center in Bethlehem, Quakertown Hospital, Sacred Heart Hospital in Allentown, St. Luke's Hospital in Bethlehem, and Warren Hospital in Phillipsburg, New Jersey.

All Blue Cross organizations are nonprofit, community-oriented, voluntary health care prepayment plans. Each is separately incorporated and locally administered but subject to the rigid standards and approval of the Blue Cross Association, which sets national policies, establishes standards, and contracts for nationwide programs such as Medicare.

Blue Cross of Lehigh Valley has a board of 15 members who live and work in the community that the organization serves. They include bankers, business and labor leaders, and college executives. To provide better communication between the administration and those the organization serves there also is a subscriber advisory committee.

Mounting costs of hospital care are a growing concern of Blue Cross. In 1981 it paid 588,969 claims at a cost of $86,344,616. This was a 22-percent increase over the previous year and represented a payout of $1.04 for every dollar taken in. Losses, covered by reserves, were $5.2 million in that single year.

The Pennsylvania Insurance Commission regulates the rates subscribers pay and must approve all rate adjustments. Blue Cross, however, also has its own programs for helping control costs. These include regular reviews to prevent, detect, and eliminate excessive use of health care benefits, pre-admission testing to reduce time spent in the hospital, planning aimed at eliminating expensive duplication of hospital services, ambulatory surgery, and home health care to reduce the length of hospital stays.

Because Blue Cross is the organization through which 85 percent of the people of the two counties it serves pay their hospital bills, the organization is increasingly concerned about cost containment. In the face of both inflation and the rapid advancement of more sophisticated medical care it strives to help those who need these services and pay for them become aware of the problem. Its goal is to help the people of the community it is dedicated to serving pay for the best hospital care available at the lowest possible cost.

BELOW
Blue Cross had its first office in Allentown on the second floor of the Hunsicker Building at 19 North Seventh Street.

RIGHT
Corporate headquarters of Blue Cross of Lehigh Valley at 1221 Hamilton Street, Allentown.

BUCKEYE PIPE LINE COMPANY

Traffic on cross-country highways and railroads in the populous Northeast is eased considerably because the millions of barrels of petroleum products needed in the Lehigh Valley region are transported safely and quietly underground by Buckeye Pipe Line Company.

The firm, with operating headquarters adjacent to one of its major pumping stations and tank-farm facilities near Macungie, Lehigh County, delivers an average of about 750,000 barrels of petroleum products and crude oil a day to approximately 80 companies. In working tanks and underground pipelines it has daily custody of over six million barrels of about two dozen grades of products and crude oil.

Buckeye, founded in 1886 by Standard Oil to gather crude oil in northwestern Ohio, has been providing dependable transportation for the industry for almost 100 years. Buckeye was a crude-oil carrier until 1945 when it expanded to transport a variety of petroleum products. Today, Buckeye is a unit of The Penn Central Corporation, with pipeline facilities in Illinois, Indiana, Ohio, Michigan, Pennsylvania, New York, New Jersey, Connecticut, and Massachusetts.

Two pipelines come into the Lehigh Valley, the original 16-inch line built in 1952 and a 20-inch added in 1975. They originate in Linden, New Jersey, where refined products are gathered from nearby refineries and marine terminals, as well as Philadelphia and the Gulf Coast via connecting pipelines, to be pumped to Macungie, a major station with more than 1.5 million barrels of tankage.

From Macungie, a system goes north via Wilkes-Barre/Scranton and Binghamton to Auburn, New York, where it branches again, one segment to Rochester and the other to serve the Syracuse-Utica area. The other system from Macungie goes west to serve Reading, Harrisburg, Altoona, Indiana, and Pittsburgh.

Movement through this transportation network, as well as that in the midwestern states, is directed, controlled, and monitored from the sophisticated Macungie complex, the hub of an intricate communications system. The flow through the pipelines is controlled not only to meet shipper demands but also to keep the distinctly different grades of product separate from each other. Buckeye accomplishes these exacting tasks with an organization of highly trained and experienced personnel. Included are professional managers and engineers,

TOP
A Buckeye employee opens a valve in the manifold area at the company's pumping station and tank farm at Macungie, Pennsylvania.

ABOVE
At Buckeye's Macungie complex, 1.5 million barrels of tankage allow petroleum products to be held until they can be redirected north and west through the firm's pipelines.

schedulers, dispatchers, quality control personnel, station and terminal operators, and a support staff.

These highly skilled people, together with the equipment they employ, allow Buckeye to deliver refined petroleum products to consumers in the Northeast and Upper Midwest at the lowest transportation cost. The pipeline industry as a whole—and Buckeye in particular—provides the safest mode of transportation available for these commodities as well as having very little, if any, impact on the environment.

J.S. BURKHOLDER FUNERAL HOME

Since 1895 the J.S. Burkholder Funeral Home has been an institution in Allentown, where its name has become the hallmark for dignified, distinctive, helpful service during a family's most poignant moments.

Established by the late J.S. Burkholder in 1895, its reputation and experience have come down through four generations, including two father-and-son teams. After the death of the founder in 1926, the business was conducted by his widow, Elizabeth Burkholder, and their son Robert L. Burkholder, a respected leader in many areas of community life. His death in 1951 again made changes necessary and Harry Mike Weber, who had been associated with him, became the managing partner under an arrangement in which the surviving members of the Burkholder family shared.

Weber acquired the business in 1971 and conducted it under the name of his predecessors and in the traditions he and they had so firmly established. When he died in 1976 his wife Mary K. Weber and their son, Michael A. Weber, a graduate of East Stroudsburg State College and Simmons College of Mortuary Science, became the owners.

Through all these years, the Burkholder practice always has been to ease the burdens and concerns of a family and to fulfill its wishes. As funerals increasingly tended to be conducted outside the home in facilities provided by the funeral director, Robert Burkholder bought the comfortable home at the north-

Early funeral equipment adjacent to J.S. Burkholder Funeral Home (at an earlier location) when most funerals in this area were held either at the family home or in a church.

The J.S. Burkholder Funeral Home has been converted from a stately old home in one of Allentown's choice residential neighborhoods.

west corner of 16th and Hamilton streets that had been the residence of one of Allentown's prominent families.

While retaining its elegantly simple decor, he converted it into a facility that was easily adaptable for funerals of almost any size. A display room, where a family may quietly make its own choice of caskets, and several slumber rooms were added. A spacious parking lot was provided across the street. The same services are available to every family, regardless of the cost of the funeral. They meet the needs of every segment of the community and the practices of all religious faiths.

The J.S. Burkholder Funeral Home is the only funeral establishment in Allentown selected for membership in the National Selected Morticians. This means that it accepts the highest standards of good funeral practice; gives full effect to the role of the clergy; respects all faiths, creeds, and customs; assures those it serves the right of personal choice and decision-making in funeral arrangements; makes funerals available in as wide a range of price categories as necessary to meet the needs of all segments of the community; and applies a standard of complete honesty in all dealings.

These are the standards and the guideposts established by the founder. They always have been the practices of the J.S. Burkholder Funeral Home.

ALVIN H. BUTZ, INC.

In the construction industry, the name of Alvin H. Butz, Inc., identifies a family that for five generations has been erecting a variety of distinctive buildings that serve the Lehigh Valley, its business and professional establishments, and the people of the community.

Solomon Butz laid the foundations for the business when he entered the building trades as a boy in his native First Ward of Allentown. Soon he was constructing houses, covered bridges (like the one spanning the Jordan Creek at what now is the Trexler-Lehigh Game Preserve), and the iron furnace in Allentown that helped meet the nation's critical needs in the Civil War period. In his turn came Solomon Butz, Jr., who, as a partner in the firm of Butz and Clader, built the addition at the rear of the old Lehigh County Court House, the former Allentown Trust building that still houses some county offices, and many other homes and commercial buildings in all parts of the city.

Alvin H. Butz joined his father as a boy and in 1928 organized the firm that bears his name. For more than 50 years

Moravian Housing for the Elderly, Bethlehem, constructed in 1978 by Alvin H. Butz, Inc.

he set an example of competence and integrity that remain the legacy of his family and its business. His son, Lee A. Butz, president of the company, is the fourth generation of the family to operate the business and his children are actively associated with him.

Projects that are testimonials to the Butz company's operations range from the $10-million tower and related facilities at the Sacred Heart Hospital in Allentown and the $8.7-million addition to St. Luke's Hospital in Bethlehem to many building and renovation projects costing less than $100,000. Its mark is on buildings erected at Lehigh University, Allentown College of St. Francis De Sales, several buildings at Lehigh Community College, and the multipurpose Life Sports Center at Muhlenberg College. It has built public schools like the distinctive

BELOW
The Fred B. Rooney high-rise tower for the elderly, Bethlehem, was built by the firm.

BOTTOM
The library is one of the facilities of the Lehigh County Community College erected by the company.

Freedoom High School in Bethlehem, the Salisbury Township Junior-Senior High School, the Eastern Northampton County Vo-Tech School, and the spacious Slatington Elementary School.

Commercial projects in recent years include the completion of the Merchants National Bank Building at Allentown's Center Square, the local office of the First Federal Savings and Loan Association of Philadelphia on the opposite corner, the $3.2-million twin-tower parking ramp for Hess's Department Store, the $8.7-million service facility for the Pennsylvania Power and Light Company and a $2-million addition to the Dial Office of the Bell Telephone Company, both in Allentown, and the $3.4-million Pocono Raceway. It built the first two wings of the B'Nai B'rith apartment complex for senior

citizens, and additions to the Phoebe-Devitt Home for the Elderly and the Southside Housing for the Aging, both in Bethlehem.

Corporate headquarters is in its own modern office building on Route 309, near the junction with Route 22, in Allentown, the site from which it operates helicopter communication between its projects. It works on the basis of competitive bids and negotiated contracts. The Butz Company pioneered the construction management approach through which, at the choice of the owners, architects and builders are chosen at the same time so they may plan together to gain advantages for their client. In 1982 *Engineering News Record* ranked Alvin H. Butz, Inc., among the 75 largest construction managers in the United States.

BELOW
The athletic facility, one of the buildings on the campus of Lehigh County Community College, Schnecksville, near Allentown, built by Alvin H. Butz, Inc.

BOTTOM
Wills Hall, housing the chapel and residence for faculty at Allentown College of St. Francis De Sales, is another example of the firm's construction work.

BELOW
The Lehigh Division Service Center of the Pennsylvania Power and Light Company, one of the projects of Alvin H. Butz, Inc.

BOTTOM
The Labuda Center for the Performing Arts, one of several structures erected by Alvin H. Butz, Inc., for Allentown College of St. Francis De Sales.

CALL-CHRONICLE NEWSPAPERS

The leader in building the Lehigh Valley into the third largest metropolitan community in Pennsylvania is the Call-Chronicle Newspapers, Inc., which through *The Morning Call*, the *Weekender*, and the *Sunday Call-Chronicle* serve all or parts of eight populous Pennsylvania counties and adjacent Warren County, New Jersey.

Established in 1895 under the leadership of the late David A. Miller, when he and the late Charles W. Weiser bought *The Critic*, a struggling daily with a circulation of 500, *The Morning Call* has become the fifth largest newspaper in Pennsylvania. Only two dailies in Philadelphia and two in Pittsburgh surpass it in circulation.

Included under the Call-Chronicle banner are *The Morning Call*, with a Monday-through-Friday circulation that in 1981 reached 121,974; the *Weekender*, a Saturday tabloid with 123,126 circulation; and the *Sunday Call-Chronicle*, which reached a 1981 peak of 160,699. The *Evening Chronicle*, a daily acquired in 1935, was merged with *The Morning Call* in 1980. Its circulation was approximately 25,000, much of it duplicated by the morning publication.

From its earliest days, *The Morning Call* has been a community-oriented newspaper dedicated to giving the area it serves the up-to-the-minute news of the state, the nation, and the world and the local news of each area it serves. To that end it publishes five daily editions, each with the detailed news of the geographical area in which it is delivered. On Thursdays it adds *Neighbors*, eight tailored tabloids with news and advertising from each of eight smaller areas.

Through the years the Call-Chronicle Newspapers have been locally owned by those directly involved in their daily management and production and for most of this time have been under the leadership of the Miller family. Weiser sold his share early because of ill health and Samuel P. Miller, who had learned the printing trade, became his brother's partner to take charge of mechanical production. When failing health forced the retirement of both brothers in 1920, their interests were acquired by others involved in publishing newspapers in Allentown. By that time the circulation of *The Morning Call* had reached 25,000, much of it in the rural areas of Lehigh County.

In 1934, with his health restored and his sons Samuel W. Miller and Donald P. Miller ready to join him, David Miller

Headquarters of the Call-Chronicle Newspapers on Newspaper Square cover a block on North Sixth Street from Linden to Turner. On one side, between Sixth and Law, are the principal operating offices, press building, distribution center, and facilities for newsprint storage.

bought a one-third interest that became available and joined the late Royal W. Weiler and Major J.C. Shumberger in building greater and better newspapers. Before Miller's death in 1958, the circulation of *The Morning Call* had tripled.

Gradually, employees were given an opportunity to buy stock in the company they were building and by the end of 1981 more than 450 of them were associated with the Miller family in the ownership either in their own names or through the Call-Chronicle Stock Savings Trust, toward which both individual employees and the firm contribute.

Together, more than 750 employees in one of the most modern and best-equipped newspaper plants in the world are at work to justify the Call-Chronicle watchword that "What's good for this community is good for its newspapers."

CAMPBELL, RAPPOLD AND YURASITS

The organization (which, with the partners, includes 11 certified public accountants and a support staff of 10 other employees) operates from its own spacious office building at 815 South Cedar Crest Boulevard on the western boundary of Allentown. The building was erected by Campbell Jr., and designed specifically for the purposes of the accounting firm, providing 6,000 square feet of office space constructed around a 900-square-foot secured concrete records vault. Extensive use of computers and word-processing equipment is employed. There also is a comprehensive library for the use of staff and clients.

Campbell, Rappold and Yurasits serves clients that include some of the largest corporations in the area, banks, brokerage firms, wholesale and retail stores, professional offices, service organizations, municipal governments and authorities, schools, colleges, churches and other nonprofit organizations, and individuals. Since the inception of the Community Chest, the company has supervised the annual campaigns as a public service.

Among the many services offered are audits, preparation of financial statements, tax returns, and estate planning. Management services include cost analyses, establishment of office procedures, feasibility studies, assistance with financial planning, the installation of accounting systems, and counseling in the area of tax shelters.

Throughout its long history members of the company and its employees have been actively involved in community affairs and have been leaders in many local organizations, including participation in and support of civic campaigns.

Campbell, Rappold and Yurasits is the contemporary generation of a partnership of certified public accountants that has been serving a broad range of clients in Allentown and across the Lehigh Valley for more than 55 years.

Established on January 1, 1926, when L. Roy Campbell (a native of Slatington and a certified public accountant) began independent practice in Allentown, the firm now includes his son Luther R. Campbell, Jr., Henry W. Rappold, Stephen J. Yurasits, Dennis S. Heller, and Dallas C. Henninger as partners.

The founder, who joined the U.S. Army Air Force after graduating from the Wharton School of the University of Pennsylvania in 1916, began his career at the end of World War I with Lybrand, Ross Brothers and Montgomery, a leading national firm of certified public accountants. He remained there until he began practice in Allentown in 1926. Through the years he practiced either individually or with a succession of colleagues, including Walter J. Levan and William L. McCollom.

The present partnership was formed May 1, 1969, with Heller and Henninger being admitted as partners six years later. The senior Campbell remained with the company until his death in March 1978.

Founder L. Roy Campbell, Sr. (1895-1978).

Partners (left to right) Stephen J. Yurasits, Luther R. Campbell, Jr., Henry W. Rappold, Dallas C. Henninger, and Dennis S. Heller.

COPLAY CEMENT COMPANY

Founded in 1866, primarily to provide the cement needed to build the Lehigh Canal, the Coplay Cement Company not only developed and patented the portland cement process in this country, but provided much of the leadership for the use of the product and the development of the industry. In addition to its original vertical kilns, now part of the U.S. Portland Cement Industry Museum, Coplay, Pennsylvania, the firm operates one of the world's most modern facilities a few miles away in Nazareth.

The company, which in its earliest years produced "natural" cement, was originated by David O. Saylor, Esias Rehrig, and Adam Woolever. As were the other plant operators who were converting the high-quality Lehigh Valley rock, the founders were concerned about the competition of portland cement, a European product being shipped to this country. In their efforts to match that product, Saylor and his associates burned local rock over a kitchen stove and had it ground in a flour mill. Their efforts soon were successful—in September 1871 Saylor obtained a patent for his process. The cement produced was used to build many important projects, which included the railroad bridges in Philadelphia which carried traffic to the Centennial Exposition of 1876. At this exposition Coplay Cement won an award for superior quality under the name of "Saylor's Portland Cement."

Two years later Saylor's portland cement was used to build Eads Jetties at the mouth of the Mississippi, the first federal

The Coplay Cement Company plant, completed in 1978, is one of the most modern in the world.

The first portland cement made in America was manufactured by the Coplay Cement Company in these vertical kilns near Coplay. They now are part of the Cement Museum maintained by Lehigh County.

project to utilize the domestic product. Architects and builders quickly learned about the product and it was used in the construction of early skyscrapers such as the Drexel Building in Philadelphia, the Woolworth Building in New York, in building New York City's subway system, and for the monumental Lincoln Memorial in the nation's capital.

The original dome kilns at Coplay had a capacity of 150 to 200 barrels of cement every 10 days, a maximum of 7,200 barrels a year. The rotary kiln of the new plant completed in 1978 has a rated capacity of over one million tons a year, the equivalent of approximately 5.3 million barrels. The firm replaced its original vertical kilns in 1888 with a group of Schoefer continuous vertical production units, and through the years was actively involved in advancing the manufacturing process both to improve the product and obtain fuel economies.

In 1966 Coplay doubled its capacity by acquiring the Nazareth Cement Company, operating it first as a subsidiary and then integrating the two companies. Subsequently the firm purchased the Egypt, Pennsylvania, operation of the Giant Portland Cement Company and the Penn-Dixie facility at Nazareth.

Societe des Ciments Francais, an international organization with headquarters in Paris, France, acquired a controlling interest in the corporation in July 1976. Although the company is French-owned, the operation is directed locally. Officers include Roger W. Mullin, Jr., chairman of the board, and George Uding, president and chief executive officer.

CROWDER JR. COMPANY

For more than 70 years, since industry began converting from steam and water power to electricity, the Crowder Jr. Company has been helping industrial and commercial enterprises throughout the Lehigh Valley and beyond to make this source of energy more useful, convenient, and economical.

The firm is unique in that it is one of the few in the United States that supplies the equipment its customers need while providing complete installation and full maintenance. Customers range from electric utilities, steel mills, and a wide range of light and heavy industries, to hospitals, hotels, commercial buildings, schools, and municipalities. It not only provides motors, control, and other industrial and electrical supplies and apparatus, but also electrical engineering, construction, and maintenance. In addition it offers fire protection service, conveyor belt service, and electrical and mechanical repair services.

The business was the idea of Harry N. Crowder, Jr., a Brooklyn-bred salesman for a steam-packing company who was so favorably impressed by the western New Jersey-eastern Pennsylvania area through which he traveled that he located in Easton in 1908, becoming a representative for manufacturers of industrial items.

He was joined in 1914 by his brother, Charles F. Crowder, and together they formed the H.N. Crowder Jr. Company with three employees and headquarters at 235 Ferry Street, Easton. The following year the firm signed a contract with the Westinghouse Electric Corporation for the sale of electric motors and controls, thus taking the first step in the electrification of Lehigh Valley industry. In 1918, through the influence of Westinghouse, a small branch was opened in Allentown—moving to 444 Union Street a year later. The company was incorporated in 1920 and Ernest W. Kuhnsman, now the chairman of the board, became its secretary and general manager.

During the Depression, when electrical construction was reduced, Crowder obtained the complete lines of many of the country's leading manufacturers. The Allentown plant soon tripled its original size, a new facility was opened in 1944 at 624 Lehigh Drive, Easton, and in 1952 a service center was built at 1107 Eaton Avenue, Bethlehem.

A modern 45,000-square-foot corporate headquarters, with sales, electrical construction, and warehousing facilities, was completed in 1972 in the Allentown Queen City Airport Industrial Park. As the demand for electrical and mechanical

TOP
One of the substations built by the Crowder Jr. Company is a 69-KV unit for the Pennsylvania Power and Light Company.

ABOVE
The main offices of the Crowder Jr. Company and a sales and service facility are located in this modern building in Allentown's Queen City Industrial Park.

services continued, a 40,000-square-foot service center was constructed in Lehigh Valley Industrial Park I, Bethlehem. Three company-owned affiliates, located in Temple and Reading, serve wide areas of Berks, Schuylkill, and surrounding counties.

The firm has 350 trained employees—many of them with more than 25 years of service. "On-call" personnel are available for emergency work 24 hours a day.

Ernest W. Kuhnsman, still active more than 60 years after he became associated with the Crowder Jr. Company, is chairman of the board of the enterprise; his son, William J. Kuhnsman, is president. Joseph E. Holaska is executive vice-president and secretary, and Carl W. Moran is treasurer.

DAY-TIMERS/DORNEY PRINTING

A company that began with a father's interest in finding a hobby for his family, and a lawyer's design for a handy book to keep track of his daily appointments and records, planted the roots of Day-Timers, a multimillion-dollar business that manufactures most of the 2,200 printed, engraved, and silk-screened products listed in its 120-page catalog. The market is 1.5 million customers in this country, Canada, and the United Kingdom.

Warren P. Dorney, a newspaper-circulation supervisor, trucked home discarded equipment and set it up in the garage at the rear of his home in the tiny village of East Texas, about 12 miles southwest of Allentown.

Attorney Morris Perkin of Allentown quickly recognized that his book, *Lawyer's Day,* would be useful to others and have wide applications. The result was a line of desk and pocket diaries, record books, and compact files that carry the Day-Timer name.

Two of Dorney's sons, Robert and William, took the printing course at Allen High School in Allentown—and did their homework in the family shop. When they entered military service in World War II, their brother Richard learned the trade from their father in the growing job-printing business. Bob became a photo-offset printer while serving in the U.S. Air

Warren P. Dorney, founder of the Dorney Printing Company, which is now Day-Timers.

Morris Perkin (1908-1976), founder of Day-Timers.

Force at Wright Field.

The family operation outgrew the garage, and the first building, a plant with about 1,600 square feet of floor space, was erected in 1949. Following the death of Warren Dorney that year, his wife Mabel and their three sons formed a partnership. Later their two daughters, Mrs. Jean Walk and Mrs. Nancy Steltz, became associated.

The firm quickly built a reputation for careful, attractive, and prompt work, producing stationery, cards, booklets, and forms for many business concerns, individuals, and institutions in the area.

In 1952 the Dorney Company began printing *Lawyer's Day,* and joined Perkin in developing an expanded family of diary-journals used by professional people in many fields, as well as other busy individuals. In time the Dorney Printing Company was merged with Day-Timers, organized by Perkin to market his product, and the incorporated line was sharply extended.

In 1971 Day-Timer became a wholly owned subsidiary of Beatrice Foods of Chicago, one of the 50 largest companies in the United States with annual sales of nine billion dollars.

Operations of the production company in the village of East Texas are still directed by the Dorney family, with Robert Dorney as president and general manager; William Dorney, executive vice-president; Richard Dorney, vice-president/manufacturing; and Jean Dorney Walk, vice-president/shipping fulfillment. Eight Dorney grandchildren are among the employees.

When the Dorney Printing Company outgrew the family garage in 1949, the first plant (inset) was erected. Now Day-Timers occupies all of the multi-level 275,000-square-foot plant to serve its 1.5 million customers.

EVERETT AND BUSCH, ARCHITECTS

The Lehigh Valley is dotted with impressive monuments to the prestigious work of Everett and Busch, the current generation in a continuing line of architects who for more than 100 years have been planning and supervising the construction of many landmark buildings in the area.

Established by S.A. Weishample when he came from Philadelphia in 1870 to establish practice as a civil engineer, the continuing firm has had a succession of only eight partners. Lewis S. Jacoby, who practiced independently through Lehigh County, was the first to join in a firm that did business as Jacoby and Weishampel. From 1911 until 1919, when he joined Herbert F. Everett to form the firm of Jacoby and Everett, Jacoby practiced independently. In 1929 Everett organized H.F. Everett Associates with his son Lee Everett, Paul Frankenfield, and Warren H. Oswald as partners. Gerald A. Busch, who became a project architect with the group in 1956, joined the father-and-son team as a partner in 1969 in a firm that practiced as Everett Associates. Busch took over the organization in 1977 when Lee Everett joined his father in retirement; the name was changed to Everett and Busch at that time.

A native of Reading, Busch was graduated from Muhlenberg College in 1955 and received his architectural training at Pennsylvania State University. The organization he now directs includes a staff of between 25 and 50, including architects and both professional structural and mechanical engineers. Together they put the ideas of prospective buildings through the drawing board and specification stages, then supervise the work that brings them to reality. They are members of the American Institute of Architects and the American Registered Architects. The average value of projects annually under way is $20 million.

Among the distinctive buildings with the firm's hallmark are Allentown's impressive City Hall and the U.S. Post Office across the street; three-quarters of the Sacred Heart Hospital including the tower structure, the school of nursing building, and the Robert L. Schaeffer wing of the Allentown Hospital; the Muhlenberg Medical Center; the main building of the Phoebe Home for the Aged; and Lehigh County's Cedarbrook Home.

Among the commercial buildings in Allentown are the First National Bank; the Finance America Building; the Lehigh

TOP
St. Catherine of Siena Cathedral in Allentown is one of the many area buildings designed by Everett and Busch, Architects.

ABOVE
Plans for Allentown's imposing City Hall were drawn by Everett and Busch.

Valley Blue Cross headquarters; and the Pennsylvania Power and Light Company Service Center. School facilities include Lehigh County Community College at Schnecksville; the Parkland High School and all the other schools in that area; Dieruff High School and the Allen High School Physical Education Building; and Freedom High School and the Bethlehem Catholic High School, both in Bethlehem. They designed the Allentown YMCA-YWCA, the Boys' Club, the Jewish Community Center, and the Lehigh Country Club. They are in-house architects for the Allentown-Sacred Heart Hospital Center and are designing the architecture and mechanical facilities of the 22-story PP&L tower. Through the years no project has been too large or too small for this continuing firm. None has ever been left uncompleted.

THE FIRST NATIONAL BANK OF ALLENTOWN

The First National Bank of Allentown, with 29 branches in Lehigh and three adjacent counties, is the oldest and largest bank in the Lehigh Valley. In terms of deposits, it ranks 15th in Pennsylvania and among the top 200 in the nation.

Capitalized at more than $5 million, the bank's assets on December 31, 1981, were $979,876,000 and its deposits $842,342,000. Funds under management in its trust department total $349 million.

According to a 19th-century historian, the bank was established "as the result of a citizens' movement called into being by a crying need." Founded in 1855 as the Allentown Bank, it began business with a state charter in a converted residence on Seventh Street, just north of Hamilton. Within a decade it had doubled the original capital of $100,000 and in 1865 reorganized under a federal charter as the Allentown National Bank. The following year the bank spent $1,600 for a "burglar-proof" safe.

By 1871, as Allentown's population reached 40,000, capital had increased to $500,000. A new eight-story bank and office building just north of the present bank at the northeast corner of Seventh and Hamilton streets was completed in March 1905.

Gaining strength under the strong leadership of attorney Reuben J. Butz, a leading lawyer who was the bank's president for 40 years and then became its first chairman of the board, the bank survived the financial crisis of 1929 and three years later took over the assets of the Penn Trust Company when that institution was denied permission to reopen after the bank holiday. It also joined in helping several troubled banks protect their depositors and rebuild their strength.

In 1942 it became the first Allentown bank to operate a branch when, at the request of the Comptroller of the Currency, it absorbed the former Emmaus National Bank and retained full-service banking in that community. Five years later, when the need for more banking services in the growing community became evident, it began planning another unit and in December 1949 opened the 19th Street Bank, the first branch bank in Allentown.

To serve the community more effectively, the Allentown National and the Second National Bank of Allentown, chartered in 1864, pooled resources and personnel on November 5, 1954, and created The First National Bank of Allentown. Since then it has merged with the National Bank of Catasauqua, the Macungie Bank, the Kutztown National Bank, the Northampton National Bank, and the Saucon Valley Trust Company, operating all of them as full-service branches. Convenient branches serve Allentown and Bethlehem neighborhoods and are located elsewhere in Lehigh, Northampton, Berks, and Bucks counties. In 1981 the bank concentrated all bookkeeping and data-processing operations at a specially designed and equipped operations center, a few blocks from the main bank.

Founded in response to needs expressed by the community, the bank has been meeting the increasing demands of an expanding area for more than 125 years.

Allentown National Bank, now First National, erected this building on the northeast quadrant of Center Square in 1871 and occupied it until 1905, when a taller office building was erected on the site.

Main offices of The First National Bank of Allentown on the northeast corner of Center Square, Hamilton Mall at Seventh Street.

FIRST VALLEY BANK

Founded in 1863 as the First National Bank of Bethlehem, First Valley is the city's oldest bank. Charles Luckenbach, a miller who in 1845 became Bethlehem's first burgess, led the move to organize the institution—and became its first president.

Following the bank's first anniversary, it declared a 4-percent dividend on the most recent six-month earnings. Two years later the increase in business forced a move into larger quarters at 535 Main Street, a few doors from the original location. Expanded and rebuilt several times, this was the bank's headquarters for 108 years.

The institution, which became the First National Bank and Trust Company in 1929, built its strengths through both lean and prosperous years—including the period immediately following the stock market crash in 1929. In 1932 First National was strong enough to absorb both the Bethlehem Trust Company, founded in 1906, and the Lehigh Valley National Bank, chartered in 1872.

In 1952 the bank opened its first branch office on West Broad Street; seven years later it merged with the Bethlehem National Bank.

First National became First Valley Bank in July 1969, a wholly owned subsidiary of the First Valley Corporation which was organized the same year.

Expansion moves included mergers with the First National Bank of Lansford and the First National Bank of Nesquehoning in 1971; the State Bank of Eastern Pennsylvania in Kingston and the Citizens Bank of Freeland in 1972; and the First National Bank in Bangor and the Liberty National Bank of Pittston in 1973. Twenty-nine offices now provide service in the Allentown-Bethlehem-Easton area, in the Slate Belt, the Panther Valley, the Hazleton-Freeland area, and the Wyoming Valley.

The bank, ranked 25th in Pennsylvania with assets of over $619.5 million on December 31, 1981, has its headquarters and all main-office operations at One Bethlehem Plaza, the 11-story structure at Broad and New streets. Opened in December 1974, the building was the first to be completed and occupied in Bethlehem's revitalized downtown section.

First Valley is a full-service community bank with consumer, commercial, and trust services for individuals and business

LEFT
Before it became First Valley Bank, the First National Bank of Bethlehem occupied this Main Street site for many years.

BELOW
The headquarters of First Valley Bank is located in this 11-story building erected at One Bethlehem Plaza in the center of the city, in December 1974.

organizations. From the most basic financial services to sophisticated money management, the institution has the resources, staff, and equipment to serve any size operation in its market area.

John R. Howell, formerly senior vice-president of the Girard Bank in Philadelphia, was named president of First Valley Bank and First Valley Corporation in 1976 and continues to serve in these capacities.

GENERAL ELECTRIC

General Electric brought a new dimension to the industrial life of the Lehigh Valley after the world's largest manufacturing company for utilities, industry, and the home began producing small appliances in Allentown.

The firm has been part of the community since 1946 when it bought a plant at 1801 South 12th Street, used in the war-time production of airplanes, and transferred its toaster-manufacturing operations from York, Pennsylvania. Expanding from the 67,000 square feet of floor space in the original facility to 450,000 square feet in five buildings, it added coffee percolators, waffle irons, griddles, counter-top ovens, and toaster ovens to the local production lines.

Shortly after beginning operations in Allentown with equipment brought from York and Bridgeport, Connecticut, factories, the plant was awarded armed services contracts for two- and four-slice toasters. As production increased with the introduction of new lines, facilities were expanded and the work force grew from fewer than 100 employees building two toaster models to more than 1,300 persons who are responsible for an array of models of the Allentown plant's basic products.

In 1953 a floor was added to accommodate an expanded engineering and accounting department; a year later, when the design department was moved from Connecticut to Allentown, production floor space was doubled by the construction of an addition to the main building. This move also provided increased office space. An aluminum die-cast foundry was added in 1956 to enable the factory to produce its own waffle irons and coffeemaker heating units. Later, space in a nearby building was leased for an all-electric warehouse to serve as the distribution center for products from Allentown and several of its sister plants. A new plating facility also was added.

The toaster-oven toaster, an industry first, was developed in the Allentown plant in 1956. This new concept incorporated a drawer underneath the toaster for heating or toasting bread slices, or the upper side of English muffins, and for keeping them warm. The unit also introduced a new type of heating element with the resistance wire wound on an extruded ceramic rod.

Another significant creation of the Allentown factory was the Toast-R-Oven™ introduced to the market in 1967. The forerunner of today's toaster-oven, it was designed to toast two slices of bread automatically and to bake like an oven. This innovation was the first of a long line of high-quality Toast-R-Oven™ units—some with a broil feature—General Electric manufactures in the constantly updated Allentown facility.

The plant is designed to add new houseware products to the lines General Electric has been expanding through its more than 100 years as the industry's leader.

BOTTOM
An employee performs final testing of a CTO-1000 VERSATRON™ countertop oven.

BELOW
Another employee completes and inspects glass doors for a Toast-R-Oven™.

GEORGE'S FOODLINER INC.

The huckster route that nine-year-old Danny George traveled with his father is a sharp contrast to George's Foodliner, the spacious supermarket he operates in Bethlehem's Westgate Mall.

However, as when he rode the wagon with his father and when he graduated to take his own route, Danny George has two cardinal business criteria: to offer only the highest-quality merchandise, and to give his customers fair, honest, and friendly service. These standards are obvious throughout his 30,000-square-foot store, where thousands of customers do their marketing every week.

In 1939, when George was just out of school, he began his own route in Bethlehem and its environs with a horse and wagon, selling farm produce, eggs, a few groceries, and—when weather permitted—meat from his father's butcher shop in Ballietsville. After two years in the Navy, he resumed his route; this time, however, he added some refrigerator equipment to his truck to expand his line of meat.

George was ready to open a market by 1952, and he erected a 40-foot by 80-foot building along Schoenersville Road, which opened on January 24, 1953. The business grew rapidly and expansions were made. In August 1967 George opened a new unit across the street. Later expanded to 33,000 square feet, the store was the second in the busy Westgate complex.

The facility, independent except for a merchandising affiliation with IGA, is a completely stocked market with a full line of groceries, vegetables, fruit, meats, and household goods. The meat department offers not only fresh meat cut on the premises, but sausages, hams, bacon, and other pork products smoked in George's own smokehouse.

The owner's mother, Margaret George, still operates the kitchen that supplies the delicatessen department with some 30 different homemade items. The meat and delicatessen departments cooperate in producing party trays for which the Foodliner is famous. It is famous, too, for its on-the-premises bakery that specializes in wedding cakes and pastries.

Since 1959 George has bought the grand-champion 4-H Club baby beef at the Pennsylvania State Farm Show, as well as champion and reserve-champion steers, lambs, and hogs at the Eastern Pennsylvania 4-H Round-Up.

The store's free coffee bar is always open. Every Tuesday morning when school is in session, between 200 and 250

TOP
One of the busiest spots in Bethlehem's Westgate Mall is George's Foodliner.

ABOVE
George's Foodliner has a wide reputation for its choice meats, some of which are smoked in his own smokehouse. He is the area's best-known buyer of grand champion beef and lamb at the Pennsylvania State Farm Show and 4-H Club Round-Up.

customers have "Breakfast at George's." Customer interviews are taped for later broadcast and demonstrations are given.

Danny George credits others with helping to build the Foodliner. Among them he specifically lists his wife, who for years ran the produce department; his mother; Fay Terrinoni, his secretary since his first year in operation; and the firm's employees, who number over 100. The Georges have three daughters—Susan, Ruthanne, and Danielle.

H.G.F. MANAGEMENT CORPORATION

In 1958 the H.G.F. Management Corporation was just a dream to 16-year-old Harold G. Fulmer III, working part time for one dollar an hour for the first McDonald's restaurant in the Lehigh Valley.

Today the H.G.F. Management Corporation is a reality, an empire built by a man who, before he was 40 years old, owned operations ranging from 14 McDonald's restaurants across the Lehigh Valley to the Traylor Hotel, one of Allentown's landmark hotel and apartment complexes, where his headquarters is located. Other holdings include the first McDonald's restaurant in Allentown; Evergreen Realty, owner of more than 1,000 residential rental units and more than 200 commercial properties; radio station WSAN, the pioneer broadcasting facility in the Lehigh Valley; Hamilton Printing, offering a wide range of services including full-color xerography; Ful-Mac Maintenance, responsible for repairs and upkeep of all of Fulmer's properties; the Kutztown Airport; and Sky King Airways, providing service for his companies.

Fulmer is a member of the Lehigh-Allentown Greater Community Council and plays a vital role in the rejuvenation of downtown Allentown. Harold Fulmer's 3,600 employees, most of them seasonal and part time, include 3,000 teenagers. In 25

Antique cars are a passion for Harold G. Fulmer III.

Harold G. Fulmer III poses with his memorabilia collection.

years his McDonald's restaurants and other H.G.F. enterprises have employed about 50,000 people. When employees reach the age of 25 and have been employed for the equivalent of a year, they become eligible to participate in the company's profit-sharing plan and to join its pension fund.

Known as an unpretentious millionaire whose only extravagance is antique cars, Fulmer has no reservations about sharing his wealth.

Recently he established the Fulmer Foundation, which dispenses money to needy individuals and organizations. The foundation regularly contributes to charities, subsidizes housing for the elderly, and supports educational institutions and arts in the Lehigh Valley.

Harold Fulmer is one of the most talked-about businessmen in the Lehigh Valley. His success story is backed by long hours and instinctive business timing. He is an entrepreneur whose organizational skills spill over into community concerns. As an integral part of Lehigh County's power elite, Harold Fulmer continues to stimulate positive growth in the Lehigh Valley.

R.S. HAHN & SONS, INC.

R.S. Hahn and Sons, Inc., an Easton sheet metal-fabricating firm, marked its 75th anniversary in 1979—and confidently anticipates its centennial celebration.

The likelihood of reaching that milestone early in the next century appears good. The fourth generation of the family already is active in the business, and the great-grandsons of the founder are as dedicated to their jobs as their forebear was when he set up his own tinsmith shop in 1904—after a long apprenticeship in a trade where the workmen were known as "tin knockers."

Through the years the company R.S. Hahn founded and headed during his lifetime has been fabricating custom-made metal units for industries in the Lehigh Valley, particularly those in the Easton area.

The organization's products range from roof flashings and stainless-steel sinks to heating and air-conditioning ducts for residential and industrial requirements. It fabricates parts for auto-body shops; ducts and collectors for air-pollution equipment; cyclones; pipe; heating and ventilating ducts for industries, schools, and commercial buildings; stainless-steel lagging for power plants; and maintenance pieces for all types of industrial installations.

Hahn began his apprenticeship in 1892, and a dozen years later bought the tinsmithing business of Stephen Nagle at 236 Church Street, Easton. He was one of the authors of the *National Apprentice Training Plan for the Sheet Metal Industry,* published in 1925 by the National Association of Sheet Metal Contractors.

That same year his son, Samuel, completed a sheet metal and drafting course at Carnegie Tech, and the operation was moved to larger quarters at 43-45 Sitgreaves Street. In 1931 another son, Herman—also a graduate of Carnegie Tech—joined his father and brother to form a knowledgeable and ambitious team. In the spring of 1954 the company moved to its present location at 25 North 10th Street.

Before the firm was incorporated in 1974, Herman's three sons had joined: Richard in 1960, John in 1965, and Michael in 1972. The fourth generation is represented by Richard's son, David, who joined the firm in 1979, and by Richard, John's son, who has been associated with it while completing his education.

In addition to fabricating metal to a customer's requirements,

TOP
R.S. Hahn & Sons was 20 years old when R.S. Hahn (standing closest to truck) and four of his associates had this picture taken showing the company's headquarters and its truck. Photo circa 1925.
ABOVE
Today R.S. Hahn & Sons, Inc., is located at 25 North 10th Street.

the corporation also sells and installs Lennox air conditioning and heating equipment.

Through the years Hahn's customers in the Easton area have included American Can installations; Ingersoll-Rand and Ecolaire, formerly its heat-transfer division; the Bethlehem Corporation; Taylor-Wharton; Lehigh Foundries, now Victaulic; Lafayette College and the Easton School District, for which it fabricates duct work; and many others.

HESS'S DEPARTMENT STORES, INC.

Hess's, at the turn of the century.

When Charles and Max Hess, Sr., came to Allentown in 1897 and opened their dry goods store in the lobby of the Grand Central Hotel on Hamilton Street near Ninth, they laid the foundation for a chain of full-service department stores that by early 1982 was serving 29 populous areas of Pennsylvania, New York, and Maryland and planning to move into more.

The flagship store in Allentown remains on the original site (although it has been expanded to include six shopping floors along almost a half-block of Hamilton Street), extends around the corner for almost a block on North Ninth Street, includes a nine-story service building on Lumber Street, and six decks of free customer parking with direct access to shopping floors from a twin-towered ramp along Linden Street. Most of the other stores in the Allentown area and elsewhere are in urban or suburban shopping malls.

Millions of customers shop these stores, which in 1981 posted gross sales in excess of $211 million. Goals now are 45 stores and gross sales of $400 million by 1986.

From the beginning until 1968, when Philip I. Berman of Allentown bought the business from Max Hess, Jr. (son of one of the founders and the merchandising genius whose innovations won national attention), Hess's was a single store which, with the exception of a few limited partners actively involved in its day-by-day business, was family owned. In 1979 it became the wholly owned subsidiary of the Crown American Corporation, with Berman remaining as chairman of Hess's board and Irwin Greenberg continuing as president. Frank Pasquerilla is chairman of the board and president of Crown American.

The foundation of Hess's growth is its strong policy of offering a wide variety of the highest quality merchandise for all members of the family and every part of the home at the lowest possible prices. It strives to operate full-service stores which, in addition to more than the usual number of departments, include in its flagship store The Marketplace, with a wide line of fine groceries and meats, a complete dental service, a travel agency, and a real estate center. Its Patio Restaurant is famous for huge portions of delicious food and ice cream sold only at Hess's.

To Hess's all this means sending buyers anywhere in the world in search of desired merchandise, opening an art gallery where the work of old masters and contemporary artists is displayed and sold, displaying museum-quality art throughout the store, and building an organization of the best available people. It also means special events, like gathering 60 of the nation's houseware manufacturers for a consumer housewares exposition. At the same time Hess's entertains its customers by bringing famous personalities and celebrities to meet them, and by giving craftsmen and artisans the opportunity to demonstrate their skills and sell their wares interspersed with its own merchandise. Days also are given over to churches and other community groups for their own bazaars.

As Hess's opens more of these unique department stores, other communities are learning what the Lehigh Valley long has known: Hess's is more than a department store. It is an institution.

Hess's in 1982.

JAINDL'S TURKEY FARM

Jaindl's Turkey Farm located in Orefield, Pennsylvania, is the largest independent agricultural operation in the Lehigh Valley. Producing approximately one million turkeys per year, Jaindl's also prides itself as the largest family-owned turkey business in the world. It hatches, raises, dresses, and markets its turkeys on 6,000 acres of prime farmland.

The farm was established in the early 1930s by the late John L. Jaindl. The first year John bought five turkey poults for five dollars from a local farmer. Today the business is owned by his son, Fred, who got his start when he was six years old helping to raise the turkeys. By the time he joined his father after service in World War II, the company was producing 2,500 turkeys per year and farming 60 acres. In 1965 Fred purchased the farm when it was raising and marketing 200,000 birds. John continued as general manager of the farm operation until 1980.

Jaindl's Turkey Farm is primarily a self-sufficient operation. Its worldwide renowned broad-breasted turkeys are a special breed developed by Fred Jaindl to produce up to 20 percent more white meat. They are hatched from eggs parented by 30,000 artificially inseminated breeding hens. Fifty grain farms of Jaindl's in Lehigh, Northampton, and Berks counties grow the turkey feed. In addition, the birds are processed and packaged for market in Jaindl's modern hospital-clean processing plant and then shipped in the firm's refrigerated trucks to markets in 20 states. Also, Jaindl's operates a feed mill and hatchery. Each year the feed mill produces 100 million pounds of feed for the turkeys. The hatchery operates as an egg wash center, an incubation area, and a nursery.

Often served in the White House for the holiday season, Jaindl turkeys have proudly carried the Grand Champion Brand label. The National Turkey Federation awarded the first blue ribbon to Jaindl's in 1954. They won virtually every dressed-turkey class in competition that year and for many years after.

Fred Jaindl has many other interests besides operating the farm. He is on the board of directors and the largest shareholder of the First National Bank of Allentown, the area's largest bank. He is a trustee of the Lehigh County Community College and for many years was a member of the Parkland School Board. Other business interests include Jaindl-Good Ford, Green Hills Water Company and Development, Green Acres Home Park and Sales, and Lehigh Grains. The Jaindl's four sons—Fred Jr., John, David, and Mark—are actively involved in major parts of the farm's operation.

Jaindl's Turkey Farm, located in Orefield, Pennsylvania. (Photo courtesy of Don Fraser Fiip.)

INGERSOLL-RAND COMPANY STANDARD PUMP ALDRICH DIVISION

The Aldrich Pump Plant, a division of the Ingersoll-Rand Company, is one of the Lehigh Valley's oldest industries. A pioneer with its roots in the Allentown Rolling Mills, it traces its own origins to 1845 when four men met in a downtown saloon to found an enterprise to reproduce bar iron, railroad-car axles, and similar items. That was more than 15 years before the Civil War.

The firm owes its name and the products for which it has became known around the world to Roscoe Hilton Aldrich, a young engineering graduate of the Worcester Polytechnic Institute who came to Allentown in 1902 to build pumping machinery with mine applications. Backed by several years of experience in the design and manufacture of pumps, he put a group of draftsmen to work and came up with ideas for a new industry that originated as the Aldrich Pump Division of the Allentown Rolling Mills.

Aldrich's central idea anticipated the electrification of both metal and coal mining and catered to the two fields. His first step was to design pumps to be driven by electrical motors, thus providing a speedup over steam power and giving his equipment greater pumping capacity and efficiency. Next he designed his first pumps as triplex units, with three plungers rather than the existing systems of simplex and duplex units. With the added parts working in synchronization, the products achieved a more uniform flow in the discharge pipes and reduced the liquid pulsations. With Aldrich triplex pumps and the quintuplex units that followed, mining companies had consistently less trouble with vibrations in the discharge lines that were strung vertically up mine shafts and slopes. The third major innovation was the introduction of the vertical stroke pump, a model that minimized the wear caused by the weight of the plunger and thus reduced maintenance. With this unique design and the mechanical efficiency it offered, Aldrich pumps became standard in the mining industry, in sugar mills, and in pulp and paper mills where a thinner and more uniform product resulted. Their use quickly spread across this country and into other lands.

The first pump built by Aldrich was a vertical triplex shipped from Allentown to Oaxaca, Mexico, in January 1903 for mine service. Little more than a month later the first unit for use in this country went to Salt Lake City. Today there are

This quintuplex pump built by Ingersoll-Rand's Aldrich Pump Plant is now installed on a North Sea platform pumping hydrocarbon condensates that bring oil to the surface from wells beneath the sea.

few countries in the world that do not have Aldrich pumps performing important functions.

Not content to stop with triple and quintuplex devices, the company continued designing and building high-performance equipment with seven and nine plungers to further smooth the pulsations caused by the positive displacement of the liquid. In each instance Aldrich was the first in the field to advance the state of the art.

By 1914 the pump portion of the business of the Allentown Rolling Mills had become so important that it was incorporated as the Aldrich Pump Company, a wholly owned subsidiary of the Allentown Rolling Mills. The parent organization later ceased to exist.

In the early 1930s the firm began serving the infant chemical industry by accepting the challenges of higher process pressures and fluids never handled before. The name of the company soon became synonymous with "tough pumping problems"; today it is a prime source of pumps for the chemical industry. It also has developed units to use water and chemicals to repressure oil wells that no longer can be pumped by the usual means, and is a leader in the area of secondary recovery.

In addition to its expertise with reciprocating displacement pumps, the firm also was the first to develop a close-coupled centrifugal model. Today, teamed with the standard centrifugal pump line that is built in the gleaming new Ingersoll plant (adjacent to the other operations on the original site), Aldrich continues to be the leader in manufacturing the specialized high-pressure reciprocating pumps used in mineral slurry pipelines, hydraulic processes, and chemical and fertilizer production.

The organization was acquired by Ingersoll-Rand in 1961. Subsequent improvement of plant facilities and continuing development programs have made Aldrich vertical pumps the finest and most complete line available anywhere. They are installed around the world in chemical plants using corrosive-process fluids, in fertilizer plants, on carbamate and ammonia service, on mineral pipelines handling slurries, in oil fields for high-pressure water flooding, in manufacturing plants for high-pressure hydraulic presses, and for many other general industrial applications.

The Ingersoll-Rand Company facility today, located at One Pump Place, Allentown.

During and since World War I, Aldrich has built pumps for the Navy and for passenger and cargo vessels. Its products are in use on the USS *Wasp,* the *Hornet,* and the *Enterprise,* in many cargo vessels of the American Export Lines, the Waterman Steamship Company, and the Bull Lines. They are used extensively on many of this country's submarines. Aldrich pumps also operate the water-tight doors that compartment the USS *America* and other liners.

The Holland and Lincoln tunnels were built with Aldrich pumps that forced the heavy steel shell segments through the earth and rock beneath the rivers to install the tubes through which traffic now flows.

The company, with a long list of prestigious firsts to its credit, is recognized as a pioneer in the industry. As the world's struggle for new energy sources presses forward, it is among the leaders in the development of new products for use in high-temperature coal-conversion plants. Management, engineers, draftsmen, and those on the production line are constantly in search of new and better pumping equipment to meet the challenges of the future.

L.P. AND SONS BRICKOTE COMPANY

Louis Polak is a humble and simple man, so modest that the successful company he established on the basis of patents he has held for more than 40 years is known only as L.P. and Sons Brickote Company.

Nineteen years old when he came to America in 1912 from the part of his native Austria that now is Czechoslovakia, Polak had a long and varied career before inventing the brick-coating process that preserves aging homes and buildings. Among other things, he maintained pool tables in New York, worked on a peanut farm in West Virginia, helped manufacture tires in Ohio rubber plants, served a prison term when he was caught making bootleg whiskey in Lehigh County, and had a small contracting business doing building repairs and remodeling.

The brick-coating process resulted from the request of a homeowner on Cemetery Street in Bethlehem who asked Polak to do something about the deteriorating shingled siding. He responded by putting tarpaper over the shingles, applying a scratch coat of white cement (that later would simulate the mortar) over wire lathing, then adding another layer of cement with pigments added to produce the color selected by the customer. Special tools he designed were used to inscribe lines that exposed the cement undercoat to give the wall the appearance of brick. Polak was granted a patent for his process on June 20, 1939.

The first brick-coated home attracted wide attention and orders for the work mushroomed. Through the years the company has brick-coated several thousand homes and many churches, schools, and industrial buildings throughout Pennsylvania, New York, New Jersey, and Maryland.

For 20 years, until Polak's home and the site of his operations were taken over as a redevelopment project, the firm was based in the Northampton Heights section of Bethlehem where the family lived. In 1967 their home and the company's headquarters were moved to a 100-acre property along Hellertown Route 1, near Leithsville.

Through the years L.P. and Sons Brickote has been a family-oriented business solely owned by the founder, now approaching his 90th birthday. A daughter, Mrs. Cecelia Laslo, manages the organization. A son-in-law, Charles Laslo, Sr., and a son, Thomas, are actively involved in the Lehigh Valley operation and another son, John, is in charge of the New Jersey facility based in East Brunswick. Another son-in-law, Louis C. Kozar, is sales manager. Two grandsons, Charles Laslo, Jr., and Louis Laslo, work from the Hellerton base. Two other grandsons, John Jr. and Jimmy Polak, are with their father in the New Jersey branch.

Polak and his wife Amelia, now deceased, were married in Scarbro, West Virginia, in 1918. They had 17 children.

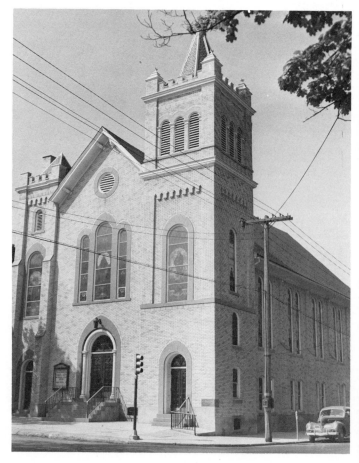

RIGHT
St. Michael's Lutheran Church at Ninth and Turner streets, Allentown, is one of the many buildings refinished by L.P. and Sons Brickote Company.

LEFT
Louis Polak, founder and owner of L.P. and Sons Brickote Company, with his patent for the brickote process.

LEHIGH CORDAGE

Lehigh Cordage is another example of a venture that in less than a score of years grew from roots planted and nurtured in Allentown to serve the public in every state and do business in other lands.

The company's products are a wide variety of rope, twine, and clothesline, most of which it manufactures, and hardware associated with its use. The rapid and solid growth is based on taking desirable products and merchandising them in a way that attracts consumers and helps retailers.

John G. Guthrie, president of Lehigh Cordage, organized the business in 1960 as Lehigh Sales and Products, a firm that wound twine into small, convenient, tangle-free packages for sale as fund raisers by Boy Scouts, junior chambers of commerce, and other community organizations. Operations were started in the basement of his home, then moved to a converted garage near 14th and Court streets. A year later the company began selling twine to the grocery trade, and as the demand increased, moved operations to an abandoned hat plant near its present location in southwest Allentown. The business was incorporated in 1965 with Guthrie's father and mother as his partners.

As the firm developed new merchandising techniques, its line increased to include a wide variety of nylon, cotton, polypropylene, sisal and manila rope, and twine in a wide range of the most desired sizes. Lehigh Cordage is now the largest supplier of cordage products to discount and home center stores in the country.

The appeal to both retailers and customers was broadened by the introduction of "The Lehigh Cordage Program," a system of convenient, in-store displays through which consumers visualize and have easy access to the rope and twine they desire. Displays from which customers make their selections range from small, specialized floor dispensers of seasonal items for hunters, fishermen, campers, gardeners, and kite flyers to large units for drugstores and supermarkets.

Open sales displays for hardware stores and building supply centers employ pegboard arrangements from 4 to 24 feet long and from 4 to 6 feet high. A typical four-foot section includes snap hooks, pulleys, and at least two dozen kinds of rope and twine, all of them packaged in lengths most desirable to the average buyer. The National Hardware Association awarded Lehigh its seal of approval for the packaging, display, and merchandising arrangements of its cordage programs.

Guthrie, a graduate of Lafayette College, served his apprenticeship with his father in a business that produced jute and synthetic yarn for carpet manufactures. His own start was in a plant established to manufacture burlap bags. The business he founded after that apprenticeship has become a multimillion-dollar operation.

The Lehigh Cordage factory at work.

Lehigh Cordage products are attractively and conveniently displayed in retail stores across the country.

LEHIGH COUNTY HISTORICAL SOCIETY

The Lehigh County Historical Society provides leadership for a variety of activities through which those interested in this area may research and preserve its heritages to give this and succeeding generations a more complete knowledge of them.

Organized in 1904, the Society is a nonprofit educational and cultural group of more than 1,200 members with an active guild of 500 women who raise funds and serve as guides.

Among its tools are the five historic properties it owns and operates as period museums, a library of local history and genealogy, programs cooperating with schools, a hardbound biennial publication encouraging members to do individual research and add to the permanent record of local history, and forums for the discussion of historical subjects. A professional staff coordinates these activities.

The properties, restored by the Society, filled with appropriate period furnishings and open to the public, include:

Trout Hall, at Fourth and Walnut streets, Allentown, a splendid 18th-century Georgian country residence completed in 1770 by James Allen, son of Allentown's founder, as a summer residence. Its park setting includes the Trout Hall Garden Theatre, a Georgian-style bandshell completed in 1981.

The George Taylor House, at Front and Poplar streets, Catasauqua, built in 1768 as a summer home by this pioneer eastern ironmaster, a signer of the Declaration of Independence, and today a National Historic Landmarks property.

The Troxell-Steckel House in Egypt, a German medieval-style farm house with a Swiss bank barn, built in 1755-56 by John Peter Troxell. The barn is a farm museum with exhibits of 18th- and 19th-century implements, antique carriages, and sleighs.

The Frank Buchman House at 117 North 11th Street, Allentown, a Victorian row house with appropriate furnishings, the boyhood home of the founder of the Moral Rearmament Movement which waged a worldwide campaign for peace based on standards of absolute honesty, purity, unselfishness, and love. It is a showcase for many of his personal effects and mementos.

The Reninger House at Fifth and Walnut streets, Allentown, a townhouse of the Civil War period with

Trout Hall, the country residence built by James Allen, son of Allentown's founder, in 1770, is one of the historic homes maintained as a museum by the Lehigh County Historical Society.

most of its furnishings from the Victorian era. One room will house a major library of Lincolniana bequeathed to the Society and other Civil War items.

The Scott Andrew Trexler II Memorial Library, administered by the Society, is housed in the Old Courthouse. Holdings include some 6,000 items, including an extensive collection of genealogical records. Two librarians supervise its increasing public use.

The General Harry C. Trexler Museum of Indian artifacts has its own spacious room in the old courthouse.

The Lehigh County Museum, established and operated by the county, has dedicated space on the first floor of the old courthouse to changing exhibits, and displays many of the Society's treasures. Furnishings in all the houses have been augmented by the Guild, which in 20 years has had many fundraising events for this purpose.

The Society aims at 2,000 members and additional corporate affiliates during the 1980s.

LEHIGH STRUCTURAL STEEL COMPANY

An aerial view of Lehigh Structural Steel's 39-acre plant along the Lehigh River.

A Vierendeel truss, 18 feet deep and weighing 83 tons, used to support a 30-story bank building in New York City.

Workmen in Allentown and Bethlehem have a long-standing partnership that has fabricated more than 1.5 million tons of steel for projects of every kind in all the 50 states, the District of Columbia, and 28 foreign lands.

The Allentown partner is the Lehigh Structural Steel Company. It uses steel produced in Bethlehem mills and fabricates it for buildings, bridges, and electric generating plants in the eastern United States and for towers which support television transmission antennae or carry electrical lines in all parts of the world.

Founded in 1919 by Robert L. Kift, W.H. Mohr, and T.R. Mullen, the company has its roots in the former Allentown Rolling Mills, one of the earliest iron works in the area. Through the years it has become one of the 10 leading independent structural steel fabricators in the nation.

In the early 1980s Lehigh Structural fabricated 30,000 tons per year of steel for buildings, bridges, and power plants. As one of the largest tower suppliers in the United States, the firm is capable of producing 40,000 tons of these structures a year, galvanizing them in its own plant.

Many major buildings in cities all along the coast from Miami to Boston were built with Lehigh-fabricated steel; so were many of the bridges that carry the highways between the Lehigh Valley and New York City. Along the way are the Jersey City Medical Center, powerhouses of the Public Service Electric and Gas Company, and all of the bridges in the vicinity of the Lincoln Tunnel, including the long, high bridge over the Passaic River with some girders 22 feet deep.

There are well over 100 buildings in New York City with the Lehigh label on their structural steel. Included are the planetarium, the Fashion Institute of Technology, the Aviation Trades School, part of the Museum of Natural History, the Stock Exchange building, and many hospitals, office buildings, and apartment complexes that tower on the skyline. The bridge connection to the Bronx from the Tri-boro Bridge is made up of curved work also produced by Lehigh.

In 1982 the company set a new record when it sent the heaviest single unit of structural steel ever delivered to New York over the George Washington Bridge, a 118-ton girder, 94 feet long, for the New York City Convention Center. Lehigh fabricated 7,000 tons of steel for that project.

The Kift-Mullen Foundation, into which Lehigh annually contributes 5 percent of new earnings before taxes, was established in 1949. It helps support and preserve private institutions serving the public interest by making annual cash gifts to hospitals, colleges, and universities, most of them in the Lehigh Valley. The foundation also grants scholarships to qualified students selected by the colleges.

LUTRON ELECTRONICS

Adjustments in a control cabinet for a large custom-built dimming system manufactured by Lutron Electronics Inc. are being made by Jim Yorgey, one of the company's sales-application engineers.

Executive offices, engineering facilities, and manufacturing operations of Lutron Electronics Inc. are situated in this sprawling plant near Coopersburg, Lehigh County.

An innovative design for a light dimmer to replace cumbersome and costly rheostats is the foundation on which Lutron Electronics Inc. has been built. In 20 years that design has been expanded into a multimillion-dollar company that adds several new products a year to the more than 600 it already manufactures and markets around the world.

The Lutron line ranges from a dimmer that replaces a wall switch in any room of a house to equipment for controlling lighting in different areas of the largest hotel ballrooms. It includes systems for incandescent, fluorescent, and high-intensity lighting in residential, commercial, and industrial installations; speed controls for fans and power tools; and equipment for utility monitoring centers where lighting varies and may require rapid changes. The organization's products are used in installations from the White House to palaces in Saudi Arabia, and in the offices of the most prestigious banks and corporations.

Controls designed and manufactured by the firm save users of electricity up to 50 percent of their lighting costs. Long before the energy crisis, Lutron's emphasis was on energy conservation.

These space-age products evolved from the small dimmer designed for incandescent lights designed and patented by Lutron in 1961. The first units were briefly manufactured by the fledgling enterprise in a corner of the Rodale Manufacturing Company's electrical-products plant in Emmaus. Initially only three people were involved in their design and production. It wasn't long before the firm moved into its own facilities and started on a successful trek to the number one position in the lighting control industry.

In 1970 Lutron moved to its present 36-acre site near Coopersburg. The corporation's headquarters and technical center, sales and administration offices, a complete engineering laboratory with UL testing equipment, and production, warehousing, and shipping facilities are housed there. The firm also operates a manufacturing plant in Puerto Rico.

To maintain its position as the technological leader in light control, the corporation has a staff of more than 30 engineers designing, testing, and developing new products. Its consensus management philosophy embodies free and open discussion of problems, their solution, and the course of action to be taken.

Lutron believes it must make a social or economic contribution, continue the health and integrity of the firm, and maintain good relationships between its employees, its customers, and the community.

Executives of the privately owned organization include Joel Spira, president and director of research; John F. McKiernan, vice-president/sales; John E. Longenderfer, vice-president/engineering; Don A. Mershon, vice-president/personnel; Robin Moseley, assistant to the president; and John F. Forney, controller.

H.T. LYONS INC.

H.T. Lyons Inc., a mechanical-contracting and engineering operation, is one of the youngest of the Lehigh Valley's major industrial firms. It has, however, accumulated an impressive list of prestigious clients that include a high percentage of repeat customers.

The company, now operating from its own conveniently located plant in the Colony Drive Industrial Park in East Allen Township, Northampton County, is three miles from the Allentown-Bethlehem-Easton Airport, and just minutes away from the industrial areas of the Lehigh Valley. It designs,

H.T. Lyons Inc. has its offices and shops in this modern industrial park building in suburban Northampton County.

installs, and services air conditioning and heating installations, plumbing, process piping, and sheet metal fabrication for commercial and industrial establishments, schools, and hospitals.

Ted Lyons, who has an engineering degree from Duke University and a master's degree in business from the Wharton School of the University of Pennsylvania, worked as a mechanical engineer from 1969 (when he completed his military service) until he established his own business in rented quarters at 10th and Linden streets, Bethlehem. The firm's rapid growth led to building its own modern headquarters and plant in the more centrally located and accessible industrial park.

From the outset, the policy of H.T. Lyons has been to meet the broad spectrum of the mechanical-contracting and engineering requirements of its customers. The comprehensive service it provides ranges from feasibility studies, through design, engineering, and construction, to long-range maintenance and servicing agreements. The service division with its own fleet of 10 fully equipped trucks is available on a 24-hour basis.

The organization's strong design capability, with in-house registered professional engineers, relieves customers of the need to rely exclusively on their own engineering departments, or to engage outside consultants. The result is fast, accurate design and cost information.

To be in a position of recommending what in its judgment will best meet the customer's needs, the firm specializes in no specific equipment brands.

The type of work for which the corporation is responsible is not generally visible. It is critical, however, to many operations and important to all for the comfort it provides. Lyons has been responsible for air conditioning, heating, and plumbing for the Good Shepherd Home Rehabilitation Center and the First National Bank Computer Center, for extensive installations at the Allentown Hospital, the Muhlenberg Medical Center, the Allentown-Sacred Heart Hospital Center, and St. Luke's Hospital. A long list of industrial work includes installations for Alpo Dog Food, Bethlehem Steel, Boise Cascade, Tarkett, General Electric, Western Electric, the Pennsylvania Power and Light Company, and the Bell Telephone Company.

Ted Lyons, the founder of the company, is its president, treasurer, and chief operating officer. Normally, the firm employs approximately 120 engineers, technicians, craftsmen, and support staff.

Ted Lyons (left) with a craftsman at the press brake, one of the large machines in the company's sheet metal-fabricating department.

MACK TRUCKS, INC.

Mack Trucks, Inc., has been a part of Allentown since 1905, when Jack and William Mack, Brooklyn wagonmakers who in 1900 built a gasoline-powered sight-seeing bus for use in Brooklyn's Prospect Park, took the suggestion of their brother, Joseph, and acquired a large foundry building on South 10th Street. The business was incorporated in February 1905 "for the purpose of manufacturing motors, cars, vehicles, boats, locomotives, automobiles, and machine and hardware specialties of every description." Jack was the first president; Joseph was treasurer.

During the following months Mack had orders for buses from many parts of the country, and completed the first one for the New England Tally-Ho Company for sight-seeing service in the Boston area. By year's end it had built 50 buses and produced its first trucks. Within six years the young company was this country's largest producer of trucks over three tons in capacity, then rated as heavy duty.

In its early years Mack merged with the Saurer Motor Company, organized in Wall Street to build a Swiss-designed truck in Plainfield, New Jersey, and the Hewitt Motor Company, which built smaller trucks, to become the International Motor Company. In 1922 it became the Mack Manufacturing Company and later Mack Trucks, Inc.

The highly successful Mack AB line was introduced in 1914, and shortly thereafter the firm began producing the heavier-duty Mack AC. This is the truck that became a legend in its time and was manufactured continuously for 24 years, from 1915 to 1939, the longest production record of any American motor vehicle. Used by American and British forces in Europe during World War I, these trucks, with snub-nosed hoods, resembling bulldogs in both appearance and tough performance, became known to the men who used them as "Bulldog Macks." The appellation grew to encompass all Mack trucks and became the company's symbol.

In the late 1930s Mack discontinued the AC and AB models to expand into higher-capacity ratings. It also began a new era for the industry by pioneering the dieselization of heavy-duty truck-tractors, producing its first diesel in 1938.

The following year, when the Army ordered 535 military trucks for troop transportation and towing heavy equipment, Mack again went into war production. Among some 30,000 heavy-duty trucks it built for America and its Allies were the powerful six-wheelers, prime-movers used for hauling

LEFT
John M. "Jack" Mack, founder and first president of Mack Brothers Motor Car Company which subsequently became Mack Trucks, Inc.

ABOVE
The famous Mack AC "Bulldog," with the longest production run of any American motor vehicle (circa 1921).

searchlights and sound detectors and for towing anti-aircraft guns; general-cargo trucks, used on every front to carry supplies from the beachheads to the advancing invasion forces and to bring back the wounded and prisoners; and the Army's biggest prime-movers, the massive T-8 tank transporters.

Between 1953 and 1956, before discontinuing the manufacture of buses in 1960, the firm introduced a popular new series of cab-over-engine tractors in both four- and six-wheel models, powered with a wide choice of engines. Production of the F Series was begun in 1962. It featured the Mack Thermodyne engines, three cab lengths with regular or deluxe sleepers, and many new conveniences for drivers.

Mack revolutionized the trucking industry in 1966, with the Maxidyne engine—featuring relatively constant horsepower and fuel efficiency. With it came Maxitorque, a five-speed transmission designed to match the horsepower characteristics of the engine. A 325-horsepower Maxidyne V-8 diesel was introduced in 1970. The Econodyne, an engine with even greater fuel efficiency, cooler operation, and easier serviceability, was added to the line in 1981.

A $43-million plant in Hagerstown, Maryland, opened in

1961, is where Mack engines, transmissions, and rear-axle carriers are designed and manufactured. Because all the principal components of the corporation's trucks are produced by its own workers in its own plants, "built like a Mack" is a generic expression of quality and durability.

Expanding production facilities in the Lehigh Valley, the organization dedicated a $10-million Engineering Development and Test Center on a 62-acre tract in Allentown's Queen City Industrial Park in 1975; that same year it opened a new $25-million plant on a site near Macungie, in Lower Macungie Township. This operation produces the complete line of fire-fighting equipment Mack has been building since it delivered the first motor-propelled hook-and-ladder in 1910 and the first motorized pumper in 1911.

In 1965, when Zenon C.R. Hansen began his nine-and-a-half-year tenure as president, Mack moved its executive offices from Montvale, New Jersey, to Allentown, and began construction of its six-story World Headquarters building. The corporation became part of Signal Oil and Gas, now the Signal Companies, in 1967. Renault of France holds a 20-percent ownership of Mack, marketing a line of medium-duty diesel trucks through the extensive Mack distribution system. The company's foreign assembly operations, administered by Mack International, are located in 10 overseas nations with a network of more than 100 distributors in some 80 countries.

Mack's newest high-technology truck, introduced late in 1982, is the first American-built truck with an all fiberglass cab. It offers many features that provide weight-saving efficiency.

Early in the 1980s Mack expects to reach its next objective: the .5 million-mile engine which will operate for 500,000 miles, with only routine maintenance before an overhaul is necessary. Its engineers already have set their sights on a logical long-range objective of the million-mile engine.

The operations of Mack Trucks, Inc., are directed by Alfred W. Pelletier, chairman of the board and chief executive officer; and John B. Curcio, president and chief operating officer.

World Headquarters of Mack Trucks, Inc., Allentown.

MERCHANTS NATIONAL BANK

The first office of the Merchants National Bank was in the basement of the Will H. Koch Clothing Store on the same corner the bank occupies today. Business, however, was conducted on the first floor of the then-new YMCA Building, a few doors away.

The Merchants National Bank's main office on the southwest corner of Seventh and Hamilton streets, the hub of the Hamilton Mall.

Merchants National Bank had its origins late in 1900, when 12 Allentown businessmen met in the offices of a young lawyer to talk about the need for another financial institution. After two years of planning they met again on January 21, 1903, and elected Mayor Fred E. Lewis the first president. His salary was set at $42 a month.

Three months later, on March 30, the bank was opened on the first floor of what then was the YMCA building on Center Square and within an hour $100,000 was deposited. In just three years deposits reached one million dollars.

From the outset the Merchants Bank was determined to set precedents and establish banking services new to the area. It was the first to open a savings department, the first to issue bank books, the first to accept deposits of only one dollar, and the first to guarantee an interest rate regardless of the amount deposited.

By 1921, when assets were more than $6.6 million, it moved a few steps from the first location to its new building on the present site, the southwest corner of Seventh and Hamilton streets.

A merger with the Citizens Trust Company on January 7,

1929, spurred the growth of the Merchants Bank's assets to more than $11 million. No record gains were made during the years of the Great Depression, but even during that period the bank's assets never dropped below $10.5 million.

During the 1940s Merchants Bank introduced another major service by initiating consumer lending. In 1949 it began a new era by opening its first branch office in a new building at Tilghman Street and Ridge Avenue. The bank's branch system expanded rapidly; today it includes 25 offices and operations extending south to Coopersburg, north to Schnecksville, west to Fogelsville, and east to Palmer Township and Wilson Borough. Included are eight drive-up and 11 walk-up windows in high-traffic areas. Many offer 24-hour service through the automated tellers the bank has been installing since 1980. The widespread facilities and their increasing use required centralization and led to a new modern operations center in Queen City Industrial Park. It was completed in 1975.

Since the 1960s Merchants Bank has monitored the wide field of electronic processing to provide more efficient record keeping and offer greater customer convenience. In 1982 it became the first bank in the Lehigh Valley to experiment with a new Pay-By-Phone system that allows communication with Merchants Bank computers for payment to third parties. That same year stockholders overwhelmingly agreed to create a one-bank holding company, known as Merchants Bancorp, Inc. This was the first step in positioning itself to take advantage of new market opportunities resulting from changes in the competitive environment and to expand even farther geographically.

The bank employs 488 full-time and 108 part-time staff members. At the end of 1981 its assets were $613 million.

MODERN INSULATION COMPANY

The claim founder Albert E. Roba is proud to make for Modern Insulation Company, which he founded in 1952, is that in 30 years it has saved its customers millions of dollars in heating costs.

A pioneer in energy conservation, the firm has insulated more than 13,000 homes, apartment buildings, churches, and other facilities across the Lehigh Valley. Most have been older buildings that never had been insulated, or in which additional protection was warranted by rising fuel costs. Modern has cut these costs up to 50 percent by installing top-quality fiberglass insulation.

Al, a Navy veteran who was graduated from Muhlenberg College in 1949, established his business on November 26, 1952, when he opened an office in his Bethlehem home and a warehouse at 1725 East Susquehanna Street, Allentown—the location where the firm has centered its headquarters and operations since 1962.

At the beginning Al sold his ideas by going door to door in a widening area. Then he had one truck, four employees, and a part-time helper. Today the organization serves an area within a 70-mile radius of Allentown with four trucks, 14 employees, and four part-time helpers. The bright orange trucks that have become its trademark are familiar throughout the territory.

Close management and direct supervision of all Modern Insulation Company installations are provided by Albert E. Roba, founder and president of the enterprise, and his son, Gerald Roba, vice-president.

This is one of the thousands of homes that have saved energy costs with insulation installed by the Modern Insulation Company.

Quality work and personal supervision have made the company one of the largest home-insulation operations on the East Coast.

In addition to the thousands of homes it has insulated, Modern has helped cut heating costs for prominent structures that include Christ Lutheran and Redeemer Lutheran churches in Allentown; Holy Ghost Roman Catholic Church and the Moravian Chapel in Bethlehem; fraternity houses, dormitories, and other buildings at Lehigh University; Trout Hall, Taylor House, and the Troxell-Steckel House, 18th-century stone buildings owned by the Lehigh County Historical Society and operated by it as museums; the Kemmerer Museum and Moravian Museum in Bethlehem; and the Allen Organ Company's world sales center in Macungie.

Al's son, Gerald, who grew up in the business, became a member of the firm following his graduation from Penn Morton College in Chester in 1971. He is now vice-president with major responsibilities in sales and service. He and his father are the ownership team that provides close direction and management control of every installation. Together with experienced workmen and the highest quality materials, they are responsible for the continuing growth of the firm and customer satisfaction with its work. The founder's wife, Bernadine, is corporate secretary.

NESTOR'S SPORTING GOODS STORE

A departmentalized store where sportsmen can shop leisurely for equipment to pursue their favorite sport and receive advice from experienced personnel, Nestor's Sporting Goods Store originated when Peter Nestor (then a schoolteacher in Whitehall Township and an active sportsman) opened a small shop in Cementon.

At the time he and his wife moved the operation to MacArthur Road in 1952, it was the second retail establishment on the strip which today, with two major malls and many retail stores and service establishments, is one of the busiest shopping districts in the Lehigh Valley. The original 160-square-foot building, now the gun shop, has been expanded to 21,000 square feet on a property that covers four acres and provides adequate off-highway parking space.

While still a teacher, Nestor bought trout, deer, and pheasants and stocked them through the Lehigh Valley to encourage interest in fishing and hunting. He introduced local sportsmen to exciting new fishing experiences in places like Canada and Alaska by lending them films of sports in those areas, some taken on his own trips. When it became evident that the Lehigh River was being cleaned up so that fish could survive, he proved it by planting tagged trout and rewarding fishermen for

Peter Nestor, founder of Nestor's Sporting Goods Store, on one of his early game-stalking walks.

bringing them in—results demonstrating that 70 percent of these fragile fish survived encouraged sportsmen's organizations to assume the responsibility for stocking. Fishing along the Lehigh was rejuvenated and other game fish were caught.

Nestor's also has two highly specialized divisions. Wilderness Travel Outfitters, opened in 1974 in a building adjoining the main store, stocks sophisticated lightweight equipment for backpackers, canoeists, and mountaineers. The stock is aimed at equipping self-propelled adventurers for anything from a day or two in the woods to an extended trek into totally new areas. Its wares range from lightweight canoes, kayaks, tents, and backpacks to a line of convenient, tasty dehydrated food. The knowledgeable staff includes a forest ranger who spends nine months of the year in the shop.

The Warming Hut, a specialty ski shop housed in its own building and staffed with experts on ski equipment, techniques, and locations, was established in 1977.

Now president, Peter M. Nestor joined his father and mother in the firm in 1973 after graduation from Ricker College in Maine where he was a member of the ski team and Outing Club. His mother Helen, who had an active role from the beginning of the company, is the secretary/treasurer, and his wife Karen is assistant treasurer. Although the founder has for the most part retired from the active operation of the business, he continues to offer valuable advice to his son. He enjoys spending much of his time with his grandsons.

Peter M. Nestor, president of Nestor's Sporting Goods Store, in the highly specialized Wilderness Travel Outfitters shop that is part of the diversified operation on MacArthur Road, Whitehall Township.

NORTHAMPTON COUNTY HISTORICAL AND GENEALOGICAL SOCIETY

The Northampton County Historical and Genealogical Society is the organization primarily responsible for gathering and preserving information and artifacts that give this generation, and those that will follow, a picture of how their forebears in Northampton County lived and what they accomplished.

Until it was incorporated in 1910 and rented the old stone schoolhouse at Church and Sitgreaves streets in Easton, the Society met in the Easton Public Library. The historic schoolhouse was developed as a museum to house the William J. Heller collection of antiques and historical artifacts related to the area.

Many additions to the museum's collections made additional space imperative, and in 1928 the old Mixsell homestead at Fourth and Ferry streets, a two-and-a-half-story, federal-style home built by Jacob Mixsell in 1833, was given to the Society by his granddaughters, Emilie Mixsell Lalor and Mary Mixsell. In 1948 Mary C. Illick donated the adjacent house. It now is used as the library, which includes approximately 1,500 volumes dealing with local history and genealogy, maps, deeds, letters, and manuscripts.

A small landscaped garden, laid out in the 19th-century manner and including a patio and small fountain, adjoins the museum. It was the gift of the Forks of the Delaware Garden Club, whose members maintain the shrubbery and trees planted near the house.

The museum displays many fine examples of antique furniture, pewter, pottery, glass, silver, china, dolls, needlework, and Pennsylvania-German folk art. Among its treasures is the earliest-known depiction of Easton, an oil painting created in 1810 by an unknown artist. Another scene is of Easton-Neston, the estate in Northamptonshire, England, for which the city is named. A collection of watercolors of Easton and vicinity, painted about 1840 by Mary Maxwell McCartney, and local 18th- and 19th-century portraits and landscapes are included in the exhibition.

The museum also exhibits weapons and military equipment from colonial times through World War I, early fire-fighting equipment used in the area, and the Carl J. Aicher collection of Delaware Indian artifacts.

The Society's objective is to expand these collections, and to promote better citizenship by disseminating information about

LEFT
The Northampton County Historical and Genealogical Society has its headquarters and museum in the former Mixsell homestead at Fourth and Ferry streets, Easton. The home was built in 1833. The library is in adjacent property.

ABOVE
Mrs. Hilton Rahn, Jr. (left), and Mrs. Lillian Meade Decker are shown in the Doll Room of the museum admiring the late 19th-century doll collection.

the history and traditions of the people of Northampton County. It holds quarterly meetings with lectures and historical programs, and publishes occasional books and pamphlets dealing with local history.

Work of the organization is supported by the contributions of some 300 members, by an endowment fund, and by an annual appropriation from Northampton County.

RODALE PRESS INC.

The single product of Rodale Press Inc. is information designed to encourage Americans to be more self-reliant, more informed, and healthier in every sense of the word.

It distills this product from the efforts of a staff of journalists, health and technical writers, and agricultural and food researchers, as well as its own experimental efforts into new crops, agriculture, and nutrition. The results are marketed in a half-dozen magazines with a combined circulation of close to six million copies, in two newsletters, in 35 to 50 books published each year, and through a new electronic publishing division that has begun producing TV programs for networks and cable companies.

The first Rodale magazine was *Organic Gardening and Farming*, now *Organic Gardening*. Introduced in 1942, its aim was to help those anxious to produce their own food without pesticides or herbicides, either in small home gardens or on larger farms. Since then it has expanded into a home-food systems publication.

Later periodicals include *Prevention*, first printed in 1950 and now the largest health magazine in the world, which focuses on helping people take control of their own health and prevent disease; *Bicycling*, added in 1978 when Rodale bought *Bicycling* and *Bike World* and combined them into a single magazine directed toward the bicycling enthusiast; *The New Farm*, instituted in 1979 to help farmers produce more economically by cutting chemical inputs; Rodale's *New Shelter Magazine*, featuring do-it-yourself information on improvements to homes and properties; and a 1982 addition, *Spring Magazine*, a lifestyle magazine for active women who are concerned with well-being and improving quality of life.

The company also publishes two health and fitness-oriented newsletters—*Executive Fitness Newsletter*, a semi-monthly issue; and *Body Bulletin*, a monthly sold to firms for distribution to their employees.

Rodale Press was founded by the late J.I. Rodale, a brilliant idea man and New York accountant who came to Emmaus when he and his brother, Joe, brought the Rodale Manufacturing Company from New York to the Lehigh Valley community. His first publication was his own humorous pamphlet. His first book was *The Verb Finder*, a directory for students, writers, and others.

When J.I. Rodale died in 1971, his son, Robert, became chairman of the board and chief executive officer of the organization that now has over 800 employees—700 of whom work in Emmaus. Other employees operate the 305-acre Rodale Research Center in Maxatawny, near Kutztown, and are in sales, graphics, and editorial offices in New York, Chicago, and Washington.

Part of the profits of the company, which in the year ending August 31, 1981, had a gross revenue of $98 million, always are plowed back into new projects. One of these is The Cornucopia Project, a million-dollar study of the U.S. food system designed to encourage local and regional production and marketing. The latest is The People's Medical Society, an effort to improve this country's troubled health care system.

The library wing of the Rodale Press building is part of this modern complex in a park setting at 33 East Minor Street, Emmaus.

The Rodale Research Center is on a picturesque farm in Maxatawny, a few miles west of Allentown, and combines both contemporary and traditional farm buildings. Testing and experimentation are conducted here.

SACRED HEART HOSPITAL

The significant periods of growth of Sacred Heart Hospital closely parallel events that shaped the city of Allentown and the greater Lehigh Valley throughout much of the 20th century.

The acute care, medical-surgical community hospital, which will admit over 13,000 patients annually after the completion of the 1982-84 building expansion project, was established in 1912 in the tiny rectory on Pine Street behind Sacred Heart Church. Six Missionary Sisters of the Sacred Heart from Hilltrup, Germany, responding to an urgent plea from Monsignor Peter Masson, came to Allentown to care for the poor and the sick, many of whom were victims of a diphtheria epidemic raging in the city.

The personal nursing care of the Sisters was deeply appreciated by many town residents. From the outset, the hospital projected an identity of compassionate caring that still permeates the medical, nursing, and support staffs of the contemporary Sacred Heart Hospital at 421 Chew Street in the heart of Allentown.

The health care needs of the community grew rapidly, and to meet those needs the magnificent estate at Fourth and Chew streets, the home of the deceased Judge Edward Harvey of the Lehigh County Court, was purchased in 1913.

Eleven Sister nurses moved into the renovated Harvey Mansion, which contained 33 patient beds, in 1915. The year 1919 saw the third major step in the development of Sacred Heart Hospital with the addition of a wing adjoining the Harvey Mansion. Completion of the wing, despite the restrictions of a wartime economy, gave the city of Allentown its first fireproof, all steel and concrete hospital.

As early as 1916 Sacred Heart Hospital organized its own school of nursing with the first class graduating in 1919. For decades the school enjoyed one of the finest reputations in nursing education in the East. The last class of 50 nurses graduated in 1980. Today there are over 2,000 school of nursing alumni located throughout the nation.

The Right Reverend Monsignor Leo Fink succeeded Monsignor Masson as rector of Sacred Heart Church and director of the hospital. His dynamic leadership during the '30s, '40s, and '50s spearheaded the dramatic growth of the mid-town medical complex.

The Trexler Memorial wing was added to the hospital in 1947. It was dedicated to General Harry Clay Trexler, a great friend of Monsignor Fink, and a loyal benefactor of the hospital.

ABOVE
The center-city, Catholic, community hospital is characterized by a careful blending of contemporary and traditional, both in architecture and philosophy.

LEFT
The Harvey Mansion at Fourth and Chew streets, the first Sacred Heart Hospital (1915).

With the completion of the Pasteur Memorial Building in 1957, the hospital continued to respond to the changing times and growing health care needs of the community.

The next major construction took place in 1976, the Bicentennial year, during which the Doctor Henry Kozloff Ambulatory Center and the modern seven-story Trexler Tower were dedicated. At the time of the dedication The Morning Call wrote editorially that "Sacred Heart has grown from modest beginnings in 1912 and there have been many notable changes and improvements since. One thing hasn't changed—the hospital's philosophy. Its church sponsors, its administrators, its doctors, nurses, and staff remain devoted to the principle of providing the finest in patient care. . . . These buildings have a rich heritage because of the many persons who have developed them and used them for so much community good."

As it has in the past, Sacred Heart Hospital, with its special dimension of caring, will continue to be in the vital center of the region's health care environment. It will be a very special presence on the horizon for many years ahead, responding to the needs of the people it is always ready to serve.

SARCO COMPANY

The Sarco Company, which will celebrate its 75th anniversary in 1985, has an international reputation for the line of automatic valves and controls it manufactures for industrial and commercial users of steam for energy sources. Principal products of the Allentown-based company are steam traps, temperature and pressure regulators, pipeline strainers, air eliminators, and humidifiers.

Founded by Clement Wells, an Englishman who came to America in 1908 to sell bicycle spokes, carbon dioxide recorders, flue gas testers, and other products for the German firm of Sanders-Rehder, the firm has been marketing its own products since 1910. Sarco is a contraction of the name of the enterprise Wells represented when he came to the Lehigh Valley and which for a while manufactured some of the equipment his own business designed and sold.

Shortly after World War I, Sarco began a new program for manufacturing its products in this country by arranging with the Roller-Smith Company of Bethlehem to act as a subcontractor in the production of its expansion traps and temperature regulators. In 1935 Wells started his own manufacturing operations in an abandoned silk mill at Clewell and Itaska streets in Fountain Hill. Turret lathes, drill presses, punch presses, and other equipment used at the Roller-Smith plant were transferred to the new site and supplemented by second-hand machinery purchased from a Philadelphia broker. When the plant opened there were 47 employees, most of whom had come over from Roller-Smith.

In 1962, after a number of expansions, Sarco finally ran out of space in Fountain Hill and built a new plant along 26th Street Southwest in the industrial park surrounding the Queen City Municipal Airport in southwest Allentown. The first building covered 110,000 square feet and additions built in 1965 and 1975 expanded it to 160,000 square feet of plant and

The Sarco Company plant is located on 26th Street Southwest, Allentown.

This old advertisement from the Sarco Company illustrates that the firm has been calling attention to saving energy and preventing industrial waste since 1922.

office space. Employment there is usually about 400.

Sarco is the only corporation that manufactures six types of steam traps, including thermodynamic, thermostatic, float traps, bucket traps, bi-metallic, and liquid expansion devices. It produces cast-iron, cast-steel, and cast-brass strainers from one-half-inch to 18-inch sizes. The strainers are designed to prevent foreign particles from reaching the steam traps. Steam regulators made of both cast iron and steel also are among its products. Many of the basic castings are produced by foundries in the Lehigh Valley.

In 1964 Sarco became a part of White Consolidated Industries of Cleveland, a $2-billion diversified corporation, one of the largest in the country.

Sarco has U.S. sales offices in Long Island City; Kenilworth, New Jersey; Philadelphia; Chicago; Houston; and Los Angeles; and a Canadian subsidiary, Escodyne Limited located in Orillia, Ontario. Its line also is marketed by domestic and international sales representatives.

SERVICE ELECTRIC CABLE T.V., INC.

Access to the advantages of television has been widely expanded by the pioneering accomplishments of John Walson, Sr., who laid the foundation for the nationwide cable television industry and whose Service Electric Cable T.V. corporation now extends into approximately 200,000 homes in more than 160 Pennsylvania and New Jersey communities.

Walson, who gave up the study of medicine for electrical engineering, began his career as a Pennsylvania Power and Light Company (PP&L) service lineman and, with his wife, also operated an electric appliance store and repair service in Mahanoy City. In 1947 he added television sets to his wares and, because signals from Philadelphia were difficult to receive in the mountainous area, erected an antenna on a 70-foot utility pole on New Boston Hill, on the outskirts of the town. The surplus Army wire he strung from the antenna site to demonstrate the sets in his store also were connected to several homes enroute in June 1948. By adding more antennae and boosters to serve more customers, he built the first cable TV system in the United States. During the first years, with the permission of the PP&L whose poles he used, the lines were extended to serve over 1,000 homes. CATV companies throughout the nation now serve more than 22 million subscribers.

In 1979 both Congress and the National Cable Television Association recognized Walson as the founder of the industry. He served as a director of both national and state cable television associations.

Walson's company also pioneered the three-channel system, the five-channel system using adjacent channels, the importation of distant channels by using microwave technology, and the use of coaxial cable in the industry. His organization was CATV's first microwave operator. In 1972 he joined Time Inc. in launching Home Box Office, the first successful pay television venture in America, and became a charter affiliate of Prism in September 1976. His firm manufactures its own amplifiers and related products in Mahanoy City. Walson also has a separate microwave company serving 27 cable systems in Pennsylvania. Service Electric was the first cable television operator to originate local color TV programs featuring Lehigh Valley news and sports.

In 1958 Walson purchased a small cable company in Bethlehem and began service in the Lehigh Valley. Operations quickly expanded into other area communities and in 1959 the firm extended its lines into Allentown. The main receiving site for the area is a 200-foot tower on Gauff's Hill, Salisbury Township. Microwave television signals also are received at mini-sites throughout the valley and transmitted by cable.

John Walson's idea—largely due to the energy he poured into it—has grown into a multimillion-dollar, singly owned corporation that has become an important local service and one that laid the foundations for millions throughout America to enjoy better television.

John Walson, Sr., chairman of the board of Service Electric Cable T.V., Inc., pioneered cable television in the United States when he brought signals broadcast from Philadelphia across these mountains in June 1948 to serve Mahanoy City, Pennsylvania, the community in the background.

C.M. STAUFFER INSURANCE AGENCY

The C.M. Stauffer Insurance Agency has been serving the Lehigh Valley community since 1915, when it was established to write insurance required under the Workmen's Compensation Act approved that year by the Pennsylvania Legislature.

Founded by Roy M. Vanwagenen and Clarence M. Stauffer, the firm was selected by the Maryland Casualty Company of Baltimore to be its agent for workmen's compensation insurance in Lehigh County and a broad surrounding area in eastern Pennsylvania. To cover the extensive territory, the firm had some 50 sub-agents to write the policies and collect the premiums in the six counties within its jurisdiction.

As Vanwagenen and Stauffer expanded its casualty business, the firm became the agent for other highly regarded companies. Currently they include Maryland Casualty, the Security Insurance Group, Millers Mutual Insurance, White Hall Mutual, the Royal Insurance Group, Insurance Company of North America, the St. Paul Insurance Group, and the Home Insurance Group.

The organization's first offices were in the Heinz Building on Hamilton Street. In 1932, when Vanwagenen moved to Tulsa, Oklahoma, to become resident manager for the Maryland Casualty Company, the business became the Clarence M. Stauffer Agency and moved to the Commonwealth Building.

Clifford L. Roehrig, a nephew of both Stauffer and Vanwagenen, began a career of more than 40 years in the business when he joined Stauffer in 1932, shortly after his graduation from Muhlenberg College. Early in 1946, following Stauffer's death, he and his aunt, Elizabeth Stauffer, joined in a new partnership. When Mrs. Stauffer died in July 1959, Roehrig became the sole proprietor of the agency his two uncles had established and which he helped build for more than 25 years.

Roehrig's son, C. Bruce Roehrig, entered his father's business after completing his studies at Muhlenberg in 1966; in 1975 he purchased the agency from his father to establish a single proprietorship, and in April 1981 he moved his office to a completely remodeled barn at 102 Springhouse Road in South Whitehall Township.

The company writes a full line of casualty, fire, and marine insurance, 90 percent of it in the commercial field, for manufacturing companies, wholesale, retail, and service enterprises, and institutional clients. Its years of experience, the

In 1975 C. Bruce Roehrig became sole proprietor of the C.M. Stauffer Insurance Agency, located at 102 Springhouse Road in South Whitehall Township.

variety of companies the agency represents, and the broad lines of insurance it offers make the firm an insurance counselor on whom its clients have learned to depend.

TARKETT

When Tarkett acquired the floor-covering operations of the GAF Corporation in 1981, the Swedish Match group became heir to the traditions of an organization whose vinyl floor coverings have a hard-to-match record of service in homes, offices, and business establishments across the country.

The plant in Whitehall Township, northeast of Allentown, is an important component of the group. Established by the Sandura Company in 1947 when it moved its facilities from Paulsboro, New Jersey, to a building in Fullerton that had been used for war production, the plant more than doubled in size during the next decade until it covered 537,000 square feet under one roof. In 1965 the operation was purchased by the Ruberoid Company and in 1967 merged with the GAF Corporation, which since 1842 has been supplying a variety of products to major industries and many professions.

The Whitehall operation established some significant firsts in the industry. In 1948 it was the first to produce vinyl flooring in widths greater than six feet and in 1957 again was the first to expand that dimension to 12 feet. The first flooring with a vinyl wear layer, modern sheet vinyl flooring as it is known today, was made in Whitehall. The first 12-foot-wide rotogravure print cylinders were engraved in the plant and, when Tarkett took over, it still was the only plant in the flooring industry equipped to engrave wide, heavy-duty rotogravure print cylinders from start to finish .

Tarkett's Whitehall operation begins with the raw materials and carries them through the modern plant to the finished Gafstar vinyl flooring. The felt base, produced in the plant, is coated with polyvinylchloride on which the rotogravure cylinders engraved there print the many patterns and designs, six col-

The manufacturing plant of Tarkett in Whitehall Township.

Vinyl floor covering is printed on huge rotogravure presses in the Tarkett plant in Whitehall Township.

ors at a time. After the printed flooring comes from the presses, the patterns are sealed in under a thick layer of clear polyvinylchloride and then pass through a four-zoned oven with temperatures up to 400 degrees Fahrenheit to complete the bonding process. This helps provide a clear, tough-wearing layer that is easy to clean and adds to the resilience. Some of the flooring also is given an extra urethane coating that provides a higher gloss and requires only damp mopping.

In-plant designers create the hundreds of patterns for the various coverings. Their resources include ideas from customers, retailers, distributors, and suggestions from employees. Shows for the trade determine the designs that are put into production. Research and development on new flooring products are also conducted at the Whitehall plant.

Among the most important operations in the plant is the work of its quality-control group, working closely with the production department at every step in the process. It is involved with raw-material testing, print standards, and color control through the printing process, thickness of the vinyl wear layer, laminating strength, and the detection of defects that are removed after a close visual inspection of every foot of the finished product.

Production normally includes about 75 designs in more than 300 colors and shades in widths up to 12 feet. It includes both rugs of varying sizes and roll goods cut to the customer's requirements. More than 2,300 different items of yard goods and rugs are warehoused at the plant to expedite the orders of customers.

Tarkett's head offices for operations in this country are at Parsippany, New Jersey. Vincent Ujcic, a veteran of the former GAF operation, is manager of the Lehigh Valley plant.

M.W. WOOD ENTERPRISES, INC.

The Wood Company story began in 1939, when Milton W. "Scotty" Wood opened a small family restaurant to bring good value and fair prices to the residents and business people in the area of Allentown's Center Square.

Today, with a staff of 3,900, the firm is still guided by the founder's principles as approximately 30 million meals are served annually in colleges, hospitals, nursing homes, businesses, and industry in a two-state area.

Several groups comprise the Wood Company. The Food Service division operates more than 100 units. Everything from fine dining to cafeteria meals to snack bar menus are available at the clients' requests. The Chef-Aide division, a cost-efficient central commissary, supplies meats, seafood, prepared vegetables, and drink syrups to unit kitchens and commercial clients. Enhancement Resources specializes in housekeeping management and institutional laundry while the J's Group brings quality fast-food to the general public.

Steady and controlled growth has been the by-word for the corporation's success. Expansion began in 1948, when Muhlenberg College contracted with Wood to feed the basketball team. Soon the college asked Wood to manage its entire food-service operation. Lehigh University followed in 1951. After more than 30 years, both are still Wood clients. Over 39 dining services and snack bars are managed for colleges and universities by the Wood Company today.

The Hospital Group was created in 1961, when Easton Hospital and Muhlenberg Medical Center brought Wood food service to their patients. A half-dozen other hospitals in eastern Pennsylvania have joined their ranks because of Wood's innovative approach to service. Working with the client, Wood has introduced the quality of restaurant-type service for hospital patients with attractive menus, extensive selections, and wine service.

The Wood Company began serving the Good Shepherd Home in 1965. Now the Nursing Home and Health Care Group consists of more than 40 public and private facilities in Pennsylvania and New Jersey. Working with the client and the community, Wood recently opened a kosher kitchen for Bethlehem's Leader II nursing home and rehabilitation center. The kitchen is a first in the area.

Education plays a vital role in the growth of the firm. Man-

LEFT
Chairman of the board Milton W. "Scotty" Wood opened a restaurant on Allentown's Center Square in 1939. It was the first building block for the Wood Company of today, which now boasts over 3,200 employees.

ABOVE
During the early days the firm was best known for "catering for all occasions." Today the Wood Company is an umbrella for four different groups: Food Service, Chef-Aide, Enhancement Resources, and the J's Group.

agers take part in company-sponsored training programs to bring a unique degree of professionalism to individual units. The corporation, recognizing the importance of the registered dietician, is in the vanguard of the industry by offering a new educational program. Wood is the first food-service business in the nation to receive accreditation from the American Dietetic Association to sponsor an internship program for registered dieticians.

People are the company's most valued resource. Many within the organization enjoy long and profitable careers. An excellent case in point is executive vice-president Wilbur J. Blew, an important guiding force within Wood's management, who joined in 1956 as a first line supervisor.

The corporate headquarters at 3320 Hamilton Boulevard, Allentown, is centrally located to all clients. Founder "Scotty" Wood, now chairman of the board, and his son, Robert C. Wood, president, both believe in maintaining a personal touch and personally visit the sites they serve. To help serve those clients better, an expanded computer center recently opened in Trexeltown.

To know the needs of the clients and meet those needs fairly and consistently—those are the goals of the Wood Company.

WARREN W. YORK & CO., INC.

Warren W. York & Co., Inc., the principal office located at 931 Hamilton Mall, Allentown, was founded in 1927 by Warren W. York as a sole proprietorship. York was the eastern Pennsylvania sales representative for F.J. Lisman Corporation, a major New York Stock Exchange firm, and he conceived the idea of a regional securities firm located in the heart of the fast-growing central eastern Pennsylvania area. Robert V.H. Harned became associated with the firm in 1928. The stock market crash of 1929 and the Depression of the early 1930s actually gave the young enterprise an excellent opportunity to develop an investment-minded clientele. With the addition of salesmen and the opening of branches in Easton, Scranton, and Harrisburg during that decade, Warren W. York & Co. gained a solid footing in developing what was to become a fully integrated brokerage business.

The war years were weathered profitably, and in 1946 the business was incorporated with York as president and Harned as executive vice-president. New branches were opened in Altoona and Johnstown and a trading and clearing office was established in New York City.

An unfortunate accident involving the company plane resulted in York's death in 1948; Harned succeeded him as president. Warren W. York & Co. became a member of the Philadelphia Stock Exchange the following year and the newly reorganized firm expanded aggressively, particularly in the field of underwritings and marketing of Pennsylvania municipal securities.

With established over-the-counter stock-trading facilities and an industry-recognized research department, the company expanded its services with a department for financial planning to include insurance products and tax shelters. Subsequently, Warren W. York & Co. became a nationally recognized full-service investment firm whose organization and capital make it the largest in the state outside of Philadelphia and Pittsburgh.

During the past decade, the corporation originated and co-managed in excess of $300 million municipal bond financings. In the same 10-year period, it participated in municipal syndicates throughout the state representing over $5 billion of debt financing for the state and its political subdivisions.

In 1979 William F. Greenawald, with over 20 years of experience in the securities business, was elected president.

The chief executives at Warren W. York & Co., Inc. (from left to right), are William F. Greenawald, Leland E. Smith, and Robert V.H. Harned.

With young, enthusiastic personnel directing its affairs and over half a century of experience and integrity of management to support it, Warren W. York & Co. has the diversification of product, strength of organization, and adequacy of capital not only to meet today's challenges, but also to better serve its clients in the years ahead.

Owned solely by its key personnel and capitalized at over $2.7 million, the firm currently maintains branch offices in Scranton, Harrisburg, and Sunbury and employs over 70 people. For more information about Warren W. York & Co., Inc., phone 432-4311.

PATRONS

The following individuals, companies, and organizations have made a valuable commitment to the quality of this publication. Windsor Publications, the Lehigh County Historical Society, and the Northampton County Historical and Genealogical Society gratefully acknowledge their participation in *The Lehigh Valley: An Illustrated History.*

Allentown Art Museum
Allentown Business School*
Allentown Pneumatic Gun Company*
Americus Hotel*
Appel-Jeweler, Inc.*
Thomas A. Armbruster, Inc.*
B & M Provision Company*
Ballietsville Inn*
The Besecke Group*
Beyer-Barber, Inc.*
Binney & Smith Inc.*
Bixler's, America's Oldest Jewelers*
Blue Cross of Lehigh Valley*
Ray C. Bracy Construction, Inc.
Brown, Fulford and Munsie, Inc.*
Buckeye Pipe Line Company*
J.S. Burkholder Funeral Home*
Alvin H. Butz, Inc.*
Call-Chronicle Newspapers*
Campbell, Rappold and Yurasits*
Coplay Cement Company*
Crowder Jr. Company*
John B. Curcio
Day-Timers/Dorney Printing*
Eastern Industries Inc.
Everett and Busch, Architects*
FinanceAmerica Corporation
The First National Bank of Allentown*
First Valley Bank*
Mr. & Mrs. C. Thomas Fuller
Funari & Brogna Company
General Electric*

George's Foodliner Inc.*
H.G.F. Management Corporation*
R.S. Hahn & Sons, Inc.*
Charlotte Treichler Harris
Hess's Department Stores, Inc.*
Holiday Rent-A-Car
Ingersoll-Rand Company*
    Standard Pump Aldrich Division
Jaindl's Turkey Farm*
Jeras Corporation
Keystone Savings Association
Charles L. Knecht III, M.D.
John L. and Ann C. Krajsa
L.P. and Sons Brickote Company*
Lehigh Cordage*
Lehigh Structural Steel Company *
Lutron Electronics *
H.T. Lyons Inc.*
Mack Trucks, Inc.*
Merchants National Bank*
Miers Insurance Agency
Modern Insulation Company*
Nestor's Sporting Goods Store*
Alfred W. Pelletier
Conrad W. Raker
Rodale Press Inc.*
Sacred Heart Hospital*
Sarco Company*
Service Electric Cable T.V., Inc.*
C.M. Stauffer Insurance Agency*
Tarkett*
George Taylor Chapter, Daughters of the American Revolution
Lecha Thal Chapter, Daughters of American Colonists
M.W. Wood Enterprises, Inc.*
Warren W. York & Co., Inc.*

*Partners in Progress of *The Lehigh Valley: An Illustrated History.* The histories of these companies and organizations appear in Chapter 8, beginning on page 159.

LIST OF SOURCES

The sources listed here do not include all the books, articles, manuscripts, and other materials used in compiling this history. Had the list been completely inclusive, it would have been nearly as lengthy as one of our chapters. We hope, however, that the works listed here will prove useful to those whom this volume stimulates to engage in their own historical research.

GENERAL SOURCES

Alderfer, E. Gordon, *Northampton Heritage* (Easton, 1963).

Condit, U.W., *History of Easton, Pennsylvania from Earliest Times to the Present* (Easton, 1885).

Federal Writers Project, *Northampton County Guide* (Bethlehem, 1939).

Heller, William J., *History of Northampton County* (Easton, 1920).

Henry, M.S., *History of the Lehigh Valley* (Easton, 1860).

History of Northampton County, 1752-1877 (Philadelphia, 1877).

Jordan, J.W., *Historic Homes and Institutions of the Lehigh Valley* (New York, 1905).

Lehigh County Historical Society, *Proceedings* (Allentown, 1908 to present).

Levering, J.M., *History of Bethlehem, 1741-1892* (Bethlehem, 1903).

Mathews, Alfred, and Hungerford, Austin W., *History of the Counties of Lehigh and Carbon* (Philadelphia, 1884).

Roberts, Charles R., et al., *History of Lehigh County* (Allentown, 1914).

Rupp, I. Daniel, *History of Northampton, Lehigh, Monroe, Carbon, and Schuylkill Counties* (Harrisburg, 1845).

Vadasz, T.P., "History of an Industrial Community: Bethlehem, Pennsylvania, 1741-1920" (unpublished Ph.D. dissertation, College of William & Mary, 1975).

Wood, Ralph, ed., *The Pennsylvania-Germans* (Princeton, 1942).

Yates, W. Ross, *Bethlehem of Pennsylvania* (Bethlehem, 1976).

———, *History of the Lehigh Valley Region* (Allentown, 1963).

CHAPTER I

Brinton, D.G., *The Lenape and Their Legends* (Philadelphia, 1885).

Farb, Peter, *Man's Rise to Civilization: The Cultural Ascent of the Indians of North America* (New York, 1978).

Heckwelder, J.G.E., *History, Manners, and Customs of the Indian Nations Who Once Inhabited Pennsylvania* (Philadelphia, 1876).

Kent, B.C., et al., *Foundations of Pennsylvania Prehistory* (Harrisburg, 1976).

Miller, Benjamin L., ed., *Lehigh County, Pennsylvania: Geology and Geography* (Harrisburg, 1941).

Wallace, A.F.C., *King of the Delawares: Teedyuscung, 1700-1763* (New York, 1949).

Weslager, C.A., *The Delawares: A Critical Bibliography* (New Brunswick, 1978).

———, *The Delaware Indians: A History* (New Brunswick, 1972).

———, ed., *Delaware Indian Symposium* (Trenton, 1972).

Wiley, Gordon R., *An Introduction to American Indian Archaeology* (New York, 1966).

CHAPTER II

Barba, Preston, *They Came to Emmaus* (Emmaus, 1959).

Chidsey, A.D., *A Frontier Village: Prerevolutionary Easton* (Easton, 1940).

Knauss, J.O., *Social Conditions among the Pennsylvania-Germans in the Eighteenth Century* (Lancaster, 1922).

Lemon, James T., *The Best Poor Man's Country: A Geographical Study of Early Southeastern Pennsylvania* (New York, 1976).

Northampton County Historical Society, *The Scotch-Irish of Northampton County* (Easton, 1926).

Meyers, Richmond, *Northampton County in the American Revolution* (Easton, 1976).

Tolles, Frederick B., *Meeting House and Counting House* (New York, 1948).

Wallace, P.A.W., *Conrad Weiser, 1696-1760* (Philadelphia, 1945).

Wolfe, Stephanie Grauman, *Urban Village: Population, Community, and Family Structure in Germantown, Pennsylvania, 1683-1800* (Princeton, 1976).

CHAPTER III

Barba, Preston, *Pennsylvania-German Tombstones* (Allentown, 1954).

Breyvogel, S.G., *Landmarks of the Evangelical Association*

(Reading, 1888).

Brumbaugh, G. Edwin, "Colonial Architecture of the Pennsylvania-Germans" in Pennsylvania-German Society, Proceedings XLI (1933).

Dornbosch, Charles H., Pennsylvania-German Barns (Allentown, 1958).

Fabian, M.H., The Pennsylvania-German Decorated Chest (New York, 1978).

Fletcher, Stevenson W., Pennsylvania Agriculture and Country Life, 1640-1940 (Harrisburg, 1950).

Gilbert, R.W., Pennsylvania-German Wills (Allentown, 1950).

Lehigh County Registrar of Wills, Wills, 1811-1860.

Long, Amos, The Pennsylvania-German Farm (Breinigsville, 1972).

Northampton County Registrar of Wills, Wills, 1752-1860.

Reinert, G.F., Coverlets of the Pennsylvania-Germans (Allentown, 1948).

Shelley, D.A., The Fraktur Writings or Illuminated Manuscripts of the Pennsylvania-Germans (Allentown, 1961).

Stapleton, A., Flashlights on Evangelical History (York, 1908).

Stoudt, J.J., Consider the Lilies, How They Grow: An Interpretation of the Symbolism of Pennsylvania-German Art (Allentown, 1937).

————, Pennsylvania-German Folk Art: An Interpretation (Allentown, 1948).

CHAPTER IV

Archer R.F., History of the Lehigh Valley Railroad (Berkeley, 1977).

Bartholomew, Craig, "Anthracite Iron Making and Industrial Growth in the Lehigh Valley," in Lehigh County Historical Society, Proceedings XXXII (1978).

————, A History of Lower Macungie Township (East Texas, Pa., 1976).

Bogen, Julius I., The Anthracite Railroads (New York, 1927).

Brzyski, Anthony J., "The Lehigh Canal and Its Effect on the Region Through Which It Passed," (unpublished Ph.D. dissertation, New York University, 1957).

Coffin, Selden J., The Men of LaFayette, 1826-1893 (Easton, 1891).

Davies, Edward J., "The Urbanizing Region: Leadership and Urban Growth in the Anthracite Coal Regions, 1830-1885" (unpublished Ph.D. dissertation, University of Pittsburg, 1977).

Folsom, Burton W., Urban Capitalists: Entrepreneurship and City Growth in the Lehigh and Lackawanna Valleys, 1800-1920 (Baltimore, 1981).

Fritz, John, Autobiography (New York, 1912).

Hellerich, Mahlon H., "The Development of Allentown,

1811-1873," in Lehigh County Historical Society, Proceedings XXXII (1978).

History of the Lehigh Coal and Navigation Company (Philadelphia, 1840).

Jones, Chester L. The Economic History of the Anthracite Tidewater Canals.(New York, 1908).

Kaufman, David B., "Helffrich on Fogelsville during the Civil War," in Lehigh County Historical Society, Proceedings XXXII (1978).

Kulp, Randolph, Railroads in the Lehigh River Valley (Bethlehem, 1962).

Lambert, J.F., and Reinhard, H.J., A History of Catasauqua (Allentown, 1914).

Lehigh County Court of Common Pleas, Case Files, 1843-1845.

Ohl, Albert, History of Upper Saucon and Center Valley (n.p., 1952).

Reichard, William J., "Civil War Letters, 1862-1863," in Lehigh County Historical Society, Proceedings XXII (1958).

Richardson, Richard, Memoirs of Josiah White (Philadelphia, 1873).

Skillman, D.B., Biography of a College, Being a History of the First Half-Century of the Life of Lafayette College (Easton, 1932).

The Story of the Old Company (Easton, 1941).

Temin, Peter, Iron and Steel in Nineteenth Century America (Cambridge, 1970).

The Thomas Iron Company, 1854-1904 (New York, 1904).

Weaver, E.A., Owen Rice: Christian, Scholar, Patriot (Germantown, 1911).

White, Josiah, Josiah White's History Given by Himself (Philadelphia, n.d.).

Williams, David G., "Iron Mining—Ironton Area" in Lehigh County Historical Society, Proceedings XXII (1958).

————, "Lehigh Canal System, Lehigh Coal and Navigation Company," in Lehigh County Historical Society, Proceedings XXII (1958).

Chapter V

Bossard, J.H., The Churches of Allentown—A Study in Statistics (Allentown, 1918).

Commonwealth of Pennsylvania, Annual Reports of the Factory Inspector (Harrisburg, 1889-1910).

Holben, Ralph, Poverty with Relation to Education (n.p., 1923).

Lehigh County Quarter Sessions Court, Dockets 1811-1900.

Lehigh County Court of Common Pleas, Case Files, 1870-1930.

Newspapers: Allentown Evening Chronicle
Allentown Democrat

Allentown Critic
Allentown Morning Call
Allentown Item
Catasauqua Dispatch
Lehigh Valley Daily News
Macungie Weekly Progress
Northampton County Quarter Sessions Court, *Dockets, 1810-1900.*

Chapter VI

Allentown Board of Trade, *Descriptive History of the City of Allentown* (Allentown, 1896).

——————, *Past, Present and Future of the City of Allentown* (Allentown, 1886).

Allentown Police Department, *Souvenir Programs* (Allentown 1924, 1926, 1928).

Benner, Nolan P., "The General and His Captain," unpublished manuscript, private collection.

Brandes, Stuart, *American Welfare Capitalism* (Chicago, 1976).

Brody, David, *The Industrial Worker in America* (New York, 1980).

——————, *The Steelworkers: The Non-Union Era* (New York, 1960).

Carnegie, Andrew, *The Gospel of Wealth.* (Cambridge, 1962).

Dorney, Oliver, "The Dutchman Remembers," unpublished manuscript, Lehigh County Historical Society.

Fink, Leo G., *Memoirs of General Harry Clay Trexler* (New York, 1935).

Gobron, L.C., *Souvenir of Allentown 1916* (Allentown, 1916).

Hessen, Robert, *Steel Titan: The Life of Charles M. Schwab* (New York, 1975).

Horne, A.R., *Pennsylvania-German Manual* (Kutztown, 1875; Allentown, 1896, 1905).

Klein, H.M.J., *Cedar Crest College, 1867-1947* (Allentown, 1948).

Kulp, Randolph L., ed., *History of the Lehigh Valley Transit Company* (Allentown, 1966).

Lehigh County Court of Common Pleas, *Naturalization Dockets.*

Lehigh County Recorder of Deeds, *Charter Dockets.*

Lehigh County, *Juvenile Court Dockets.*

McQuade, Jean P., and Orpe, Frank, *Dare to Be Brave* (Center Square, Pa., 1977).

Morrison, T.M., *Coopersburg Survey* (Easton, 1914).

Northampton County Court of Common Pleas, *Naturalization Dockets*; Recorder of Deeds, *Charter Dockets.*

Ochsenford, S.E., *Muhlenberg College* (Allentown, 1892).

Richards, H.M.M., "A History of Muhlenberg College, 1916-1962," unpublished manuscript, Muhlenberg College.

Rosenberger, H.T., *The Pennsylvania-Germans, 1865-1891* (Lancaster, 1966).

Shankweiler, F.L., *Men of Allentown* (Allentown, 1917, 1922, 1951).

Stiegler, Ernie, *Men of Allentown 1970* (Allentown, 1970).

Wynkoop, Ronald, *The Golden Years: Old Time Easton and Philipsburg* (Easton, 1970).

Chapter VII

Allentown-Lehigh Chamber of Commerce, *Worlds of Living* (Allentown, 1977).

Call-Chronicle Newspapers, *Clipping Files.*

Lehigh-Northampton Joint Planning Commission, *Population and Housing* (Allentown, 1963).

Muir, Sara, et al., *Leaders of Lehigh 1980* (Allentown, 1980).

INDEX

PARTNERS IN PROGRESS

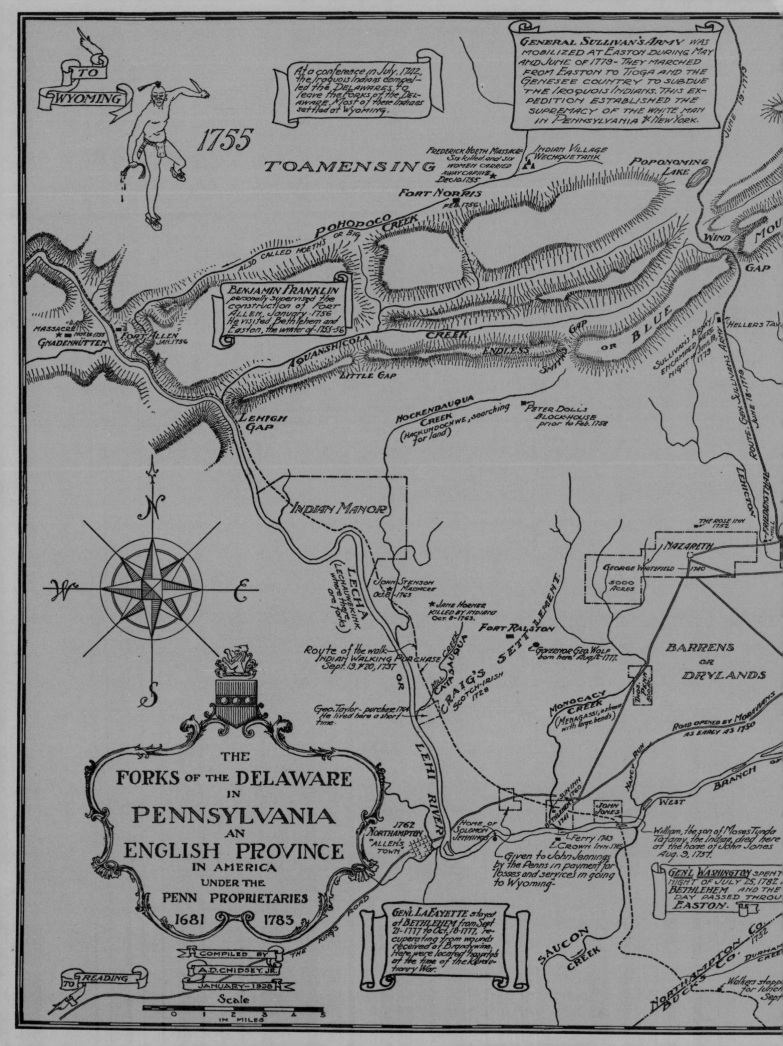

TO WYOMING

1755

At a conference in July, 1742, the Iroquois Indians compelled the Delawares, to leave the forks of the Delaware. Most of these Indians settled at Wyoming.

GENERAL SULLIVAN'S ARMY WAS MOBILIZED AT EASTON DURING MAY AND JUNE OF 1779 - THEY MARCHED FROM EASTON TO TIOGA AND THE GENESEE COUNTRY TO SUBDUE THE IROQUOIS INDIANS. THIS EXPEDITION ESTABLISHED THE SUPREMACY OF THE WHITE MAN IN PENNSYLVANIA & NEW YORK.

JUNE 19, 1779

TOAMENSING

FREDERICK HOETH MASSACRE Six killed and six women carried away captive Dec. 10, 1755.

Indian Village Wechquetank

POPONOMING LAKE

FORT NORRIS FEB. 1756

POHOPOCO CREEK also called HOETHS OR BIG CREEK

WIND GAP

MOU

HELLERS TAV.

Sullivan's Army Encamped here night of June 18, 1779

BENJAMIN FRANKLIN personally supervised the construction of FORT ALLEN, January 1756 He visited Bethlehem and Easton, the winter of 1755-56

AQUANSHICOLA CREEK

ENDLESS GAP

SMITHS GAP

OR BLUE MTS.

Route Gen. Sullivan's Army June 18, 1779

MASSACRE Nov. 24, 1755 GNADENHÜTTEN

FORT ALLEN Jan. 1756

LITTLE GAP

FRIEDENSTHAL MILL

LEHIGH GAP

HOCKENDAUQUA CREEK (Hackundochwe, searching for land)

PETER DOLL'S BLOCK-HOUSE prior to Feb. 1758

LEHICTON

THE ROSE INN 1752

INDIAN MANOR

LECHA (LECHAUWEKINK, where there are forks)

JOHN STENSON MASSACRE Oct. 8, 1763.

JANE HORNER KILLED BY INDIANS Oct. 8, 1763.

FORT RALSTON

CRAIG'S SETTLEMENT

NAZARETH

GEORGE WHITEFIELD 1740

5000 ACRES

BARRENS OR DRYLANDS

Route of the walk INDIAN WALKING PURCHASE Sept. 19 & 20, 1737

MILL CREEK

CATASAUQUA CREEK

CRAIG'S SETTLEMENT Scotch-Irish 1728

E Governor Geo Wolf born here Aug. 12, 1777.

INDIAN SCHOOL

Geo. Taylor - purchase 1764 He lived here a short time.

MONOCACY CREEK (MENAGASSI, a stream with large bends)

Road opened by Moravians as early as 1750

NANCY RUN

WEST BRANCH

THE FORKS OF THE DELAWARE IN PENNSYLVANIA AN ENGLISH PROVINCE IN AMERICA UNDER THE PENN PROPRIETARIES 1681 1783

1762 NORTHAMPTON "ALLEN'S TOWN"

LEHI RIVER

HOME OF SOLOMON JENNINGS

SUN INN 1760

BETHLEHEM 1741

Ferry 1743 CROWN INN. INS.

JOHN JONES

William, the son of Moses Tunda Tatamy, the Indian, died here at the home of John Jones Aug. 3, 1757.

Given to John Jennings by the Penns in payment for losses and services in going to Wyoming.

GEN'L WASHINGTON SPENT NIGHT OF JULY 25, 1782 IN BETHLEHEM AND THE DAY PASSED THROU EASTON.

COMPILED BY A.D. CHIDSEY, JR. JANUARY - 1938

THE KINGS ROAD

GEN'L LAFAYETTE stayed at BETHLEHEM from Sept. 21, 1777 to Oct. 18, 1777, recuperating from wounds received at Brandywine. Here were located hospitals of the time of the Revolutionary War.

SAUCON CREEK

NORTHAMPTON CO. 1752

BUCKS CO.

DURHAM

Walkers stopped for lunch Sept.

70 READING

Scale 0 1 2 3 4 5 IN MILES